FOOD LOVERS' SERIES

FOOD LOVERS'
GUIDE TO
RHODE ISLAND

The Best Restaurants, Markets & Local Culinary Offerings

1st Edition

Patricia Harris & David Lyon

gpp

Guilford, Connecticut

D0830521

Editor: Amy Lyons
Project Editor: Lauren Brancato
Layout Artist: Mary Ballachino
Text Design: Sheryl Kober
Illustrations by Jill Butler with additional art by Carleen Moira Powell and MaryAnn Dubé
Maps: Melissa Baker and Alena Joy Pearce © Morris Book Publishing, LLC

ISBN 978-0-7627-8361-8

Printed in the United States of America
10 9 8 7 6 5 4 3 2 1

All the information in this guidebook is subject to change. We recommend that you call ahead to obtain current information before traveling.

This book is dedicated to hungry travelers everywhere.

Contents

Recipes, 249

Appendices, 273

About the Authors

Patricia Harris and **David Lyon** are coauthors of Globe Pequot Press's *The Meaning of Food, Food Lovers' Guide to Massachusetts, Food Lovers' Guide to Montreal, Food Lovers' Guide to Vermont & New Hampshire*, and *Food Lovers' Guide to Boston*. They have written about Vermont cheese, Belgian beer, Tahitian *poisson cru*, New Hampshire hot dogs, Neapolitan pizza, Maine lobster, and Spanish elvers for such publications as the *Boston Globe, The Robb Report, Westways*, and *Cooking Light*. They chronicle their travel adventures and culinary explorations on HungryTravelers.com.

Acknowledgments

We would like to acknowledge the skills, hospitality, and generosity of everyone in the food business in Rhode Island. We are especially thankful to the cooks and chefs who shared their recipes for this volume, and to Naomi King for sage advice on adjusting them for home cooks. We offer a memorial salute to the late Laura Strom for conceiving the Food Lovers' series, and thank Amy Lyons for letting us take such an active role in the much-expanded series that she envisioned and made happen. We also want to thank project editor Lauren Brancato for shepherding this manuscript to publication.

Introduction: Rhode Island—A Little State Divided by a Great Big Bay

There are a few things you should know about eating in Rhode Island: A New York System wiener is usually washed down with coffee milk. Clams go with everything. And it doesn't matter if there's an "h" in the spelling of jonnycakes or not, as long as they're made with stone-ground white cornmeal.

For such a small state (only 1,214 square miles), Rhode Island has more than its share of gastronomic quirks. Where else will you find three kinds of clam chowder?

That clams figure so prominently in the Ocean State shouldn't be a big surprise. The shoreline of Little Rhody stretches for 384 miles, and quahogs (*Mercenaria mercenaria*) inhabit the muck of the entire intertidal zone. The Algonkian tribes who first settled Rhode Island ate the clams and used the shells for everything from cooking tools to hard currency. When the English moved in, they

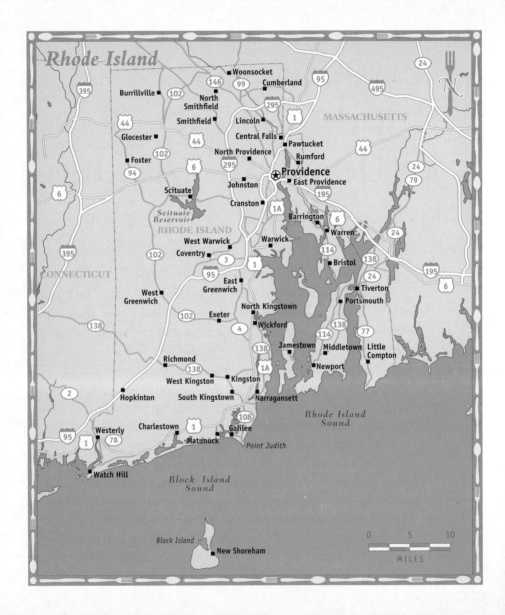

took to clams (and corn) in a big way. Nearly 400 years later, there is hardly an establishment either on the coast or inland that does not serve quahogs (also known as hard-shelled clams) on its raw bar, steamed, chopped into clamcakes, in marinara sauce, on pizzas or linguine, or in a casserole spiced with some Portuguese *chouriço*. The stuffed clam—usually a large "chowder" quahog minced up with onion and bread stuffing, shoved back in the shell and baked—just might be Little Rhody's contribution to American handheld cuisine. It is almost never actually called a stuffed clam; it is a "stuffie."

Rhode Island's commercial fishing industry is centered around the Port of Galilee, just west of Point Judith. Big and small boats alike land scallops, lobster, squid, cod, flounder, tuna, halibut, and swordfish, and some of the state's best restaurants for simple fish preparations flank the port. All in all, the commercial catch each year is worth more than $200 million at off-the-boat prices. The largest catch by volume is tender squid for calamari, which probably explains why every bar with a fryolator serves fresh fried Point Judith calamari, preferably with fried hot pepper rings. The most valuable catch, on the other hand, is lobster.

Not all the food in Rhode Island is caught; much of it is grown. The upland soils in the northern half of the state are thin, glacial till, but they nonetheless yield bountiful harvests of apples, blueberries, and other fruit, as well as a modicum of row crops. The soils in the southern half of the state are rich and loamy glacial outwash plain, and the cold New England climate is tempered by proximity to the ocean. Farms along the southern tier produce copious crops of tomatoes, peppers, corn, cucumbers, melons, and squashes. Look for their riches at farmstands, folding tables on the roadside, and on the menus of the state's best restaurants. The coastal growing zone has even proved hospitable to European wine grapes (*Vitis vinifera*), and the state's small wineries have begun producing wines to be taken seriously.

Farm-to-fork dining has taken hold throughout the state, but nowhere more noticeably than in the two main cities of Newport and Providence. With its historic connections to New York yachting, Newport attracts a clientele that expects accomplished fine dining and has the wherewithal to pay for it. Providence is less seasonal and less a tourist destination than Newport. It was once a great factory town, and the portable lunch cart was actually born here in the mid-19th century. It has, in fact, been reborn in Providence as part of a very healthy food-truck scene. The classic roadside diner grew out of the lunch cart tradition, and Providence retains two beauties. You'll find even more just north of the city in the Blackstone Valley and down in South County. Along with serving egg breakfasts and burger lunches, diners help keep the jonnycake tradition alive.

As a manufacturing center, Providence was also a magnet for immigration, especially southern Italians who flooded into the city from the late 19th century into the 1920s. The state's largest and most cohesive Italian-American community is still found on Federal Hill in Providence, which is a touchstone shopping and dining neighborhood. The Federal Hill diaspora into the rest of Rhode Island strongly influences the culinary offerings of its restaurants and bakeries. One principally Rhode Island manifestation of Italian-American cuisine is the pizza strip—a block of pan pizza usually eaten at room temperature as a quick snack. Restaurants high and low almost inevitably offer either eggplant or chicken parmesan—or both.

But a funny thing is happening in Rhode Island dining, as new immigrants bring new flavors to the table. Some of the state's most interesting food is appearing in little ethnic restaurants in the old mill towns of the Blackstone River Valley. Right now, Colombian, Mexican, and Peruvian cooks in Woonsocket, Central Falls, Pawtucket, and North Providence are laying the groundwork for the next great cuisines to enter the local mainstream.

All those ethnic influences are balanced by more traditional culinary training, and the Providence campus of Johnson & Wales University was a pioneer in schooling chefs. JWU also helped create a culinary awareness in Providence that put the small city in the national foodie vanguard. Although the two most famous Rhode Island chefs (Johanne Killeen and George Germon) studied art at the Rhode Island School of Design before opening Al Forno, many of the state's top chefs first sharpened their knives and their palates at JWU.

Given its rich food culture and multitude of flavors, it is sometimes hard to believe that the entire state of Rhode Island is smaller than the land area of Anchorage, Alaska, and only twice the size of Houston, Texas. It is proof that big tastes come in small packages.

How to Use This Book

Rhode Island may be small, but it still has a number of distinct regions. We have divided the state into seven chapters to make it easier for touring—and for looking things up. The two largest metropolitan areas of Providence and Newport stand alone. We joined the former industrial mill towns north of Providence with the farm country west of those towns as a chapter we call "Blackstone Valley & Northwest Rhode Island."

South of Providence, the state is cleft by Narragansett Bay. The metro Providence area as it continues down the west side of the bay is captured in a Cranston-Warwick chapter. Filling out the west bay coverage is the South County chapter, which also contains a section about dining on Block Island. The chapters for the east side of Narragansett Bay begin with an East Bay chapter covering East Providence, Barrington, Warren, and Bristol. Farther south, the Newport County chapter takes in all of Aquidneck Island not within Newport's borders as well as Tiverton and Little Compton on the east side of the Sakonnet River. Each chapter is packed with wonderful places to visit as you're passing through, and other establishments that are destinations in themselves. Alas, space does not permit us to include every worthy spot.

Each chapter includes a map of the region, which can help you plan trips to do your own exploring. While you're on the road, be sure to check chapters for adjacent areas—a terrific surprise might await just a few miles away. Farmstands and farm stores are seasonal by nature, and we've done our best to identify when they're open. Still, it's always a good idea to call ahead.

Because we have sliced and diced the regions into manageable portions, we have listed entries in just a few categories:

Foodie Faves

These are principally restaurants and more casual eateries (such as diners and fish shacks) that represent some of the best dining in the region.

Specialty Stores, Markets & Producers

This section of each chapter is devoted to places where you can get all the wonderful ingredients to prepare a great meal or a picnic and the shops where you can purchase the kitchen hardware to turn provender into repast. The category also includes pastry shops, bread bakeries, and coffee roasters.

Farmstands, PYOs & Wineries

Farmstands can range from a card table and a hand-lettered sign at the end of a driveway to a year-round store that offers honey, jam, pickles, breads, and maybe even flowers in addition to fresh fruits and vegetables. We could not possibly include every farm selling a few cucumbers from a table by the mailbox, but we have tried to include many that are open for longer seasons. Pick-your-own produce and fruit operations are included in this category. With its ocean-tempered climate, Rhode Island is on the way to becoming a significant producer of vinifera wines, so the wineries are found under this heading.

Farmers' Markets
Many Rhode Island farms have been in the same families for generations, and farmers' markets are essential venues for meeting the people behind your dinner. Farmers selling at the markets often feel they must offer something special—something you cannot get from the local grocery store. That may be an heirloom fruit or vegetable, an unusual ethnic varietal, or the assurance that the food you buy is free of chemicals. Because the number of farmers' markets continues to proliferate, it's always a good idea to double-check times and locations by checking the website of the Rhode Island Department of Agriculture at dem.ri.gov/programs/bnatres/agricult/pdf/rimarkets.pdf.

Price Code
Each restaurant carries a price code to give you a rough approximation of what you will spend. We chose to base the code on dinner entree prices. As a general rule, double the figure to estimate the cost of a 3-course meal with a glass of wine. The codes represent the

majority of dinner entrees; most restaurants will have a few dishes that are less expensive and a few that are more expensive. Note that many restaurants set a price for fish dishes (lobster, especially) that depends on market price. The cost of lunch is almost always lower.

$	under $15
$$	$15 to $25
$$$	$26 to $40
$$$$	more than $40 or prix fixe

Keeping Up with Foodie News

Farm Fresh Rhode Island, farmfreshri.org. This nonprofit organization tries to keep track of farms and markets, and often serves as a direct sales link between farmers and chefs. Various affiliates offer workshops for youth as well. The website can be difficult to navigate but includes a blog with food-related news.

GoLocalProv.com. This online print and video site covers both breaking news and lifestyle features for Providence and, by extension, all of Rhode Island. Local food and dining coverage can be very useful.

Newport Life Magazine, newportlifemagazine.com. The "Taste" department of this giveaway is filled with news about food, restaurants, and cooking.

Providence Journal, providencejournal.com. The state's major newspaper has the best coverage of Rhode Island restaurants as well as farms and fishermen. See the "Food Blog" to isolate each week's stories.

Providence Monthly, providenceonline.com. Short takes on the website do a good job keeping up with comings and goings in the restaurant scene.

Providence Phoenix, providence.thephoenix.com. Free weekly entertainment tabloid reviews restaurants and bars, sometimes with breathless prose.

Quahog.org. This website bills itself as "the definitive Rhode Island road trip." It offers a distinctly opinionated point of view on everything from Rhode Island folklore to restaurants serving New York System wieners. Sometimes irritating, sometimes exasperating, and sometimes amusing, it's the primo Rhode Island enthusiasts' site.

Rhode Island Monthly, rimonthly.com. Rhode Island is small enough that the city magazine format works well to cover the whole state. Restaurant reviews at *Rhode Island Monthly* tend to go into a little more depth than at the state's newspapers.

South County Living Magazine, southcountylivingmagazine .com. This giveaway lifestyle magazine published seven times a year in Wakefield often focuses on restaurants and other subjects of interest to foodies.

Rhode Island Food Specialties

Rhode Island has a food lexicon all its own, some of which seems inscrutable on first encounter. For residents of big states, here are some Rhode Island delights that you probably won't find at home but shouldn't miss.

New York System Wieners

Contrary to what some establishments might claim, the "wiener" (often spelled "weiner") is not just another name for a hot dog. It is a Vienna sausage that has grown up—a pale, lightly smoked sausage that is thinner than a hot dog. In the "New York System," the sausages are placed in soft buns like a hot dog, and topped with mustard, a "secret recipe" meat sauce, minced white onion, and celery salt. In a classic New York System, the condiment trays sit between the grill and the service window, allowing grill cooks to stack buns on their forearms and load each with a wiener before passing them over the counter or through the window. New York System wiener joints traditionally kept long hours, feeding barflies through a window on the street after the bars closed, but many now open just for breakfast and lunch.

Jonnycakes

These simple griddle cakes consist of little more than stone-ground white cornmeal and enough milk or water to make a batter.

Although they taste nothing like pancakes, jonnycakes are popular at breakfast topped with maple syrup. They can also be served with savory dishes. They are also known as johnnycakes or, among NPR fans, as "journey cakes." All stories about their origins should be taken with a grain of salt. For a recipe, see p. 253.

Stuffies

Baked stuffed clams (almost always called "stuffies") usually consist of chowder clams minced up very fine with onions and bread stuffing, shoved back in the shell, and baked. They're often sold cold as a snack and have neither a pronounced clam flavor nor many chewy bits. A lot of places buy them precooked, so if you find a spot that makes them on the premises, be sure to try them.

Clamcakes

Most non–Rhode Islanders are surprised the first time they order a clamcake in the Ocean State, often assuming that the restaurant forgot the clams. Nope. They are usually very finely minced. But the kicker is that clamcakes are not patties—they are fried balls of dough, which are also popular without the clams as "doughballs." Many diners like to dunk their clamcakes into Rhode Island clam chowder.

Clam Chowder

Rhode Island sometimes seems caught between a rock and a hard place, that is, between New England and New York, and nowhere is this truer than in clam chowder. New England clam chowder usually has milk or cream and butter, and is often thickened with a roux. Manhattan clam chowder has a tomato-broth base. Rhode Island clam chowder—sometimes called clear chowder—is more of a tan color, since it has neither milk products nor tomato. It tends to be brinier and have a more pronounced clam flavor. Many establishments serve all three versions. For a great recipe for Rhode Island clam chowder, see p. 251.

Quahog

Pronounced *KO-hog,* this is the Algonkian name for the hard-shelled clam that goes by the Latin moniker of *Mercenaria mercenaria.* Small ones are called littlenecks, slightly larger ones cherrystones, and big ones are known as chowder clams. The two smaller grades often show up at raw bars, and the littlenecks are used extensively in Italian dishes such as *spaghetti alle vongole,* clam pizza, clams *zuppa,* or littlenecks and *chouriço.* The often-tough chowder clams are cut up for chowder, clamcakes, and stuffies.

Coffee Milk

Let the rest of the world drink chocolate milk. Rhode Islanders prefer to lace their moo juice with coffee syrup to make coffee milk. Ideally, the syrup should be Autocrat, produced by the old-time

Providence coffee roaster. The ratio of syrup to milk is a matter of taste, but coffee milk is usually *very* sweet.

Cabinet

To much of America, this is a milk shake—that is, a mix of milk, syrup, and ice cream. A "milk shake" in Rhode Island (or in the rest of New England, where a cabinet is known as a "frappe") is just milk and syrup. (See "coffee milk," above.)

Lemonade

Thanks to Angelo DeLucia, who founded Del's Lemonade in Cranston in 1948, Rhode Islanders think that lemonade is a concoction of crushed ice, sugar, and lemons, known elsewhere as an "Italian ice."

Providence

Providence may be the best food city its size in the US. With a population of 178,000, it is home to the original campus of Johnson & Wales University with its highly influential culinary arts program. Johnson & Wales–trained chefs run many of its restaurants, yet the Providence dining style steers away from white-linen fine dining. Under the influence of the groundbreaking Italian restaurant **Al Forno** (see p. 18), Providence became a leader in developing a distinctively American approach to casual but serious dining that parallels the French bistro and the Italian trattoria.

As elsewhere in Rhode Island, Providence restaurants owe a debt to Italian-American cooking as it developed in immigrant communities. Federal Hill was a magnet for Italian immigration between 1870 and 1910, and remains the purest concentration of Italian-American culture in the state, complete with great bakeries, *salumerias*, pizzerias, and restaurants. Befitting Providence's role in the broader American culinary vanguard, the neighborhood's old-school Italian-American restaurants are slowly giving way to more modern and stylized dining establishments that serve contemporary

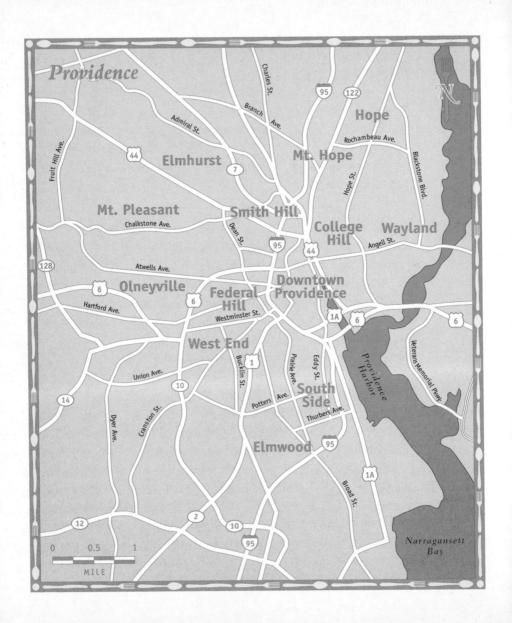

Italian cuisine based on the products of the fields and harbors of Rhode Island.

In addition to Johnson & Wales, Providence is also home to the Ivy League Brown University, cutting-edge creative arts Rhode Island School of Design, as well as Catholic Providence College and the public Rhode Island University. The students give the city a youthful air and an enthusiastic clientele for bakery-cafes, coffee shops, hipster bars, and late-night eateries. Weekend brunch is a very significant meal in Providence, especially in the West End and neighboring parts of Federal Hill.

Foodie Faves

Abyssinia, 333 Wickenden St., East Side, Providence, RI 02903; (401) 454-1412; abyssinia-restaurant.com; Ethiopian; $–$$. Abyssinia, a pioneer Ethiopian and Eritrean restaurant in Providence, wisely chose authenticity over assimilation. You need know only two Ethiopian words: *injera* (the sourdough bread made from the tiny teff grain well tolerated by celiacs) and *berbere* (the spice blend similar to North African *ras el hanout* but with a stronger kick of hot red pepper) to select among the dishes of stewed meat and vegetables. The menu also includes a number of vegan dishes that grew out of the Ethiopian Orthodox Christian prohibition against flesh of all kinds on Wednesdays, Fridays, and all of Lent. The *injera* serves as both bread and chief eating utensil. Teas and herbal infusions are the main drinks, but Abyssinia is also BYOB.

Adesso on the Hill, 139 Acorn St., Federal Hill, Providence, RI 02903; (401) 521-0770; adessoonthehill.com; Italian; $–$$. This successor to the College Hill restaurant Adesso, which won a following for its Cal-Ital cooking before closing under unclear circumstances, brings back the Neapolitan-style pizza and the sauce-heavy pastas with al dente fresh vegetables that made its predecessor so loved. A lot of the sauces are rich tomato-cream versions, and many of the pasta plates are augmented with generous servings of beef tips or shrimp. Not exactly Italian, but too fond of fresh veggies to qualify as traditional Italian-American, Adesso gives good value on dishes straight out of 1980s Atlantic City. Order a bottle of Chianti, speak up to be heard over the din, and enjoy.

Al Forno, 577 S. Main St., East Side, Providence, RI 02903; (401) 273-9760; alforno.com; Italian; $$–$$$. Chef-Owners Johanne Killeen and George Germon opened Al Forno in 1980 and almost immediately vaulted Providence into national attention as a great eating city. Their interpretations of rustic Italian cuisine from many different regions are tempered by an insistence on adapting

recipes to New England provender. Al Forno's signature is the smoke and heat of a wood fire, whether the oven where the pasta casseroles are baked or the charcoal grill where meats and pizzas are finished. In fact, Al Forno pioneered the grilled pizza in Providence and it remains one of the most popular segments of the menu.

JOHANNE & GEORGE BY THE BOOK

Cucina Simpatica (Harper Collins, 1991), the first cookbook by Johanne Killeen and George Germon, contains recipes for some of the signature dishes at their restaurant **Al Forno** (see p. 18), including clams Al Forno, roasted vegetables, grilled pizzas, and the baked pastas that put the restaurant on the culinary map. Fans had to wait 15 years for their encore *On Top of Spaghetti . . .* (William Morrow, 2006). "Pasta is the food we love best," the couple writes in the introduction to this volume full of recipes for baked and fresh pastas and sauces. We especially love the simple pasta and sauce pairings that the couple whips up for themselves after a busy night in the restaurant. Even at their most relaxed, Killeen and Germon can't help but innovate with such pairings as tomato, cinnamon, and mint or olives, thyme, and lemon—for sauces that come together in the time it takes to boil water and cook pasta.

We've always been fond of the Italian sausages roasted with grapes and balsamic vinegar and served with garlicky mashed potatoes. A true gastronomic landmark, Al Forno was one of the first American restaurants to prove that casual dining can nonetheless be world class.

Ama's, 3 Luongo Sq., West End, Providence, RI 02903; (401) 421-2200; Japanese; $–$$. Named for the female Japanese pearl divers, Ama's serves Japanese-styled Rhode Island food. Raw seafood leans more towards raw bar than sashimi (the oysters are invariably great), but owner Mike Sears also has a way with pickled vegetables and perfectly cooked beautiful miniature veggies in the Japanese manner. The bar stocks sake, plum wine, and beer. Having only 20 seats means that Ama's feels a bit like a hidden find—except on nights when there's a line of would-be diners spilling out into the square.

The American, 311 Iron Horse Way, Valley, Providence, RI 02908; (401) 865-6186; 311ironhorseway.com; Traditional American; $$–$$$. Located in the corner of the 1885 red-brick factory building of the Locomotive Works (later the American Locomotive Co.), this gallant throwback to classical American dining is a smart, high-ceilinged room with massive windows (and equally massive drapes) and a menu that could have been served at Delmonico's in its pre-Prohibition heyday. There are steaks and chops to be sure, but you can also order a succulent roast half chicken, a classic American meat loaf, or a more modern lobster mac and cheese. Other hints of modernity slip in, like the Steakhouse Bacon appetizer of slices of molasses-braised pork belly fried to order. The menu may hark back to the Gilded Age, but the modest prices mean that you don't have to be a robber baron to dine here.

Andino's Restaurant, 171 Atwells Ave., Federal Hill, Providence, RI 02903; (401) 421-3715; andinositalianrestaurant.com; Italian; $$–$$$. If you're not careful walking by, Anthony Andino may draw you into a conversation and before you know it, you're inside

Andino's eating the famous snail salad made with chunks, not slices, of sea snails with olive oil, red onion, roasted red peppers, celery, and olives. If you're in for a penny, you're in for a pound, so you order veal medallions with artichoke hearts, pepperoni, and sliced sweet red peppers. Frank Sinatra croons on the sound track, and the portions look like they were designed by an Italian grandmother who thinks you're too thin. As Anthony Andino says, "A lot of restaurants here are eclectic or New Italian. But if you're looking for your mother's food, it's here."

Angelo's Civita Farnese, 141 Atwells Ave., Federal Hill, Providence, RI 02903; (401) 621-8171; angelosonthehill.com; Italian; $. No one will ever accuse Angelo's of jumping on the New Italian bandwagon. A Federal Hill favorite since 1924, Angelo's proudly serves the dishes of Italian immigrants from Sicily, Campania, Calabria, and Puglia. That means plates like long-stewed tripe, panfried eggplant with red gravy and mozzarella, and a veal parm that's been hand-pounded in the kitchen until it's wide enough to cover the plate. The Antignano family has run the place from the beginning, and they keep the prices as much a throwback as the food. This is bargain eating of solid red-sauce cooking.

Aspire Seasonal Kitchen, Hotel Providence, 311 Westminster St., Downtown, Providence, RI 02903; aspirerestaurant.com; New

American; $$–$$$. Always the suave spot for downtown dining, Aspire changed direction slightly in 2012 when new chef Gregory Krol focused the menu on seasonal, local ingredients. In fact, the menu describes Aspire as serving "Rhode Island cuisine." We're not quite sure when cornmeal-crusted fried shrimp with an ancho pepper honey mustard sauce entered the canon of Ocean State cooking, but the dish makes a seriously good appetizer. Krol has a rooftop garden for herbs and a few vegetables, so he can give a completely local touch to a more traditional dish like baked cod with oven-roasted potatoes and summer vegetable succotash. In summer, try for an outdoor table among the twinkling lights of the patio.

Bacaro, 262 Water St., East Side, Providence, RI 02903; (401) 751-3700; bacarorestaurant.net; Italian/New American; $$–$$$. Bacaro parlays great views, slick design, and a wine-bar approach to Italian dining into a unique alternative to most of the Providence Italian restaurants. Diners are encouraged to make a meal of charcuterie from the *salumeria* with a bottle of wine. This is called the "Bacaro Experience." Some of the entrees take pleasant liberties with Italian (and Italian-American) tradition. The highly popular "crispy chicken," for example, consists of crunchy cooked chicken pieces with buttered noodles and Parmigiano Reggiano—over *pasta e fagioli!*

Better Burger Company, 215-217 Thayer St., College Hill, Providence, RI 02906; (401) 228-7373; betterburgercompany.com; Casual American; $. Providence hasn't escaped the burger craze by any means, but Better Burger is definitely a cut above. Angus steak burgers are available in three sizes, but we suggest paying a little more for the grass-fed "Farmer's Burger" or the free-range "Farmer's Lamb Burger." Even vegetarians have a choice between a vegan mixed-vegetables patty and a falafel burger (chickpea patty with hummus). In effect, BBC is the Brown campus neighborhood's counter to the golden arches.

Blount Clam Shack and Soup Bar, 371 Richmond St., Downtown, Providence, RI 02903; (401) 228-7746; blountretail .com; Seafood; $–$$. Blount Fine Foods claims to be the largest producer of clam chowder in New England and the largest producer of lobster bisque in the country. You can try both at the company's faux fish shack restaurant, along with such other classics as a lobster salad roll or a whole-belly clam roll. The chefs put haddock to particularly good use in a fried haddock sandwich, a haddock Reuben (with swiss cheese, coleslaw and tartar sauce), and a haddock BLT. Stop by the refrigerator case on your way out for a dizzying choice of soups to heat up at home, including scallop and bacon chowder, fire-roasted vegetable, and butternut squash and apple. For other seasonal locations in East Providence and Warren, see p. 145 and p. 154.

Bravo Brasserie, 123 Empire St., Downtown, Providence, RI 02903; (401) 490-5112; bravobrasserie.com; French/Casual American; $$–$$$. Hardly a brasserie (beer is mostly an afterthought), Bravo

is nonetheless a particularly good buy for a *croque monsieur,* scallops wrapped in bacon, or *moules frites*. Mussels, in fact, are a house specialty. The appetizer bowl of steamed mussels with spicy chorizo and charred onions even comes with a healthy serving of excellent grilled Tuscan bread.

Brickway on Wickenden, 234 Wickenden St., East Side, Providence, RI 02903; (401) 751-2477; brickwayonwickenden.com; Casual American; $. And you thought hipsters didn't get up for breakfast! With a youth culture vibe that echoes the late '60s and a menu of "omlets," egg plates, and pancakes at dynamite prices, Brickway is always bustling in the morning. Lunch service, which begins at 11 a.m., emphasizes overstuffed wraps, including the Ocean State Roll-Up of grilled chicken, bacon, lettuce, tomato, avocado, and ranch dressing.

Broadway Bistro, 205 Broadway, Federal Hill, Providence, RI 02903; (401) 331-2450; broadwaybistrori.com; New American; $$. Nominally on Federal Hill, this smart little neighborhood bistro really belongs more to the hipster West End than the Italian enclave. With dishes like ribs and grits or roasted asparagus with homemade bacon for appetizers and plates like Atlantic cod cakes or lamb loin chops with minty cottage cheese among the entrees, we could eat here every night. Prices are particularly sweet for such thoughtful, inventive cooking.

Cafe Nuovo, 1 Citizens Plaza, Downtown, Providence, RI 02903; (401) 421-2525; cafenuovo.com; Mediterranean/New American; $$$. Outdoor plaza dining makes this perhaps the perfect restaurant during Waterfire, the warm-weather arts nights with floating fires on the city's rivers and canal. The magic of the night combines with expertly executed high-end food to create a truly memorable experience. Pasta and risotto choices are restrained, and many diners prefer the grill fare, comparable to any good steak house. The "composed dishes," as the menu puts it, speak with a French accent, from the cassoulet and slow-braised lamb shank to the Dover sole and bouillabaisse.

Camille's, 71 Bradford St., Federal Hill, Providence, RI 02903; (401) 751-4812; camillesonthehill.com; Italian; $$$. Established in 1914 on Atwells Avenue, Camille's is the oldest restaurant surviving on Federal Hill. While many of its compatriots offer the restaurant version of southern Italian and Italian-American home cooking, Camille's focuses on fine dining as you might experience it in southern Italy. The *crudo* menu alone—small plates of mostly raw, sushi-grade fish with bright accompaniments—is one of the best around. A typical *crudo* dish, for example, might be yellowfin tuna belly with Sicilian blood orange and its zest, saffron-infused flying fish roe, and a drizzle of pomegranate balsamic vinegar. For an entree, consider the brined grilled pork chop with vinegar peppers and garlic sauce or the famed house lasagna layered with Bolognese sauce, ricotta, mozzarella, sausage, and meatballs.

Capriccio, 2 Pine St., Downtown, Providence, RI 02903; (401) 421-1320; capriccios.com; Continental; $$$–$$$$. This formal cousin to **Cafe Nuovo** (see p. 25) sits a little farther downriver and lacks the outdoor dining, but it's hard to beat for sheer old-fashioned formality. The food is classic, from pan-seared *foie gras* with fresh berries to steak Diane (flattened filet mignon with mushrooms, shallots, and brandy). Prices reflect that tuxedoed elegance, but the restaurant also offers a bargain priced pre-theater 3-course prix fixe of more conventional Italian fare (you have to show your tickets).

Caserta Pizzeria, 121 Spruce St., Federal Hill, Providence, RI 02903; (401) 621-3618; casertapizzeria.com; Italian/Pizza; $. Gourmet pizzas may be all the rage, but Caserta, which opened in 1953 and offers a simple, no-nonsense menu, continues to hold its own with old-fashioned pies. Pizzas can be topped with cheese, pepperoni, mushrooms, olives, anchovies, or any combination thereof. The toppings may be limited, but the chefs apply them liberally and the large rectangular pies with 12 pieces are great for a crowd. For a change of pace, try Caserta's own invention, the "Wimpy Skippy," a spinach pie stuffed with cheese and pepperoni.

CAV, 14 Imperial Pl., Downtown, Providence, RI 02903; (401) 751-9164; cavrestaurant.com; New American; $$–$$$. This Jewelry District stalwart has a striking decor of African and Asian art, all of it for sale and none of it relating culturally to the sophisticated, contemporary plates of food. The kitchen makes some inspired pairings, like lychee fruit with Atlantic salmon or pan-seared chicken breasts with pears poached in red wine. The lower-priced bistro entrees are freshly conceived riffs on some classics—ravioli filled with caramelized onions served with an arugula pistachio pesto, for example, or mussels with a spicy *arrabbiata* sauce. You can enjoy the same amazing decor at lunch while chomping on a wrap, a deli sandwich, a burger, or a modest serving of lemon zest risotto.

Centro Restaurant and Lounge, 1 W. Exchange St., Downtown, Providence, RI 02903; (401) 228-6802; centroprovidence.com; Italian; $$–$$$. Chef Ryan Escudé prowls the state looking for top seafood and produce for this central Italian restaurant in the Westin Hotel. Although Centro is the hotel's service restaurant (they do breakfast and room service), the elegant room feels like a stand-alone establishment. With dinner entrees such as black-pepper-flecked pappardelle with braised beef cheek and mushrooms of the season, Centro is popular with locals for a special night out. But it's also possible to enjoy the setting and a more casual meal of pizza and antipasti such as crabcakes, rolled eggplant stuffed with ricotta, or flash-fried Point Judith calamari.

Chez Pascal, 960 Hope St., East Side, Providence, RI 02906; (401) 421-4422; chez-pascal.com; French/New American; $$$.

The motto at Chez Pascal is "French-influenced, New England grown," and that winning combination takes form with a great selection of pâtés, charcuterie, and cheeses as small plates, escargots with garlic butter and parsley brioche as an appetizer, and imaginative meat and fish dishes. One of the better French–Rhode Island combos might be sauteed bluefish fillet with caramelized fennel, a rice cake, and a "bouillabaisse sauce" (really a catch-of-the-day fish stew). For those who need a French fix on the go, the restaurant has the **Hewtin's Dogs** food truck (see p. 35), which sells sausages, a few sandwiches (the bacon-wrapped meat loaf with fig compote is a special winner), and some superb hot dogs. If you don't spot the truck by the image of a dachshund in striped sweater and beret emblazoned on the side, just look for the long, patient line of customers.

Cook & Brown Public House, 959 Hope St., East Side, Providence, RI 02906; (401) 273-7275; cookandbrown.com; New American; $$. Self-consciously modeled on a European gastropub, Cook & Brown comes across as fully New American, thanks to Chef-Owner Nemo Bolin's love of produce from local farms and fish from docks stretching from Galilee north to Maine. While some plates are familiar in the New American bistro lexicon (pan-seared day-boat scallops, butter-poached Maine lobster), others are welcome departures—like the appetizer of grilled smoked beef tongue served with a cabbage-daikon slaw. Bolin even accommodates diners on a budget by including a cheeseburger with caramelized onions on the dinner menu and by offering multicourse tasting menus on weekends for $50 or so.

Cuban Revolution, 50 Aborn St., Downtown, Providence, RI 02903; (401) 331-8829 and **Cuban Revolution at the Plant,** 60 Valley St., Olneyville, Providence, RI 02909; (401) 632-0649; the cubanrevolution.com; Cuban; $–$$. With murals of Fidel Castro and Malcolm X, Marilyn Monroe, and John F. Kennedy, Cuban Revolution seeks to channel the 1960s and promote lively political debate. But it's OK if you simply want to enjoy the Latin vibe and dig into a plate of *picadillo* (ground pork with cinnamon, tomatoes, olives, raisins, and almonds), a bowl of shrimp and corn chowder, or a Cubano sandwich. At the Plant, DJs on Thursday and live music on Friday and Saturday obviate the need to talk anyway.

The Dorrance, 60 Dorrance St., Downtown, Providence, RI 02903; (401) 521-6000; thedorrance.com; New American; $–$$. This terrific bar and restaurant demonstrates the up side of a down economy. Located in the soaring ground level of a 1901 Beaux-Arts landmark building in the heart of downtown, the Dorrance gives dining a kind of majesty that was long missing from Providence's haute comfort food restaurant scene. Frankly, it feels like a grand Parisian bar-cafe, with the high ceilings, giant windows, and stained glass. The room may be regal, but the welcome is warm and service is relaxed and friendly. The menu, with a mix of a few small plates and a few larger ones, is a fine expression of contemporary American bistro food. Start with sautéed Rhode Island squid or beef tartare on Ritz crackers with Sichuan spices, before tucking into roasted dry-aged duck with beets and kohlrabi or suckling pork with baby turnips and rhubarb. The wine list ventures far beyond the usual suspects to provide a range of tastes and prices.

Duck & Bunny, 312 Wickenden St., East Side, Providence, RI 02903; (401) 270-3300; theduckandbunny.com; Eclectic; $. By all reason, Duck & Bunny shouldn't work. A cupcake and crepe shop with a line of good wines by the glass and artisanal beers? We can understand the espresso coffee drinks—that goes with cupcakes. But a cigar menu? (To be enjoyed on the outdoor porch.) The classy barroom gives way inside to a warren of cute small rooms that the owners call a "snuggerie." That cuteness should be strike three, but Duck & Bunny is a winning and inviting place in spite of it all. (Part of that is due to staff who really understand hospitality.) What pulls it all together? High quality and fine service in all the venial sins. The chocolate salt caramel cupcake is worth an extended stay in purgatory.

Eddie & Son Diner, 74 Dorrance St., Downtown, Providence, RI 02903; (401) 621-4118; Casual American; $. This marvelously old-fashioned place is a mainstay for downtown workers looking for quick—and filling—breakfasts and lunches. In classic diner style, those breakfasts feature eggs, home fries, and corned beef hash, along with a variety of three-egg omelets. Top choices for lunch are the Italian-American standbys such as chicken cutlet parmesan, baked macaroni (with meatballs or sausage), and baked stuffed eggplant. Closed Sat and Sun.

El Rancho Grande, 311 Plainfield St., Olneyville, Providence, RI 02909; (401) 275-0808; elranchogrande restaurant.com; Mexican; $. It's been about 40 years since Maria Meza immigrated to the United States, but fortunately she has not lost her taste for the epony-mous mole sauce and other dishes of Puebla, one of the wellsprings of great Mexican cuisine. El Rancho is a warm and welcoming place to sample the subtle spices and hints of chocolate in a true mole poblano, which Meza serves with chicken-stuffed enchiladas or over a chicken breast. You might start your meal with guacamole poblano (which adds tomatoes, red onions, jalapeño peppers, and cilantro to the avocado) and end with a crepe filled with guava jam and topped with vanilla ice cream.

Fidas Restaurant, 270 Valley St., Valley, Providence, RI 02909; (401) 351-9369; Casual American; $. With an authentic New York System setup and red-and-aqua laminate interior that could only come out of a Zippy the Pinhead fevered dream, this edgy hipster stopover serves a solid wiener (mild meat sauce), triple-decker club sandwiches, and good fried chicken. It also has complete fountain service, including cabinets.

Flan y Ajo, 225A Westminster St., Downtown, Providence, RI 02903; (401) 432-6656; flanyajo.com; Spanish; $. Tapas always taste best when you're standing at a bar, elbow-to-elbow with other customers and eyeing their plates to decide what you want to try next. So don't despair if you can't snag one of the few stools or outdoor tables at this tiny spot. Just wriggle your way to the bar for a *bocadillo* (small sandwich) of tuna and red pepper or smoked salmon, goat cheese, honey, and capers for lunch. You'll want to return in the early evening for a round of tapas, such as chicken or ham croquettes, shrimp in garlic, *boquerones* (white anchovies) on olive oil crackers, or *patatas bravas,* the Spanish bar food classic of roasted potatoes and spicy tomato sauce. Flan y Ajo serves light lunch Mon through Fri and tapas Tues through Sat. BYOB.

Foo(d) at AS220, 115 Empire St., Downtown, Providence, RI 02903; (401) 831-3663; as220.org; New American/Vegetarian Friendly; $. AS220 is a nonprofit organization devoted to supporting and nurturing Providence's artists and arts community. This laid-back cafe adjacent to an art gallery certainly nourishes their bodies with an eclectic neo-hippie menu that ranges from African peanut soup to grilled tofu and garlic hummus, or from panfried mushroom barley risotto cakes to slow-roasted chile-rubbed pork. After you place your order at the counter, you'll probably have time to peruse the artwork before your food is delivered to your table. Be sure to check the schedule of events—music, poetry slams, fashion shows, and more—before you leave. Much of the food, by the way, is sourced locally and the conversations at adjacent tables are often fascinating.

Geppetto's Grilled Pizzeria, 57 DePasquale Sq., Federal Hill, Providence, RI 02903; (401) 270-3003; geppettospizzeria.com; Italian/Pizza; $. Despite the name, Geppetto's offers a variety of soups, pastas, and other entrees. But most diners opt for a grilled pizza, which is best enjoyed at an outside table when weather permits. Toppings can be overly elaborate for our taste (such as steak, red peppers, onions, lettuce, mozzarella, cheddar cheese, and ranch dressing), though many diners find the grilled chicken, pesto, diced tomatoes, caramelized onion, and crumbled feta cheese to be a winning combination. We think that the delicate crust (white or whole wheat) is best served by the restrained, classic pairing of cheese and tomato.

Gracie's, 194 Washington St., Downtown, Providence, RI 02903; (401) 272-7811; graciesprovidence.com; New American; $$$. Gracie's was one of Providence's earliest farm-to-table restaurants, and owner Ellen Gracyalny and chef Matthew Varga continue to promote local flavor in the heart of the city, steps from Trinity Rep. They even maintain a 1,000-square-foot garden on a nearby rooftop to supply the kitchen with salad vegetables, tomatillos, fennel, alpine strawberries, and the like. Since the move from Federal Hill to Washington Street in 2005, Gracie's has won a solid following for

THE ORIGINAL ROAD FOOD

It's really only fitting that Providence is a big player in the current craze for food trucks. The first recorded mobile lunch cart got its start here in 1872, when Walter Scott hooked up a small freight wagon to a horse, parked it in front of the *Providence Journal* offices at night, and began selling food to the late-night newspaper workers. Records show he served ham sandwiches, boiled eggs, buttered bread, and pie—each item for a nickel. For 30 cents, customers could get a plate of sliced chicken.

Another 19th century stalwart, the Haven Brothers Diner (originally a horse-drawn wagon) opened for business in 1888. Now owned by the Giusti clan, it operates at the corner of Dorrance and Fulton Streets in downtown from 4:30 p.m. to 5 a.m., selling burgers, hot dogs, and sandwiches from its window.

The city boasts two-dozen-plus food trucks, many of which gather at lunchtime on Washington Street between City Hall Park and Kennedy Plaza, barely a block from the Haven Brothers haunt. Most Providence food trucks focus tightly on a single item or at least a

special-occasion dinners. Most entrees are straightforward preparations that highlight the ingredients—like roasted Atlantic halibut with a terrine of summer squash, garlic confit, and roasted peppers in vinegar sauce. A modest 3-course prix-fixe is available nightly, but many opt instead for the 5- or 7-course tasting menus.

single cuisine. Like No Udder claims to be the world's first all-vegan soft-serve ice cream truck. Poco Loco Tacos serves . . . tacos. Hewtin's Dogs Mobile specializes in hot dogs. Fancheezical sells a variety of grilled cheese sandwiches and some great riffs on tomato soup. The Plouf Plouf Mobile Bistro might be the most ambitious of all, serving "rustic French scratch cuisine" cooked to order. That could be a grilled hanger steak with hand-cut Belgian-style fries, a grilled organic duck burger, fresh lobster on a brioche with tarragon and wild mushrooms, or even roasted snails in puff pastry.

The trucks go where the hungry diners are, so look for them to congregate on lower Weybosset Street, on Thayer Street on College Hill, and around popular bars at closing time. The best way to know where they are and what's on special is to follow their tweets. The food and dining staff at the *Providence Journal* have even put up a Twitter feed that captures more than a dozen trucks. Find it at twitter .com/#!/projoblogs/food-trucks.

Harry's Bar & Burger, 121 N. Main St., East Side, Providence, RI 02903; (401) 228-7437; harrysbarburger.com; Casual American; $. This gastro-burger joint is worth seeking out for the quality of the burgers, the selection of craft beer on tap, and the chummy cheek-by-jowl ambience of the crowded dining rooms. Harry's serves its burger as a pair of sliders, making it possible to cook to order without long waits. The menu informs that burgers are "not cooked to your preference." They're served well-done, but not at all dry. The simple Harry's Classic with toasted potato roll, grilled onion, lettuce, and a pickle is everything a burger should be. The M.O.A.B. (Mother of All Burgers) adds cheese, bacon, mushrooms, and fried onion strings. Salt and pepper fries are a good accompaniment, though variations that pile melted cheese and homemade chili on the fries are available for diners who can't just let a good thing be.

Hemenway's Seafood Grill & Oyster Bar, 121 S. Main St., East Side, Providence, RI 02903; (401) 351-8570; hemenwaysrestaurant .com; Seafood; $$–$$$. The seafood equivalent of a steakhouse, Hemenway's can be very seductive indeed in the summer when patio dining is available on the river. All the New England classics are here, from fried clams to steamed lobster, but Hemenway's also serves a lot of sustainably farmed fish (salmon, arctic char, rainbow trout) and flies in such high-end treats as Alaskan king crab legs. The restaurant has become a special-occasion standard in Providence—the place to mark a graduation with a big lobster or celebrate as a family with the seafood tower. The kitchen also does a beautiful job with the lobster ravioli from **Venda Ravioli** (see p. 59), presenting them with a chiffonade of fresh basil, charred tomato coulis, cooked lobster meat, and basil oil. Rib eye, filet mignon, and New York strip steaks are also available for diners less enamored of seafood.

Jacky's Waterplace & Sushi Bar, 200 Exchange St., Downtown, Providence, RI 02903; (401) 383-5000; jackyswaterplace.com; Asian; $$–$$$. Something of an anomaly on the East Coast, Jacky's Waterplace brings the razzmatazz of a big Hong Kong (or Las Vegas) restaurant to the bluff above Waterplace Park. Chef-Owner Jacky Ko (who also has **Jacky's Galaxie** restaurants in Bristol, Cumberland, North Providence, and Johnston, see p. 86 and p. 147) has a flair for the dramatic and an exuberant way with Asian food of many national origins. Jacky's Waterplace is the kind of place to come with a friendly crowd, order lots of scorpion bowls, mai tais, and Singapore slings, and munch the night away on platters of maki rolls while a few in the group take turns slurping surf clams and savoring smoked eel.

Julian's, 318 Broadway, Federal Hill, Providence, RI 02909; (401) 861-1770; juliansprovidence.com; New American/Vegetarian Friendly; $–$$. Perhaps the primo hipster hangout at the intersection of Federal Hill and the West End, Julian's is insanely popular for Sunday brunch. One of the more inventive egg dishes is the "Israeli breakfast" of eggs poached in a spicy tomato sauce with home fries and garlic bread. Vegan dishes such as carrot cake pancakes, cinnamon orange vegan french toast, and tofu scramble are especially popular. The kitchen tries to be carnivorous and vegan at the same time, leading to a dinner plate that offers either house-made corned beef or house-made corned seitan with fingerling potatoes, maple-glazed carrots, and stout-braised cabbage. Imagination reigns supreme, often to good effect. Balsamic cherry-glazed sirloin steak with sweet corn–pine nut polenta and asparagus in brown butter might sound as if too many lilies are being gilded, but the flavor combinations turn out to be novel and successful.

Kartabar Restaurant, 284 Thayer St., College Hill, Providence, RI 02906; (401) 331-8111; kartabar.com; Mediterranean; $$. Kartabar is one of the best places on College Hill to keep up with the European soccer leagues, courtesy of the big-screen televisions that seem eternally tuned to one match or another. When you get hungry, the pan-Mediterranean menu offers everything from a Caprese salad to tabouli, from grilled kebabs to a filet mignon literally stuffed with blue cheese. Many of the patrons are ex-pat college students, so you can learn to say "The ref's a @#$%#^^!" in any of several languages.

La Laiterie Bistro, 184-188 Wayland Ave., East Side, Providence, RI 02906; (401) 274-7177; farmsteadinc.com; New American; $$–$$$. Founded in 2006 by chefs Matt and Kate Jennings at the height of the 100-mile diet craze, La Laiterie is a farmhouse bistro in the city—conveniently attached to a heck of a cheesemonger (**Farmstead,** see p. 61). Since almost everything is sourced from New England, menus have a distinctly seasonal cast, with lots of asparagus and peekytoe crab in the spring, the gastronomic holy trinity of corn/tomatoes/basil in the summer, and squashes and hearty greens in the fall. Look for roasted root vegetables over the winter. The locally raised meats and New England cheeses—and the local catch—keep the menu stoked with protein in all seasons. That can mean dishes as homey as roast beef with dumplings and fried garlic or as inventive as grilled Rhode Island squid and octopus with bitter citrus and charred cucumber. At any rate, start the meal with a house pâté. Beer and wine, surprisingly, are mostly imported. For Matthew Jenning's recipe for **Farmstead's Macaroni with Heirloom Tomato Sauce and Fresh Chevre,** see p. 259.

The Liberty Elm Diner, 777 Elmwood Ave., South Side, Providence, RI 02907; (401) 467-0777; libertyelmdiner.com; Casual American; $. Don't be put off by the industrial neighborhood and small rutted parking lot of this 1947 Worcester diner a few blocks from Roger Williams Park & Zoo. The Guy Fieri stencil tag on the door should tip you that the Liberty Elm takes its food and its history seriously and welcomes a little pop culture notoriety. All the bona fides you'd expect of a locavore restaurant hold true here as well: locally roasted fair-traded coffee, cage-free eggs, **Kenyon's Grist Mill's** (see p. 190) white cornmeal for the Johnny Cakes (as the menu spells them), preservative-free bacon and sausage from New England smokehouses. . . . Even the soda pop (**Yacht Club,** see p. 107) comes from Pawtucket. A frequent special is the Wicked Awesome Meatloaf Sandwich made with Angus beef from Blackbird Farm in Smithfield and topped with local pea greens. Ever since Fieri taped a segment of *Diners, Drive-Ins, and Dives* here, the Liberty Elm has offered "Guy's Turkey Sandwich" of sliced turkey breast (roasted in-house) with pea tendrils, herbed mayonnaise, and sliced tomato on thick slabs of toast. In fact, it's hard to go wrong at the Liberty Elm—especially when the service is as warm and friendly as that offered by waitresses in Raymond Chandler novels.

Local 121, 121 Washington St., Downtown, Providence, RI 02903; (401) 274-2121; local121.com; New American; $$. When the former Dreyfus Hotel was converted into artists' live-work space in 2005, the lower levels became a multi-space establishment with a live music venue, a bar with DJ entertainment, and a separate fine dining room. In keeping with the name, most of the food comes from New England farms, fishing boats, and cheesemakers, so menus tend to be highly seasonal. The kitchen doesn't balk at heavy spicing, though, serving Matunuck littleneck clams with hot andouille sausage, or pork shoulder roast with a smoked peach and onion cobbler. Most wines are European or Californian, but a handful of New England whites are also available.

Loie Fuller's, 1455 Westminster St., West End, Providence, RI 02909; (401) 273-4375; loiefullers.com; New American/French, $$. A fave with other local chefs, Loie Fuller's serves bold food in an unabashedly Art Nouveau setting. The murals, wood-framed curved mirrors, and other decorative details are perhaps intended 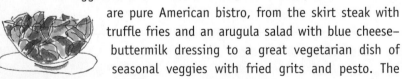 to suggest a fin-de-siècle French decadence, but the flavors are pure American bistro, from the skirt steak with truffle fries and an arugula salad with blue cheese–buttermilk dressing to a great vegetarian dish of seasonal veggies with fried grits and pesto. The wines are predominantly French; Rhône and Loire Valley value wines take up the lion's share of the list. They're typically hearty, unfussy wines—a perfect pairing with the food. Loie Fuller's also offers a very popular weekend brunch that includes pillowy beignets dusted with sugar as well as a barbecued brisket version of eggs Benedict.

Los Andes, 903 Chalkstone Ave., Valley, Providence, RI 02908; (401) 649-4911; losandesri.com; Peruvian; $. Peruvian food is all the rage in Los Angeles and New York these days, and a visit to Los Andes will show you why. Think of it as high-altitude Spanish food with South American provender. Many of the meats are marinated before cooking, and many more are prepared with some version of Andean *aji* pepper, a fruity chile related to the habañero and Scotch bonnet. Some culinary historians suggest that *ceviche* originated in Peru. The fruity, spicy version at Los Andes consistently wins over diners who don't otherwise like fish. If you're undecided, just order the mixed grill (*parillada de los andes*), which comes with rice, cheese, and yuca—or any of the specials. Be on the lookout for the frequent special, *arroz con pato*—a rice plate with duck confit and roasted duck breast finished in a mango-vodka glaze.

Louis Restaurant, 286 Brook St., College Hill, Providence, RI 02906; (401) 861-5225; louisrestaurant.org; Casual American; $. Opened just after World War II, Louis has become a breakfast institution on College Hill, catching both the early risers and those who've been out all night. (It opens at 5 a.m., closes after lunch at 3 p.m.) Fruit-filled pancakes are one of the morning specials, with flavors changing with the seasons. (It's worth visiting in the fall for the pumpkin pancakes, or so the regulars say.) This is American comfort food, mixing culinary traditions willy-nilly. One of the lunch specialties, for example, is the barbecued chicken cheese ravioli topped with marinara sauce. A limited selection of wine and beer is also available, but most regulars savor the bottomless cup of coffee.

Mi Ranchito Restaurant, 1516 Westminster St., West End, Providence, RI 02909; (401) 331-6584; Guatemalan; $. A bilingual public school teacher who moonlights as a *barista* steered us to this place that is popular with her students and their families. Sure enough, when we arrived, almost every table was filled with Spanish speakers who were talking and laughing as they ate plates of *carne adobada* (marinated park) with rice and beans, chicken or beef fajitas, and fried red snapper. Servings, by the way, are very generous, so be careful not to fill up on the chips, salsa, and much-praised guacamole.

Mill's Tavern, 101 N. Main St., East Side, Providence, RI 02903; (401) 272-3331; millstavernrestaurant.com; New American; $$. The old-fashioned tavern setting of oak-paneled circular booths with leather upholstery hardly prepares an unsuspecting diner for the sharply focused contemporary cooking by Chef Edward Bolus. The wood-burning oven supplies plates like roast duck over Himalayan red rice or local rabbit braised with stone fruits. Bolus always has stovetop dishes on tap as well, including variants of seared scallops, pasta with fresh vegetables, and pan-roasted Scottish Atlantic salmon. A bargain prix-fixe menu is offered daily.

Newport Creamery, 673 Smith Ave., Smith Hill, Providence, RI 02908; (401) 351-4677; newportcreamery.com; Casual American; $. Is it written into the Rhode Island zoning laws that every neighborhood must have a Newport Creamery? It sometimes seems that way. Like its siblings, this one does a fine job with family-pleasing soups, salads, sandwiches—and great ice cream.

New Rivers, 7 Steeple St., East Side, Providence, RI 02903; (401) 751-0350; newriversrestaurant.com; New American; $$–$$$. This pioneer in New American dining (founded in 1990) passed to a second generation of owners in 2012 when longtime sous chef Beau Vestal and cook Elizabeth LaMantia took over from Pat Tillinghast. The focus on local flavors didn't miss a beat in the transition, as Vestal had long ago assumed most of the charcuterie and butchering duties. He even makes his own *lardo* from local pigs, serving it with olive oil, a garlic crostino, and roasted cherry tomatoes. New Rivers remains one of the best places in Rhode Island to order the chicken—a mustard- and lemon-infused half bird served with pickled red onion and fennel, crispy bacon, a lemon pan sauce, and fingerling potatoes cooked in duck fat. (Our knees go weak just thinking about it.)

Nick's on Broadway, 500 Broadway, Federal Hill, Providence, RI 02909; (401) 421-0286; nicksonbroadway.com; New American; $$–$$$. Compact and stylish, Nick's gets slammed at weekend  brunch (no reservations), but fans don't mind standing in line for homemade sausages and house-cured bacon, or eggs Benedict on house-baked buttermilk biscuits. Dinner is so local that the menu tells you the pedigree of every vegetable and all but the maiden name of the lemon-roasted chicken. House charcuterie also figures prominently at dinner. The 4-course tasting dinner is a bargain, as are wine pairings. Nick's enthusiastic preparations of good local foods make dining a kind of celebration.

Olneyville New York System, 20 Plainfield St., Olneyville, Providence, RI 02909; (401) 621-9500; olneyvillenewyorksystem .com; Casual American; $. "When this place opened, hot dogs were a dime, coffee was 5 cents, and a movie ticket was 12 cents," the old-timer at the next stool told us the last time we took seats at the counter and ordered a couple of hot wieners. In this location since 1953, Olneyville opened in the 1930s when Greek immigrants Nicholas and Anthony Stevens split off from their relatives at **Original New York System Hot Weiners** (see p. 45). The much-lauded wieners are cooked in vegetable oil and served with mustard, onion, celery salt, and meat sauce flavored with a secret spice blend. They are still a good deal and are best accompanied by a side of french fries and a tall glass of coffee milk. For other locations in North Providence and Cranston, see p. 45 and p. 121.

Original New York System Hot Weiners, 424 Smith St., Smith Hill, Providence, RI 02908; (401) 331-5349; Casual American; $. With its great Art Deco neon sign, its tiny window above the grill for serving on the street after closing time inside, and its record of having employed David Byrne in the early 1970s pre–Talking Heads, this wiener spot has about all the pop culture cred that any one place can handle. The restaurant opened July 12, 1927, and the staff claims that any number of famous people (Louis Armstrong included) have stopped in over the years for a few late-night dogs. ONYSHW is a big proponent of the thin, small wiener made of pork and veal in a natural casing and lightly smoked like a sausage. One of the grill men scoffs at the by-the-yard sausages that some system wiener places use. "Those aren't wieners," he says. "They're hot dogs." This Smith Hill stalwart stays open until after the bars close, but shuts indoor service a half hour early. On the weekends that can be as late as 2:30 a.m.

Pane e Vino, 365 Atwells Ave., Federal Hill, Providence, RI 02903; (401) 223-2230; panevino.net; Italian; $$–$$$. Owner Joseph DeQuattro opened this fresh-market Italian spot in 2002, and it remains a favorite among knowledgeable Providence diners. The main dinner menu blends the traditions of northern Italy (especially wood-grilled meat and fish) with some of the best-loved Roman dishes like *bucatini all' amatriciana* and pasta with the anchovy-garlic-caper-olive *puttanesca* sauce. On weekdays from 5 to 7

WALK LIKE AN ITALIAN

The bakeries, shops, restaurants, and cafes on Federal Hill all exude Italian warmth and hospitality, but it can still be fun to visit with an insider who knows everybody and can expound on the fine points of the foodstuffs and cuisine. Chef Cindy Salvato leads 3-hour walking tours of some of the bakeries, wine merchants, butcher shops, and specialty food stores that give Federal Hill its Italian accent. Samples, of course, are included. For more information, see savoringrhodeisland.com. For Salvato's recipe for Pasta with Italian Tuna, Snap Peas, Lemon, and Toasted Bread Crumbs, see p. 267.

p.m., Pane e Vino offers a bargain-priced 3-course trattoria menu of Italian-American dishes like baked eggplant parmesan and penne in red sauce with sausage and a big meatball.

Parkside, 76 S. Main St., East Side, Providence, RI 02903; (401) 331-0003; parksideprovidence.com; New American; $$–$$$. One of the pioneers of Providence's rebirth as a dining destination, Parkside feels like it's always been here on the Providence riverfront, drawing the downtown business crowd at lunch and a lively dining and drinking scene in the evenings. Many of the bistro classics are available on either the lunch or dinner menus (*steak-frites*, beef bourguignonne, and even suckling pig cassoulet), but the big French Rotisol rotisserie really sets Parkside apart. Ducklings, chickens, and racks of pork ribs, and (of course) whole suckling pigs go on the spit for slow and even roasting. The crisp duck served with bourbon and sour cherry demi-glace, mashed celeriac, and crunchy green beans could make you think you're eating in the French countryside.

Potenza Ristorante & Bar, 286 Atwells Ave., Federal Hill, Providence, RI 02903; (401) 273-2652; walterpotenza.com; Italian; $$. Chef Walter Potenza was born and raised in Abruzzo, and Potenza Ristorante has one of the most purely Italian menus on Federal Hill. Although Potenza strays occasionally to specialties of the Veneto and Le Marche, most of the dishes on the menu are classically Abruzzese—representing both the rugged mountains and the bountiful shore. All the pasta is made fresh daily, and Potenza embraces Rhode Island seafood. A perfect fusion of Abruzzo and coastal New England is his *astice:* ravioli filled with lobster tail meat, topped with New Bedford scallops, and served in the lobster-cream sauce named *aurora* for its sunrise colors. With 48 hours' notice, the restaurant will also prepare a special meal of Jewish-Italian Sephardic cooking, or meals based on Italian regional specialties. Options for these meals can be found on the restaurant's website. For the chef's cooking school in Cranston, see p. 126. For Chef Potenza's recipe for **Screppelle m'busse,** see p. 261.

Providence Oyster Bar, 283 Atwells Ave., Federal Hill, Providence, RI 02903; (401) 272-8866; providence oysterbar.com; Seafood; $$. Neptune himself would feel at home in this seriously handsome bar with a good list of cocktails and martinis, a lot of modest wines by the glass, an outstanding raw bar, and popular sushi. The menu is at its best during "appy hour" (4 to 6:30 p.m.), when most of the items are finger food. Alas, so many people know this that the place tends to be packed before emptying out a bit when the dinner menu comes into effect. For the evening, you might start with the fried oysters served with corn puree and pico de gallo, then move on to roasted day-boat cod with Roma tomatoes and a garnish of shrimp.

Red Stripe, 465 Angell St., East Side, Providence, RI 02906; (401) 437-6950; redstriperestaurants.com; New American; $$. Located in the Fox Point section of the East Side, Red Stripe calls itself an American brasserie, which is another way to say "gastropub" but with more emphasis on the food. The kitchen dabbles in international cuisines with Americanized versions of paella, Portuguese fisherman's stew, and English-style stout-battered fish-and-chips. Some of the best dishes may be the most American, including meat loaf, grilled rib eye steak, and lavender-scented pressed chicken (aka "brick chicken"). Prices are reasonable and frugal diners can save even more by ordering from the sandwich corner of the menu.

Rick's Roadhouse, 370 Richmond St., Downtown, Providence, RI 02903; (401) 272-7675; ricksroadhouseri.com; Casual American/ Barbecue; $. This sister establishment to **Harry's Bar and Burger** (see p. 35) lays on the faux down-home aw-shucks a little thick, but the kitchen does a sterling job with baby back ribs and Texas-style brisket, and the smoked chicken mac and cheese is downright inspired. Seating is not quite outdoors, but close, as the garage-style doors of the restaurant roll up to let in the sunshine and fresh air. Beware: Tuesday night features karaoke.

Rue Bis, 95 South St., Downtown, Providence, RI 02903; (401) 490-9966; therue.com; Casual American; $. This breakfast and lunch spot at the edge of the Jewelry District across the street from the Children's Museum is a great place to enjoy a breakfast burrito or one the famous "colossal gooey sticky buns." Nicely priced hot sandwiches (such as roasted turkey, applewood bacon, cheddar cheese, lettuce, and mayo on a ciabatta bun) come with a choice of oven-baked (i.e., healthy) "fries" or an Asian cucumber salad. There's also a small pizza of the day and a few choices of calzones.

Rue de L'Espoir, 99 Hope St., East Side, Providence, RI 02906; (401) 751-8890; therue.com; New American; $$. This 1976 trail-blazer in serious eating manages to keep its edge year after year. Originally more French and Italian, the menu has drifted to the western side of the Atlantic with serious bistro dishes like pork shank braised in brown beer and served with bacon and mascarpone polenta, or a lamb burger with Granny Smith apple curry and feta.

Head chef Michael Koussa has been with the restaurant for more than 30 years, but his cooking never gets tired. Like the name of the establishment, it's always bright with hope.

Sakura Restaurant, 231 Wickenden St., East Side, Providence, RI 02903; (401) 331-6861; Japanese; $–$$. The college-town sushi bar meets the college-town coffeehouse in this Japanese restaurant that also serves udon noodle plates, rice plates, and a few tempura and teriyaki dishes. Sakura simplifies choices by offering a number of partially pre-selected sushi dinners, most under $20.

The Seaplane Diner, 307 Allens Ave., South Side, Providence, RI 02905; (401) 941-9547; Casual American; $. There used to be a seaplane depot across the street on this fairly desolate stretch of Allens Avenue, and nowadays there's a scale model seaplane mounted on the roof of the 1953 Jerry O'Mahony stainless steel diner. Well-maintained but never dolled up with *American Graffiti*–style faux nostalgia, the Seaplane is one of the rare diners that never lost touch with its roots. The menu calls the breakfast and lunch "homestyle," and they are—assuming your mom made her own corned beef hash at breakfast and deep-fried a veal cutlet for a veal parm sandwich at lunch. On Friday and Saturday nights the Seaplane serves dinner (including fresh roasted turkey, and on Fridays, seafood) and stays open until 4 a.m. to accommodate the post-bar crowd.

Siena, 238 Atwells Ave., Federal Hill, Providence, RI 02903; (401) 521-3311; sienari.com; Italian; $$. This first of two Sienas (the other is in East Greenwich, see p. 179) brings a northern Italian accent to Italian-American cooking—and does so at a bargain price for Tuscan dishes. Portions are large, service is efficient and professional, and dishes like the wood-grilled pork tenderloin marinated in amaretto are richly flavored and beautifully executed. There's also a nicely restrained selection of wood-grilled pizzas.

Spike's Junkyard Dogs, 485 Branch Ave., Mount Hope, Providence, RI 02904; (401) 861-6888; spikesjunkyarddogs.com; Casual American; $. Dave Drake launched Spike's on College Hill some years ago, naming it after his bulldog. His jumbo hot dogs with all manner of toppings became a big hit, and he began to franchise the shops. This was the first franchise, and now that the original is gone, it's the oldest Spike's still standing.

Spirito's Restaurant, 477 Broadway, Federal Hill, Providence, RI 02909; (401) 434-4435; spiritosrestaurant.com; Italian; $$. Located in the Italo-American Club but open to the public (except when reserved for special events), Spirito's is a hub of Italian-American social life in Providence. Anyone whose name ends in a vowel has been here for a wedding, a christening, a memorial, or a fund-raising event. Reasonably priced and generous plates of pasta with marinara or Bolognese sauce are augmented by the classic Italian-American treatments of chicken and veal (Parmesan, Milanese, and Florentine), baked and broiled seafood, and grilled steaks. Garlic bread accompanies all.

Tazza Caffe, 250 Westminster St., Downtown, Providence, RI 02903; (401) 421-3300; tazzacaffe.com; New American; $–$$. Open long hours, Tazza shows its coffee-shop roots best in the morning with espresso drinks and pastries. It morphs into a popular lunch spot, with soups, salads, and some excellent sandwiches, including the "Grilled Cheese3" with provolone, mozzarella, and taleggio on ciabatta. In the evening, most diners stop by for drinks and small plates. These range from mac and cheese with roasted garlic and mascarpone to a trio of bacon burger sliders served with Parmesan truffle fries to a bold grilled octopus salad with roasted peppers. Larger plates aspire to bistro chic (whole roasted Mediterranean branzino, prosciutto-wrapped monkfish, house-smoked duck breast), but the majority of diners stick to two or three small plates for the price of one large one. The Saturday and Sunday brunches are hugely popular, but who wouldn't like buttermilk beignets served with lemon curd and orange honey butter?

Temple, 120 Francis St., Downtown, Providence, RI 02903; (401) 919-5050; temple-downtown.com; Mediterranean; $$. When Executive Chef David Cardell wanted to overhaul this former locavore restaurant in the Renaissance Hotel, he consulted Mediterranean cooking superstar Joyce Goldstein for advice. The result is a temple of flavors from the countries surrounding the Mediterranean. Located downstairs in an edifice originally designed as a Masonic temple (hence the name), this dramatic restaurant serves some of our favorite comfort food, from a Moroccan lamb tagine with dried fruits and saffron or a Persian chicken tagine with pomegranates and walnuts, to grilled Greek chicken marinated in lemon and yogurt or grilled Block Island swordfish with a polenta cake. The mixologists at the bar are especially accomplished. Warm up for dinner with a Camel Ride: cognac, Grand Marnier, tangerine juice, and lemon juice.

Tini, 200 Washington St., Downtown; Providence, RI 02903; (401) 383-2400; thetini.com; Italian/New American; $$–$$$. Is it a cocktail bar? An *enoteca?* Or is it just a sleek little space to get the flavors of **Al Forno** (see p. 18) streamlined into a menu of a few dishes displayed nightly on the flat-screen TVs above the U-shaped white marble bar? Chef Darius Salko offers plates like short ribs and pasta, mushroom gnocchi, and seared scallops with beluga lentils. Head bartender Mat Aruda muddles the drinks and oversees a short list of wines by the glass sufficiently obscure that you've probably never tasted them before.

Trinity Brewhouse, 186 Fountain St., Downtown, Providence, RI 02905; (401) 453-2337; trinitybrewhouse.com; Casual American; $. Good burgers, good pizzas, passable barbecue, and even a surprisingly tasty vegetarian gumbo provide the sustenance necessary to soak up the fine ales brewed on the premises. Established in 1995, Trinity was one of the pioneer New England brewpubs, and over the years its brewmasters have perfected a long list of easy-quaffing beers, including a fruity but nicely crisp Rhode Island IPA and a thick and chewy Irish stout.

Union Station Brewery, 36 Exchange Terrace #2, Downtown, Providence, RI 02903; (401) 274-2739; johnharvards.com; Casual American; $–$$. Located in the handsome former Providence train station, this brewpub is part of the John Harvard group launched in Cambridge, Massachusetts. The pub dining menu may seem familiar, as it has all the pub grub classics, plus a few of the trendy variants, like lobster mac and cheese. Certain dishes (like the chicken potpie and the ale-battered fish-and-chips) are especially tasty and satisfying. The beers tend to be the easy-drinking sort, but you can't go wrong with the Providence Pale Ale.

Waterman Grille, 4 Richmond Sq., East Side, Providence, RI 02906; (401) 521-9229; watermangrille.com; New American; $$. About as far east as you can go in Providence without crossing into East Providence, this classy bar-restaurant at the Gatehouse offers a smart New American bistro menu with all the upscale comfort food you could ask for—from lobster mac and cheese to wood-fired Margherita pizza to barbecued short ribs and lobster corn fritters.

The outdoor deck is an especially nice amenity, weather permitting. A wide-ranging and reasonably priced menu of wines by the glass and craft beers in the bottle encourages grazing and sipping.

XO Cafe, 125 N. Main St., East Side, Providence, RI 02903; (401) 273-9090; xocafe.com; New American; $$–$$$. In an earlier incarnation under founder John Elkhay (also the man behind **Rick's Roadhouse,** p. 49 and **Harry's Bar & Burger,** p. 35), XO was a full-on steak house. With Executive Chef Simon Keating at the helm, XO still offers filet mignon, sirloin, and rib eye steaks with all the sauces and trimmings, but the focus is more clearly on plates that reflect New England farms and fisheries. The Aquidneck Farm meat loaf, for example, features local spinach and a melting pat of Berkshire Blue in the demi-glace. Tuna is attributed to Linda Greenlaw (the surviving sword-boat captain in *The Perfect Storm*). It's served in a sesame-seed crust with bok choy and a spicy miso broth. The wine list roams the globe and includes a number of excellent choices by the glass.

Z Bar and Grille, 244 Wickenden St., East Side, Providence, RI 02906; (401) 831-1566; New American; $$. This super-friendly bar is a fine place to quaff a few brews to slake your thirst, but the kitchen is the big surprise. The bistro menu is limited but choice, with dishes like pan-roasted sea bass with tomato and tarragon relish or rigatoni sauced with ratatouille, goat cheese, and herb pesto. Before 5 p.m., though, you'll have to settle for pastas and sandwiches, as the ovens aren't stoked until dinner service.

Zooma Trattoria, 245 Atwells Ave., Federal Hill, Providence, RI 02903; (401) 383-2002; trattoriazooma.com; Italian; $–$$. Neapolitan cuisine is no better (and no worse) than other Italian regional cuisines, but it certainly is distinctive and Zooma deserves a lot of credit for adhering closely to the traditions. We can't imagine how much Caputo "00" flour the kitchen goes through every week, since they use it for handmade pastas (spaghettini being the main exception) and to make their terrific Neapolitan-style pizzas. Those pies are baked in a tile-lined, wood-fired oven, resulting in a thin, somewhat chewy crust that rivals any we've tried in Naples. For a joint taste of Naples and Rhode Island, try the black-pepper bowtie pasta with local littleneck clams, olive oil, garlic, parsley, and a little minced hot pepper. Alas, the wine list does not retain the Neapolitan theme, with Campania represented by a single thirst-quenching Falanghina.

Specialty Stores, Markets & Producers

A-1 Restaurant Supply, 221 Admiral St., Smith Hill, Providence, RI 02908; (401) 421-7030; a1restaurantsupply.com. You could equip an entire commercial-grade kitchen from the used restaurant appliances in the huge warehouse and even commission A-1 to fabricate a custom stainless steel range hood and countertops.

But, it's worth a look even if you are only in the market for small appliances and gadgets such as bar blenders, skillets, baking or fish spatulas, pizza cutters (including a clever one with parallel blades to cut strips), or heavy-duty whisks. A-1 also sells cleaning products, including its own brand of degreaser.

Antonelli Poultry, 62 DePasquale Ave., Federal Hill, Providence, RI 02903; (401) 421-8739. Every ethnic neighborhood used to have a place like Antonelli where farmers brought their chickens, ducks, geese, quail, rabbits, and even turkeys to be slaughtered, processed, and sold. If you like to know where your meat comes from (hint: chicken does not come in plastic wrap on Styrofoam trays), then consider buying your birds here. The shop also has a wide range of eggs, making it a good spot to pick up quail eggs for decorative salads and duck eggs when you want to wow your guests. If you are so inclined, you can actually choose your live chicken and watch the process.

Blue State Coffee, 300 Thayer St., College Hill, Providence, RI 02912; (401) 383-8393; bluestatecoffee.com. Blue State offers good coffee with a conscience, appealing to an iPad-toting contingent of Brown students and faculty. All the beans are fair-traded, organic, and shade-grown, and the company principals travel to the source to meet the farmers. A cut of the profits is channeled to nonprofits in New Haven, Connecticut; Providence, R.I.; and Boston where the five stores are located in college neighborhoods. Roasts range from light to dark, and beans are roasted frequently and ground just before brewing to ensure an optimally fresh cup.

Bottles, 141 Pitman St., East Side, Providence, RI 02906; (401) 372-2030; bottlesfinewine.com. Rhode Island's liberal regulations regarding wine importing mean that the state has a mind-boggling variety of available labels. Bottles simplifies the process 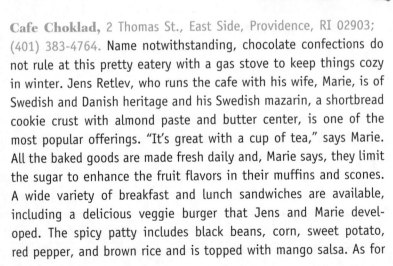 of choosing by displaying its selections by grape varietal, allowing you to weigh whether you want an Oregon pinot noir, a bargain South African pinot noir, or a real Burgundy.

Cafe Choklad, 2 Thomas St., East Side, Providence, RI 02903; (401) 383-4764. Name notwithstanding, chocolate confections do not rule at this pretty eatery with a gas stove to keep things cozy in winter. Jens Retlev, who runs the cafe with his wife, Marie, is of Swedish and Danish heritage and his Swedish mazarin, a shortbread cookie crust with almond paste and butter center, is one of the most popular offerings. "It's great with a cup of tea," says Marie. All the baked goods are made fresh daily and, Marie says, they limit the sugar to enhance the fruit flavors in their muffins and scones. A wide variety of breakfast and lunch sandwiches are available, including a delicious veggie burger that Jens and Marie developed. The spicy patty includes black beans, corn, sweet potato, red pepper, and brown rice and is topped with mango salsa. As for chocolate lovers, the shop carries Neuhaus chocolates from Belgium and "people go crazy for our brownies," says Marie.

Cafe Zog, 239 Wickenden St., East Side, Providence, RI 02906; (401) 421-2213; cafezog.com. If Phoebe had been in charge, the cast of *Friends* would have hung out at this congenial spot with a relaxed counterculture vibe, all the requisite gourmet coffee drinks and sweets (including a clever Oreo bar), and avocado and sprouts available to top any sandwich. For late risers, breakfast, including the Zog pancake special with maple syrup, walnuts, banana, and powdered confectioner's sugar, is served all day.

City Girl Cupcake, 99 Weybosset St., Downtown, Providence, RI 02911; (401) 580-1271; citygirlcupcake.com. You never know quite what to expect at City Girl, which has more than 75 cupcake flavors. "We bake every night and offer eight flavors a day," says founder Steve Smith. Those choices might include lemon, pink Champagne, lavender, chocolate coconut, or red velvet. If you can't make it to the shop, watch for the mobile cupcake carts on the streets (see p. 35).

Costantino's Venda Ravioli, 265 Atwells Ave., Federal Hill, Providence, RI 02903; (401) 421-9105; vendaravioli.com. Even in our travels to Italy, we've never encountered a food emporium as large and comprehensive as this Federal Hill landmark. In addition to the shop's own fresh and frozen pasta, you can find all the meats, cheeses, rices, and specialty oils and vinegars to make an

Italian feast at home. But cases of prepared foods—from stuffed eggplant to stuffed manicotti, cucumber salad to octopus salad— are so tempting that you may never want to cook again. There are a few tables in the deli area if you want to grab a quick sandwich (meatball, veal and peas, speck with tomato and mozzarella) and linen-topped tables if you prefer to have a server bring you a plate of ravioli or grilled sea scallops. In summer, outside tables on DePasquale Plaza are tops for people-watching. Many of the same dishes can be ordered at dinner across the plaza at Costantino's Ristorante. For Venda Ravioli's recipe for **Sweet Sausage with Spinach Penne Pasta,** see p. 263.

Crugnale Bakery, 11 Newark St., Valley, Providence, RI 02908; (401) 831-9592; crugnalebakery.com. The Valley is home base for the small network of Crugnale bakeries. The company started here in 1917 and the baking facility turns out the pizza strips, calzones, calzone loaves, breads, and pastries for all the shops. Crugnale's specialty nuggets—roll-sized pieces of dough filled with spinach and cheese, for example, or with pepperoni and cheese—are great for a quick bite. But Crugnale is probably best known for the full ring of 36 nuggets baked into a big round that can be easily pulled apart. It's great party food.

Eno, 225 Westminster St., Downtown, Providence, RI 02903; enofinewines.com. Owners Jerry and Roberta Ehrlich got the bug for the Mediterranean lifestyle when they moved their family to Tuscany in 1989. They shopped every day, which meant that the last stop before going home to cook was the *enoteca* to choose the wine. Although there's nothing the least bit rustic about this polished shop, the Ehrlich's passion for wine is evident in the range of wonderful, sometimes hard-to-find wines—as well as the bargain rack of $12 and under bottles for wine lovers on a bit of a budget.

Farmstead, 186 Wayland Ave., East Side, Providence, RI 02906; (401) 274-7177; farmsteadinc.com. "About 98 percent of our cheeses are domestic," says Thomas Perry, who often tends the cheese case in this utterly unpretentious gourmet shop. "We work directly with farms to get the best product and we are very respectful of terroir," says Perry, "but sometimes customers just want something to grate on pasta and we always carry classic European cheeses such as Parmigiano Reggiano, Manchego, and good old aged Gouda." The shop also carries a range of domestic charcuterie as well as its own pickles, jams, mustards, *mostarda,* pâtés, mousses, and scrapple, made with local pork and corn meal from **Kenyon's Grist Mill** (see p. 190). Light lunches, such as an olive oil–poached swordfish sandwich with cured olives and lemon confit, hint at the finesse of the kitchen at adjacent **La Laiterie Bistro** (see p. 38). But grilled cheese sandwiches and mac and cheese are also available.

HIGHER EDUCATION FOR THE TASTEBUDS

The College of Culinary Arts at Johnson & Wales University looms large on the Providence food scene. Each year brings an influx of eager young students who help keep the city lively. Many of those students graduate into the restaurant kitchens of Providence and the rest of New England.

For home cooks, the college offers an ambitious schedule of Chef's Choice Recreational Cooking Classes. Led by faculty members, the 3-hour classes combine demonstrations and hands-on experience and might focus on specific cuisines, such as Spanish or French, or particular foods such as pies or appetizers. Many of the classes emphasize nutrition and healthy eating, while others concentrate on seasonal foods or on preparing a knock-em-dead dinner party menu. The classes take place in the college's state-of-the-art Cuisinart Center for Culinary Excellence. Harborside Campus, Providence, RI 02905; (401) 598-2336; jwu.edu.

Gasbarro's Wine, 361 Atwells Ave., Federal Hill, Providence, RI 02903; (401) 421-4170; gasbarros.com. Antonio Gasbarro established a liquor store on Federal Hill in 1898. It's now known as Gasbarro's Wines and occupies a huge space with extensive display racks. The shop carries about 900 Italian wines (and even more wines from California), but it's also a perfect spot to buy high-end

With its displays of stoves and other appliances and exhaustive library of cookbooks and menus, the university's Culinary Arts Museum is a valuable resource for students. Many exhibits trace how both cooking and dining have evolved over the years and are equally fascinating to the general public. Anyone who has endured a cross-country flight on a bag of pretzels will be amused by the displays of menus and elegant table settings that recall the glory days of travel by train and plane. Not surprisingly in the city that was the birthplace of the lunch cart, the museum has a special interest in diners and claims to have the only permanent exhibition devoted to these uniquely American eateries. In fact, the museum houses the Ever Ready, a 1926 Worcester Lunch Car diner that last operated in Providence in 1989. It has been almost completely restored to its marble, chrome, polished wood, and tile glory. It's a far cry from the modest little Dandy Diner, also on display. Dating from 1915, this early Worcester diner features a wooden counter and 10 wobbly wooden stools. Culinary Arts Museum, 315 Harborside Blvd., Providence, RI 02905; (401) 598-2805; culinary.org.

liqueurs, grappas, and digestives, including the full selection of Poli single-varietal grappas from the Veneto.

Gourmet Heaven, 173 Weybosset St., Downtown, Providence, RI 02903; gourmetheaven.com. The salad bar at Gourmet Heaven is a favorite with downtown workers making a quick and healthy

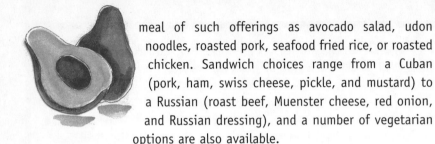

meal of such offerings as avocado salad, udon noodles, roasted pork, seafood fried rice, or roasted chicken. Sandwich choices range from a Cuban (pork, ham, swiss cheese, pickle, and mustard) to a Russian (roast beef, Muenster cheese, red onion, and Russian dressing), and a number of vegetarian options are also available.

Juniper, 229 Thayer St., College Hill, Providence, RI 02906; (401) 421-4851. Sometimes it's nice not to be confronted with too many choices when you just want a taste of something sweet. Juniper offers only three flavors of frozen yogurt: the tart original and richly fruity blueberry and strawberry. They are delicious on their own but can be enhanced with various toppings. The shop also whips up smoothies. Stick with strawberry mango—it's the most popular.

L'artisan Cafe & Bakery, 9 Wayland Square, East Side, Providence, RI 02906; (401) 331-4444. Ghassan Daou used to run a gourmet market in Montreal and has transplanted that city's chic style and international flair to this casual eatery with a great patio for outside dining. As to be expected, the bakery turns out a good croissant, while lunch and light dinner offerings run the gamut from flatbreads and baba ghanoush to chicken dumpling soup and vegetarian or Thai chicken panini. Cases along one long wall feature prepared foods—eggplant parmesan, macaroni and cheese, couscous, seafood salad—to take out or enjoy in the cafe with a glass of wine or beer.

LaSalle Bakery, 685 Admiral St., Northwest, Providence, RI 02908; (401) 228-0081; and 993 Smith St., Northwest, Providence, RI 02908; (401) 831-9563; lasallebakery.net. Open and airy spaces with cafe tables and stools and counters in the windows invite lingering. Regulars stop in for a pumpkin raisin muffin or blueberry scone for breakfast, a chicken potpie or spinach and feta croissant for lunch, or a lemon crème tart or pistachio cannoli for a late afternoon pick-up. Beautiful breads are baked with either crunchy or soft crusts, and sweets range from éclairs and nut bars to fruit tarts and cupcakes. The Elvis, for example, is a chocolate cupcake with peanut butter filling, banana buttercream topping, and toasted coconut garnish.

Meeting Street Cafe, 220 Meeting St., East Side, Providence, RI 02912; (401) 273-1066; meetingstreetcafe.com. Order at the counter and the staff brings soups, salads, and sandwiches. The cookies are such a hit with Brown students that the cafe sells eight varieties by mail order: chocolate chunk, peanut butter, oatmeal raisin, plain sugar, macadamia white chocolate, ginger spice, chewy chocolate, and a concoction the cafe calls "garbage" (coconut, oats, raisins, pecans, walnuts, almonds, and white, milk, and dark chocolate).

Nancy's Fancies Cakes, 294 Atwells Ave., Federal Hill, Providence, RI 02903; (401) 421-2253; nancysfanciescakes.com. Like all Federal Hill bakeries, Nancy's offers cannoli, but the shop really excels at gourmet cupcakes. Examples of flavor combinations, such as Oreo cheesecake, lemon meringue, and coconut dream, are on display just to spark your imagination. Select your favorite flavor of cake, filling, frosting, and topping, and watch as a custom cupcake is created before your eyes.

Palmieri's Bakery & Caffè, 64 DePasquale Ave., Federal Hill, Providence, RI 02903, (401) 861-2253; and 147 Ridge St., Federal Hill, Providence, RI 02909, (401) 831-9145. For a sense of history, seek out the Ridge Street "original" location of this bakery, established in 1901. It's a great place to enjoy a tomato, egg, and cheese sandwich for breakfast or a tuna melt or spinach pie for lunch. For a cannoli or almond cream tart with an espresso, try the cozy cafe on DePasquale Plaza in the heart of Federal Hill.

Panadería Maya, 113 Valley St., Olneyville, Providence, RI 02907; (401) 831-3326. In addition to breads and a variety of simple, not-too-sweet cookies, Maya offers filling and reasonably priced lunch fare such as chicken or plantain tamales and crunchy, rolled tacos filled with beef. Fried empanadas filled with pastry cream make a rich dessert, though neighborhood children prefer the chocolate-covered bananas on a stick. A refrigerator case holds chorizo, tortillas, cheeses, and Jarritos sodas from Mexico in such flavors as tamarind, mango, and lime.

Pastiche Fine Desserts Cafe, 92 Spruce St., Federal Hill, Providence, RI 02903; (401) 861-5190; pastichefinedesserts.com. Dessert fads may come and go, but Pastiche has maintained its focus on beautiful cakes and tarts for more than 25 years. If you're lucky, you might get a table by the fireplace in the winter to warm up with a cup of tea and a slice of lemon velvet or chocolate mousse cake, banana cream tart, or all-American chocolate layer cake. Or opt for a chocolate peanut butter brownie, apricot scone, or butterscotch crumb cake. Cakes that will serve four to 12 people are readily available; larger cakes require advance order.

risd|works, 20 N. Main St., East Side, Providence, RI 02903; (401) 277-4949; risdworks.com. This shop in the lower level of the RISD Museum features objects designed and/or made by alumni and faculty of the Rhode Island School of Design. A number of those talents have turned their attention to the kitchen and table with products that make food preparation easier (the Kaposi fruit and vegetable chopper) or simply more fun (a porcupine-shaped vegetable brush, crocodile tongs, or mouse cheese grater). Beautiful wooden cheeseboards, ceramic bowls, and wine and tea glasses make any meal more elegant.

Roma (Trattoria Roma and the Original Roma Marketplace),
310 Atwells Ave., Federal Hill, Providence, RI 02903; (401) 331-5000; romaprov.com. You can easily stock your pantry with the nice selection of Italian cheeses, dried pastas, olive oils, canned tomatoes, and other imports at Roma. But the prepared foods are also a big draw, including arancini, eggplant parm, and big meatballs of ground veal, pork, and beef. At lunch time Roma does a big business in cold and hot subs, cal-zones, and delicious brick-oven pizza. In the evening (Tuesday through Saturday) and Sunday afternoon, the same kitchen offers trattoria service at tables in an adjoining room. "It's mostly the classics," says Chef-Owner Dominic Ierfino. "You can have a nice osso bucco, a risotto, or maybe some grilled sea scallops on arugula." For Ierfino's recipe for **Spaghetti alle Vongole,** see p. 257.

Scialo Bros. Bakery, 257 Atwells Ave., Federal Hill, Providence, RI 02903; (401) 421-0986; scialobakery.com. This family-run bakery was founded in 1916 and still relies on brick ovens that were installed in the 1920s. Scialo is best known for its Italian cakes, which might range from a fairly simple butter rum cake to an elaborate cassata cake featuring sponge cake soaked in orange liqueur, layered with chocolate pastry cream and ricotta cream and

A Doughnut for St. Joseph

Sicily and Naples alike observe the same tradition of making a special pastry for the feast of St. Joesph (March 19). Called *zeppole*, or St. Joseph's cakes, they are deep-fried dough balls topped with powdered sugar and often filled with egg custard or white pastry cream. Although they were once reserved for the feast day, *zeppole* are often available in Italian bakeries throughout Providence at all times of the year.

topped with marzipan. The same ricotta cream is used to fill the cannoli shells that are fried upstairs. They are filled to order as "cannoli filling only lasts 6 hours before it makes the shell soggy," according to counter clerk Alana Grayson. One of our favorite simple snacks is the Karla cookie of shortbread encasing lemon or strawberry preserves.

Seven Stars Bakery, 820 Hope St., East Side, Providence, RI 02906; and 342 Broadway, Federal Hill, Providence, RI 02909; (401) 521-2200; sevenstarsbakery.com. Lynn and Jim Williams opened their bakery in a renovated garage on Hope Street in 2001. The couple now has three locations (including one in East Providence, see p. 158) and an off-site baking facility in Pawtucket, but still puts the same amount of care into each item that comes out of the ovens. Breads, including the immensely popular olive loaf with Kalamata and Moroccan olives, are made with a process of long fermentation for extra flavor and longer freshness. The same process enhances the Danish pastries and croissants, though we devour the inspired chocolate almond croissants so quickly that they never have a chance to get stale. Though the baking process may be different, cookies, bars, muffins, and scones all adhere to the same high standards. For a recipe for Seven Stars' **Blueberry Turnovers,** see p. 254.

Silver Star Bakery, 150 Ives St., East Side, Providence, RI 02906; (401) 421-8013. You can pick up Portuguese rolls and sweet breads in this small shop, but be sure to try one of the huge Portuguese popovers. "They're like a doughnut, but more eggy and airy with glazed sugar on top," explained the young woman behind the counter. Split one for dessert after a chicken- or meat-filled empanada.

Sin, 200 Allens Ave., Studio #2, South Side, Providence RI 02903; (401) 369-8427; eatwicked.com. Sin makes cakes for special occasions, and we can imagine that it seems like a wonderful joke to order a wedding cake from a place called Sin. But Jennifer Luxmoore and her staff are serious about their sweets, using topnotch ingredients and just enough sugar to enhance the other flavors. The baking facility in a brick building in an industrial part of town also has a small retail shop where you get an idea of Sin's style by trying a cupcake shot. "It's just one little bite, when you don't want to feel so, so guilty," says office manager Jeanne Paradiso. In fact, it will leave you plenty of room to try a lemon or lime sugar cookie, a fudgy brownie, or the shop's signature chipotle peanut butter cookie. That same chipotle also adds a bit of heat to the popular cheddar-bacon scones. For the recipe for **Sin's Brownies,** see p. 271.

Taquería El Taconazo, 500 Valley St., Valley, Providence, RI 02908; (401) 437-8808. A former roving food truck, Taconazo has found a permanent home in an industrial strip that hosts a weekend flea market. The corrugated metal building is painted the green, red, and white of the Mexican flag, and the tiny kitchen turns out all manner of tacos and *sopes* (small, soft corn tortillas with meat, onions, and cilantro, or with meat, beans, lettuce, onion, cheese, and sour cream, respectively). Meat choices include ground beef, chicken, pig's ears, beef tongue, goat, spicy pork skin, hot sausage, and chopped pork with pineapple (*pastor*). The same meats also fill gorditas, burritos, *huaraches,* tostadas, and enchiladas. On weekends, El Taconazo also serves a shrimp cocktail of shrimp and salsa in a tall glass, and slow-roasted chile-spiced *carne asada* as a dinner plate with rice, beans, lettuce, avocado, tomatoes, and tortillas. This is about as close to great Mexican street food as you can get in Rhode Island.

Tony's Colonial Food Store, 311 Atwells Ave., Federal Hill, Providence, RI 02903; (401) 621-8675; tonyscolonial.com. Tony DiCiccio left southern Italy for Providence in 1955 but never lost his taste for the foods of home. "Ninety-five percent of the items in the shop are from Italy," he says, including

cheeses, dried pastas, olive oils, vinegars, and a variety of cold cuts. Many people stop in at lunch for an eggplant parmesan or assorted cold cut and cheese grinder and perhaps leave with minestrone soup, a potato frittata, or a serving of veal and peas for dinner. Housewares, including ravioli makers, pasta cutters, espresso pots, and cheese graters share the shelves with their companion food products.

Virginia & Spanish Peanut Co., 260 Dexter St., West End, Providence, RI 02907; (401) 421-2543; vspnutco.com. This old-time nut roaster was established in 1913 by Peter S. Kaloostian. Today it's run by grandsons Peter and Robert and great-granddaughters Candace, Shelley, and Ellen. The roastery and packaging plant produces Black Bear peanut butter and snack bags of Black Bear peanuts—probably their most widely known product line. But the company extends far beyond peanuts, as it either makes or distributes all manner of nuts, bakery, and confectionery items as well as supplies for cotton candy, candy apple, and sno-cone concessions. The factory business office even functions as a mini-store for the products. The office is open weekdays all year, as well as Sat mornings Oct through Dec.

Wayland Square Fine Wine & Spirits, 210 Wayland Ave., East Side, Providence, RI 02906; (401) 351-9463; waylandwines .com. Bob Russell owns and operates this fine wine store, and what he might lack in exhaustive offerings, he makes up for by having a well-curated selection of well-priced wines. Russell encourages browsing and knows when to offer advice, and when to let you make your own mistakes.

White Electric Coffee, 711 Westminster St., West End, Providence, RI 02903; (401) 453-3007; whiteelectriccoffee.com. You can get a coffee milk here (made the same as everywhere, with supermarket syrup and milk), but the strength is espresso that, as they used to say, puts hair on your chest. It's rich and dark and creamy—and it tastes like coffee because the beans are both freshly roasted and freshly ground. Add some good sandwiches at lunch (sliced turkey on a croissant) and excellent pastries to stretch the espresso experience, and the combination equals just about the perfect coffee shop. Too bad it closes at 6:30 p.m. weekdays, 5 p.m. on weekends.

Whole Foods Market, 261 Waterman St., Providence, RI 02906; (401) 272-1690; and 601 N. Main St., University Heights

Marketplace, Providence, RI 02904; (401) 621-5990; wholefoods market.com. **Both locations are full-size versions of the Texas-based natural food market chain.**

Farmers' Markets

Broad Street Farmers' Market, 807 Broad St. Sat from 9 a.m. to noon, July through Oct.

Brown University Farmers' Market, Wriston Quad, corner of George and Thayer Streets. Mon from 11 a.m. to 2 p.m., Sept and Oct.

Capitol Hill Farmers' Market, 1 Capitol Hill, across from State House. Thurs from 11 a.m. to 2 p.m., July through Oct.

Davis Park Farmers' Market, corner Chalkstone and Oakland Streets. Sun from 10 a.m. to 1 p.m., Sept and Oct.

Fruit Hill Farmers' Market at RIC, RIC Old Alumni House lawn, Fruit Hill Avenue. Thurs from 3:30 to 6 p.m., Aug through Oct.

Hope Street Farmers' Market, Lippitt Park, 1059 Hope St. Sat from 9 a.m. to 1 p.m., June through Oct.

Hope Street Farmers' Market II, Lippitt Park, 1059 Hope St. Wed from 3 to 6 p.m., June through Oct.

Kennedy Plaza Farmers' Market, Washington Street along Burnside Park. Fri from 11 a.m. to 2 p.m., June through Oct.

Neutaconkanut Park Farmers' Market, Plainfield Street. Mon from 3 to 6 p.m., July through Oct.

Parade Street Farmers' Market, Cranston Street Armory, Parade and Hudson Streets. Thurs from 3 to 7 p.m., June through Oct.

Ship Street Farmers' Market, Brown Medical School, corner Ship and Richmond Streets. Tues from 11:30 a.m. to 2 p.m., April through Oct.

Whole Foods University Heights Farmers' Market, 601 N. Main St. Mon from 3 p.m. to dusk, May through Oct.

Wickenden Street Farmers' Market, 65 Brook St. Tues from 2 to 6 p.m., June through Oct.

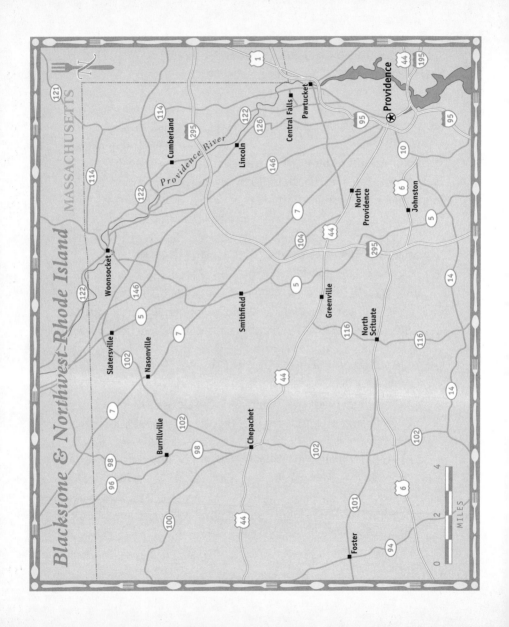
Blackstone & Northwest—Rhode Island

Blackstone Valley & Northwest Rhode Island

This chapter marries the old mill towns of the Blackstone River Valley with the open farmland and orchards of northwest Rhode Island. It is the only region in this book that does not touch upon the ocean.

America's version of the Industrial Revolution was born in Pawtucket in the Blackstone Valley. The river and its adjunct canals powered great manufacturing enterprises through most of the 19th century. Those red-brick mill towns have proven to be enduring magnets for immigration, beginning with the Irish and French-speaking Canadians in the mid-19th century, the Italians in the late 19th century, through to today's influx of Spanish speakers from Central and South America. Each wave of immigrants has left a mark on the gastronomy of northern Rhode Island, which makes this region especially interesting to broad-minded foodies. In addition to Italian-American cooking that is ubiquitous in Rhode Island, Hispanic cooking has come to the forefront—from the taco culture of Mexican street food to the more sophisticated Spanish-oriented food of Colombia.

Dining in this area is fascinating. You can find a good meal in traditional mid-20th century diner cars, in downtown lunch joints that have held on long after the mills closed, and in modest but often excellent restaurants found, of all places, in strip malls.

As you proceed west of I-295, the land opens up into broad fields often rimmed by old stone walls. This was Rhode Island's first orchard country. Indeed, a sign on Route 116 at the border of North Scituate and Smithfield calls the latter "Appleland," while pointing out that it was established in 1730. The area branched out into other crops—peaches, nectarines, pears, berries, vegetables. Although the fickle climate remains something of a challenge for viticulture, the region even boasts a few of the state's wineries.

Foodie Faves

Andrew's Bistro, 3755 Mendon Rd., Cumberland, RI 02864; (401) 658-1515; andrewsbistro.com; Italian; $$. Don't be put off by the tired strip mall—once you're inside Andrew's, all that asphalt and snarled traffic fades away. Calling the restaurant a bistro doesn't make it French, but we assume that owners Carl Amaral and Chris

Lopes wanted to emphasize a casual informality. It's a warm and welcoming place, and the extensive menu treads the line between a steak house and an Italian-American classic restaurant akin to those found on Federal Hill in Providence. All the Rhody favorites can be found among the appetizers, including fried calamari with hot pepper rings, clams casino with generous strips of bacon, and clams *zuppa* (red or white). There are also new twists on retro dishes, like a wedge of iceberg lettuce with diced tomatoes, bacon, and olives.

Bon Asian Bistro & Hibachi Grill, 1386 Atwood Ave., Johnston, RI 02919; (401) 270-0777; bonasianbistro.com; Asian; $-$$ for dining room, $$-$$$ for hibachi room. With black walls and woodwork, red upholstery and a few blue-lit Buddhas, this immense restaurant in a Johnston strip mall cannot help but impress with its stylized drama. Serving a mash-up of Thai, Chinese, and Japanese food, Bon offers a wide range of classic sushi rolls and an even wider range of its own inventions made to order. The Godzilla roll, for example, has spicy crab, avocado, and tempura flakes wrapped in eel and finished with eel sauce. Teriyaki plates and stir-fried wok combinations are popular (they're very inexpensive at lunch), but for sheer theatricality and a big night out, book seats at one of the hibachi tables where a cook prepares your dinner as

KA-BOOM!

Just when you think that you've gotten a handle on Rhode Island's many food specialties, you discover that there are some regional ones as well. Woonsocket appears to be the birthplace of the dynamite sandwich, a mix of long-simmered ground beef, green peppers, onions, and tomatoes that's served in a long sandwich roll. Like many food specialties, the origins of the dynamite are murky, but it seems to have first appeared in the 1920s among the immigrants from French Canada who worked in Woonsocket's mills. Of course, every cook adds his or her own spices and other ingredients to the basic recipe. At Castle Luncheonette, cooks add celery to the mix and make about 200 pounds a week. Castle is perhaps the best-known place to try a dynamite sandwich, though they also serve the mixture on hot dogs, hamburgers, or spaghetti. You can also find dynamites at Moonlight House of Weiners, which usually has an all-you-can-eat dynamite special one night per week. Old-timers in the Pawtuxet Valley also sometimes call a dynamite a "torpedo," a term some Rhode Islanders otherwise reserve for a cold cut and cheese sandwich on a long roll, aka a "sub" or "grinder."

Castle Luncheonette, 420 Social St., Woonsocket, RI 02895; (401) 762-5424; Casual American; $.

Moonlight House of Weiners, 32 Rathbun St., Woonsocket, RI 02895; (401) 766-5806; Casual American; $.

you watch. As an extra kick for the family, Bon offers a children's hibachi menu as well.

Chan's Fine Oriental Dining, 267 Main St., Woonsocket, RI 02895; (401) 765-1900; chanseggrollsandjazz.com; Chinese; $. The Chan clan has been serving Chinese food in Woonsocket since 1905, and has occupied this vast space that encompasses both a Chinese restaurant and a 150-seat jazz and blues club since 1965. John Chan, who's run the operation for more than 25 years, refers to Chan's as "the home of eggroll, jazz, and blues." Concert-goers have to settle for the buffet, but regular diners can order off an extensive menu of very inexpensive Chinese-American fare. Some Rhode Islanders consider Chan's the standard-bearer of Chinese food in the state; others skip the meals in favor of drinks and the show.

Cherri's State Line Diner, 195 Danielson Pike, Foster, RI 02825; (401) 647-9800; Casual American; $. True to its name, this old-fashioned roadside diner sits between the Welcome to Connecticut and Welcome to Rhode Island signs on Route 6. The original 1953 Worcester Lunch Car Company diner was narrow with unusual vertical paneling on the exterior. Over the years a back room with pine paneling and an ice cream take-out window have been added. Current owners are more focused on providing basic breakfast and lunch fare (the usual egg and sandwich suspects) than on the history of the diner, per se. Still, aficionados stop in for a meal—or one of the homemade muffins or a slice of homemade pie—just to get a gander at a style of Worcester diner unusual even in New England.

Connie & Nikki's Restaurant and Creamery, 526 Pawtucket Ave., Pawtucket, RI 02860; (401) 725-2540; Casual American; $. This little box of a building looks even smaller from the outside than it does inside. As a convenience, it features a take-out window, but if you indulge in the drive-through, you'll miss the virtual Coca-Cola museum inside. Every flat surface and wall is covered with a Coke plaque, advertising, or other bit of memorabilia. The fact that everything is spic-and-span clean saves it from becoming a candidate for A&E's *Hoarders*. Chocolate chip pancakes, three-egg omelets with home fries, and apple cinnamon muffins are some of the most popular breakfast choices, while lunch features homey comfort dishes like a meat loaf sandwich, tuna melt, spaghetti and meatballs, and, of course, burgers. And, no, Connie & Nikki's doesn't serve Pepsi products.

Country Chowder Shack, 659 Hartford Pike, North Scituate, RI 02857; (401) 934-2044; thechowdershack.com; Seafood; $. For more than 40 years this roadside clam shack in the Rhode Island countryside far from the shore has been giving inlanders their fix of Rhode Island–style clamcakes and a choice of red or white clam chowder. The menu is a little broader than that, but not much, offering fish-and-chips, fried squid rings with hot peppers, and fried strip or whole clams. Hot dogs and smaller wieners are available for folks who don't like fish, and full dinners feature fried smelts, fried scallops, fried shrimp, and lobster or seafood salad rolls. Dining is at outdoor picnic tables, and when the fish is gone, you can get ice cream for dessert. The shack is open from late March through Oct (later if the weather is warm).

Cucina & The Grille, 900 Victory Hwy., Slatersville, RI 02876; (401) 767-2444; marrarestaurantgroup.com; Italian; $–$$. Steve Marra didn't become so successful (six restaurants and counting) without understanding what people want. One kitchen serves these side-by-side restaurants. The Grille has casual fare such as grilled pizzas, wraps, burgers, nachos, and fried calamari. Cucina, on the other hand, is a fine-dining spot with a menu of veal and chicken plates, Italian takes on steak (with sautéed mushrooms or with hot pepper rings), and good basic pasta with house "gravy" with either meatballs or sausages. Italian-American seafood plates (linguine with clams, shrimp scampi, and the like) are also available. Portions are large, prices are low, and no one goes away hungry.

d carlo trattoria, 970 Douglas Pike, Smithfield, RI 02917; (401) 349-4979; dcarlotrattoria.net; Italian; $$. Surprisingly warm and cozy for a strip-mall restaurant, d carlo has serious ambitions as a fine-dining real Italian (not Italian-American) restaurant. Dishes like the pan-seared yellowfin tuna with zucchini fritters and roasted tomato aioli would be right at home on the Italian Riviera. Braised beef short ribs with a sesame-ginger twist to the spicing highlight Executive Chef Chris Kattawar's willingness to depart a little from classic Italian cooking to simply make the best dish possible. For those who just yearn for Nonna's cooking, d carlo does offer chicken or veal parmesan. The dessert menu is extensive, always featuring a fruit dish and a chocolate dish. Of course, half the diners order the addictive tiramisu.

Doherty's East Avenue Irish Pub, 342 East Ave., Pawtucket, RI 02860; (401) 725-9520; dohertys.com; Casual American; $–$$. Perhaps the Providence area's premier craft beer pub, Doherty's always has 82 brews on tap, available by the glass, the pint, or in flights of four or six 5-ounce glasses. Another 50-some are available in the bottle. The food menu is almost as broad and as international, ranging from burgers and sandwiches to Mexican-American plates, to old pub standards like mac and cheese and shepherd's pie. On weekends, Doherty's offers an especially popular brunch that features sweet plates like french toast (and vegan pancakes), all the egg classics, tofu scrambles, and a super plate of spicy Cajun roasted pork. Brunchers can also order the same sandwiches (including pulled pork braised in Murphy's Irish Stout) as evening patrons. For brunch-time imbibers, Doherty's offers the 32-ounce Champagne mimosa and the refreshing beer-mosa of Hoegaarden with a splash of orange juice and a slice of orange.

El Antojo Restaurante & Panadería, 494 Dexter St., Central Falls, RI 02863; (401) 726-6091; Colombian; $. The bakery cases full of breads and pastries could throw you off, but El Antojo is a full-service Colombian restaurant serving from morning through early evening. Locals swear by the sweet corn arepas with melted cheese, with or without accompanying scrambled eggs or bits of fried beef. For an authentic taste of the Colombian countryside, order the plantain soup with meatballs and rice. Cash only.

El Paisa Restaurant, 598 Dexter St., Central Falls, RI 02863; (401) 726-8864; elpaisa.com; Colombian; $–$$. Cesar and Donatila Zuleta have carried the torch for Colombian cooking in Central Falls since they took over El Paisa in 1978. The gigantic plates of grilled meats (*churrasco*) are famous in the local Spanish-speaking community and are perhaps the best introduction to the cuisine. Other dishes such as *mondongo* (tripe stew) and the *chicharónes* are authentic, but they are acquired tastes. The *chicharónes* are a far cry from the fried pork rinds that go by the same name in Mexico. In Colombia, they are made by rubbing the skin of pork belly with baking soda, chopping it into bite-sized pieces, then slowly rendering out the fat in a little water before allowing the meat to deep-fry in the rendered fat. The whole fried fish (*mojarra frita*) makes a slightly lighter meal, as it comes with salad and an arepa.

ENN Japanese Cuisine & Sushi Bar, 600 George Washington Hwy., Lincoln, RI 02865; (401) 333-0366; ennri.com; Japanese; $–$$$. Located out on a highway in a former auto dealership, ENN still somehow manages to cultivate a serene, very Japanese ambience once you're in the door. One of the owners is a sushi chef, while his wife often serves tables. The sushi selection is extensive, and ENN occasionally gets in giant clam or some top tuna belly (*chu* or *o-toro*)—delicacies not usual in a suburban Japanese restaurant. Many of the dishes, like the tuna belly, are market priced since they involve ingredients that fluctuate with the season, including Washugyu (American-raised Kobe-Angus-Wagyu-cross beef). Tempura and teriyaki plates are also available, but most fans of ENN prefer the sushi and sashimi combos.

Georgia's Family Restaurant, 915 Dexter St., Central Falls, RI 02863; (401) 722-7030; Casual American; $. If you want to get to know everybody in Central Falls, eat breakfast and lunch at Georgia's, where the burgers are still modest 5-ounce patties with modest prices, the egg salad oozes from the edges of a bulky roll, and all the conventional diner dinner plates (meat loaf, grilled pork chops, ham steak, open-faced turkey sandwich) are available at lunch. At breakfast (the only menu served on weekends), you can order your omelet stuffed with *linguiça,* kielbasa, pepperoni, or all three.

Jacky's Galaxie, 1764 Mendon Rd., Cumberland, RI 02864; (401) 333-4700; 449 Mineral Spring Ave., North Providence, RI 02860; (401) 354-4570; and 1 Commerce Way, Johnston, RI 02919; (401) 276-0688; jackysgalaxie.com; Asian; $–$$. Jacky Ko keeps spreading the gospel of pan-Asian dining in Rhode Island. This

Cumberland spot is comparable to his Bristol location (see p. 147). It, too, offers a good sushi bar, Asian-themed banquet rooms, and cooked menu that encompasses almost every Japanese, Thai, Vietnamese, or Chinese dish ever served in Rhode Island. The North Providence and Johnston locations have essentially the same menus but are somewhat smaller operations. For a more glamorous version of the same kind of cooking, see the related **Jacky's Waterplace** in Providence (see p. 37).

LJ's BBQ, 727 East Ave., Pawtucket, RI 02860; (401) 305-5255; ljsbbq.com; Barbecue; $–$$. Serving lunch and dinner (and brunch on the weekends), LJ's has overcome its spotty location in a Pawtucket neighborhood mall to gain a devoted following in the Providence metro area. In no small part, this is due to the popularity of the LJ's BBQ food truck that has a knack for showing up outside a bar right at closing or for finding a place to park near an outdoor music event. But if you eat only from the truck you miss the fun of bourbon flights at the bar. To sample the pitmasters' style, order the Real Deal Combo of sweet and saucy pulled pork, smoked Texas-style beef brisket, a half rack of St. Louis ribs, and a dark-meat barbecued chicken quarter.

La Cucina, 266 Putnam Pike, Smithfield, RI 02917; (401) 349-4130; lacucinari.com; Italian/Casual American; $$–$$$. Yet another ambitious restaurant tucked into a strip mall, La Cucina has feet in two worlds. On one hand, it has a lively bar section where many patrons prefer to dine, yet it also boasts a large and quite romantic dining room. The bar area sees a lot of traffic for breakfast and lunch. Breakfast is American fare like pancakes and egg dishes; lunch gets into sandwiches and Italian-American dishes like a big meatball with ricotta and tomato sauce, *pasta e fagioli,* eggplant parmesan, and linguine with red or white clam sauce. The dinner menu has a more Italian mien, with a number of grilled vegetable and meat dishes, including a plump veal chop stuffed with spinach, prosciutto, and Fontina cheese.

Modern Diner, 364 East Ave., Pawtucket, RI 02860; (401) 726-8390; Casual American; $. This 1941 Sterling Streamliner was the first diner ever listed on the National Register of Historic Places, and it's deserving of the honor. It was moved to its current site in the 1980s when downtown Pawtucket was in the throes of "urban renewal," and despite the fact that many people have to navigate illogical one-way streets to get here, the Modern is packed for breakfast and lunch. There's a standard menu of diner classics (burgers, chili, meat loaf, sandwiches, and all the eggs, pancakes, and french toast variations) but on weekends everyone orders from the handwritten specials. That might include pesto-cheese grits with eggs and home fries; an omelet with Canadian bacon, apple, and brie; or a Benedict of poached eggs on Portuguese muffins topped with *chouriço* patties and hollandaise. The diner is known for the "jimmie gimmie," a Pawtucket variant of eggs Benedict that includes two poached eggs on English muffins topped with melted cheese and bacon and served with home fries (no hollandaise).

New York Lunch, Inc., 8½ Main St., Woonsocket, RI 02895; (401) 762-9619; Casual American; $. "We're a landmark," says Joan Dupont, who runs New York Lunch with her husband John. To prove it, she points to a 1907 photograph of downtown Woonsocket that clearly shows the classic lunch counter with an earlier incarnation of a Coca-Cola sign out front. John's father bought the eatery in 1951 and now John is the keeper of the secret recipe for the meat sauce for New York System wieners. "Everyone has to get out of the kitchen when I make it," he says only half in jest. A handpainted menu board from the 1960s hangs in a side dining room for the overflow crowd. "We still serve the same food that we've had all along," says Joan. In addition to wieners, that includes other grill staples such as egg sandwiches, burgers, a tuna melt, a BLT, and the humble grilled cheese and tomato.

Newport Creamery, 568 Putnam Pike, Smithfield, RI 02828; (401) 949-2122; newportcreamery.com; Casual American; $. From modest beginnings in Middletown (see p. 236), Newport Creamery has taken its menu of family-pleasing soups, salads, sandwiches—and great ice cream—across the state. This Smithfield location is something of an anomaly, as it is built of tan brick (not red brick) and stands alone rather than being part of a shopping mall.

BLACKSTONE CULINARIA

What a great idea! Every week the Blackstone Valley Tourism Council organizes a tour to one of the region's ethnic restaurants or other dining establishments. Participants enjoy a cooking demonstration, usually followed by a meal. For information on Blackstone Culinaria and a schedule of upcoming events, check blackstoneculinaria.com or call (401) 724-2200.

Olneyville New York System, 1744 Mineral Spring Ave., North Providence, RI 02904; (401) 383-4155; olneyvillenewyorksystem .com; Casual American; $. The newest branch of this king of wie-nerdom is located on a hillside in a strip mall where you take your life in your hands driving in and out because there is no light and traffic whizzes past. Maybe that's why it has a drive-through window—for wiener fans who like living dangerously (as if eating a fried wiener weren't dangerous enough). For the original in the Olneyville section of Providence, see p. 44.

Patriots Diner, 65 Fountain Dr., Woonsocket, RI 02895; (401) 765-6900; patriotsdiner.com; Casual American; $. The chrome on the exterior is so shiny that we guessed right away that Patriots must be a modern replica of a dining car. Sure enough, it opened in 2006 as a squeaky-clean version of a classic greasy spoon. The menu hits all the right notes with breakfast all day, lots of burgers, hot open-faced turkey and roast beef sandwiches, fried fish, and a few Greek and Italian specialties. Open 24 hours.

Rasoi, 727 East Ave., Pawtucket, RI 02860; (401) 728-5500; rasoi-restaurant.com; Indian; $–$$. Located in the Blackstone Place mall next to **LJ'S BBQ** (see p. 87), this handsome Indian restaurant with saffron-colored walls and red and blue trim features an open kitchen so diners have an unobstructed view of the cooks at work. Chef-owner Sanjiv Dhar is an evangelist of Indian cuisines, even appearing on Rhode Island public television to give cooking lessons. With Rasoi (which is Hindi for "kitchen"), Dhar tries to balance simply giving diners a pleasant dinner of Indian specialties with educating them to the nuances of regional cuisines. A lot of Indian ex-pats come here to get the tastes of home, and Dhar caters to vegetarians and vegans, even offering a vegan and gluten-free buffet on Saturday. Spicing tends to be subtle at Rasoi, so diners raised on Punjab curry houses may find the food a little bland. The Sunday buffet focuses on regional Indian cuisines. Once a month or so, Dhar also offers cooking classes.

Right Spot Diner, 200 S. Bend St., Pawtucket, RI 02860; (401) 726-8910; Casual American; $. A heavily modified 1930s Worcester diner, the Right Spot was moved from East Avenue to its current outskirts location in 1975. The original diner is encrusted with add-ons, including an ice cream and take-out window. The menu hews to the classic diner formula of eggs and sweet grill dishes in the morning, sandwiches, hot dogs, and burgers at lunch. Its saving grace is that it serves the Rhode Island trinity of wieners, coffee milk, and cabinets.

River Falls Restaurant & Lounge, 74 S. Main St., Woonsocket, RI 02895; (401) 235-9026; riverfallsri.com; Traditional American; $–$$. Sharing a handsome stone mill building with the live entertainment and dance club City Side, River Falls covers all the eating and drinking bases from its list of 20 craft beers and a good burger menu to fried seafood, pasta plates, and the El Dorado rib. The El Dorado was Woonsocket's big-night-out restaurant for 30 years and was known for its specialty of prime rib rubbed with spices. Former owner Bob Pelletier shared the spice recipe with River Falls, and the classic 28-ounce El Dorado cut of prime rib is now a feature on the menu. (A 16-ounce version is also available.)

Rocco's Pub & Grub, 55 Douglas Pike, Smithfield, RI 02917; (401) 349-2250; roccospubandgrub.com; Casual American/Italian; $–$$. Rarely does the name of a restaurant describe it so well. Despite the highway-side location, Rocco's manages a credible pub atmosphere, and Chef Antonio DaCosta is flexible enough to offer a good burger menu (including chicken parm sliders!) as well as a lot of appetizer-sized dishes that go well with beer. His *pommes souf-flés,* for example, are a cross between crisp potato puffs and tender potato chips, and the accompanying Gorgonzola sauce is just salty enough to make sure you keep drinking. There's always a short list of greatest-hits pasta dishes: meatballs and sausage, Bolognese, linguine with littlenecks, and lobster macaroni and cheese.

Sam's New York System, 1031 Mineral Spring Ave., North Providence, RI 02904; (401) 722-7922; Casual American; $. This North Providence stalwart is the post–closing time wiener spot of choice for many barflies. The raw onions here are chopped coarser and the meat sauce is long-simmered, making a pair of Sam's all the way (meat sauce, mustard, onions, celery salt) something of a halitosis special. Many patrons actually favor the "steaks" of griddled shaved beef with mushrooms, onions, cheese, and peppers on a sub roll. Cash only.

Stanley's Famous Hamburgers, 535 Dexter St., Central Falls, RI 02863; (401) 726-9689; stanleyshamburgers.com; Casual American; $. We wonder if it was a coincidence that Polish immigrant Stanley F. Kryla opened this hamburger joint in 1932, the same year that Popeye cartoon character J. Wellington Wimpy first uttered his famous catchphrase, "I will gladly pay you Tuesday for a hamburger today." The Stanleyburger remains a modest patty of freshly ground beef served on a soft bun with grilled onions and sliced pickles. You can gussy it up with tomato, mushroom, bacon, cheese, or pepper, but the original with almost caramelized onion and tangy sweet pickle remains a benchmark that's a whole lot tastier than a can of spinach. For the full Central Falls immigrant nostalgia experience, ask for the fries "Quebec style." They are smothered in brown gravy and sprinkled with cheese curds. In Quebec they'd be called *poutine*. Stanley's also serves fish-and-chips, a wide variety of sandwiches, and some salads and soups. But face it—everyone comes for the burgers.

Taqueria Lupita, 765 Dexter St., Central Falls, RI 02863; (401) 724-2650; taquerialupitari.com; Mexican; $. This delightful family-run restaurant prepares authentic northern Mexican fare from scratch, including homey comfort food like *pozole* (hominy-pork stew) with red or green salsa to stir in, chicken tamales with *mole poblano* sauce, and plump burritos with a choice of meats. Besides a broad choice of juices and *batidos* (milk shakes), Lupita also has a small selection of Mexican beers.

Taso's, 1500 Atwood Ave., Johnston, RI 02919; (401) 228-3880; Casual American; $. Gyros, wieners, snail salad, eggplant parm— Taso's has it all in this strip mall location that looks like three establishments from the outside but all connects once you go in the doors. The grill section has a full New York System setup, while a complete pizza kitchen surrounded by tile stands behind the grill. Calzones are as big a part of the business as pizzas. The food is hardly fancy, and it does represent a mashup of all the Rhode Island ethnic traditions, but Taso's is known for delivering carefully cooked meals at bargain prices.

Tavern on Main, 1157 Putnam Pike, Chepachet, RI 02814; (401) 710-9788; tavernonmainri.com; Traditional American; $–$$. Built as a private home in 1760 and converted into a tavern and inn in 1799, this country stage stop is redolent of old-timey Yankee tradition. The low, beamed ceilings and wide-planked floors haven't changed much since its inception, while the wooden booths and tables are perfect examples of 20th century Colonial Revival decor. One kitchen serves both the tavern and the dining room, with a massive menu that ranges from simple fish-and-chips to a 20-ounce cut of roast prime rib. In between you'll find a lot of Italian-American plates like chicken and veal parm, seafood Alfredo, and pasta and meatballs. Straightforward colonial cuisine is offered on Sunday—roast turkey, roast stuffed chicken, baked stuffed scrod, and fried chicken or fish.

Trattoria Romana, 3 Wake Robin Rd., Lincoln, RI 02865; (401) 333-6700; trattoria-romana.com; Italian; $$–$$$. Chef-Owner Luciano Canova manages to run pizza and Italian take-out operations from this same kitchen, but it's clear his heart lies in the fine-dining Italian restaurant. Many of the best dishes hark back to his childhood growing up on a farm in central Italy—chicken sautéed with panfried eggplant, for example, or bucatini carbonara—but he also offers a long list of more refined plates like veal medallions garnished with lobster. Once inside, it's easy to forget you're in a strip mall next to a Wendy's.

Weiner Genie, 88 Higginson Ave., Lincoln, RI 02865; (401) 726-6641; Casual American; $. Breakfast and other grill fare have overtaken the wiener trade here, but Weiner Genie still has its old neon sign of a wiener with a top hat in the window. Indeed, wieners are still available at lunch and dinner, though the larger steamed hot dog is more popular. Dinner plates are especially good deals, and hit some regional favorites with fish cakes and beans, meatball with peppers and french fries, and a good old French-Canadian shepherd's pie.

Wine & Cheese Restaurant, 1861 Smith St., North Providence, RI 02911; (401) 349-3446; wineandcheeseri.com; Italian; $. Although the name of the place might suggest a post-poetry reading reception, the "cheese" is mostly on top of Italian-American entrees and pizzas, and the wine list relies heavily on California 1.5-liter varietals for wines by the glass, and very modest wines by the bottle. But this nicely upscaled pizza restaurant does a very good job with thin-crust pizzas available in 6-inch, 10-inch, and 14-inch sizes, oven-baked sandwiches, and pasta plates. A shady patio is a favorite spot for summer dining.

Wright's Farm Restaurant, 84 Inman Rd., Nasonville, RI 02830; (401) 769-2856; wrightsfarm.com; Traditional American; $. With about 1,400 seats, Wright's Farm Restaurant dwarfs every other eatery in Rhode Island—even the massive **Twin Oaks** (see p. 130). It represents the apotheosis of a distinctly Rhody phenomenon, the "family-style chicken dinner" restaurant, though the decor is more institutional than homey. The menu consists of one meal: mixed salad with Italian dressing, fresh white dinner rolls, french fries, pasta in a very sweet marinara sauce, and "oven-baked" chicken. Each diner gets a half chicken to start, though seconds are available on everything. The rule of the game is that if you don't request seconds, you can take home whatever you don't eat. The chicken is slowly cooked—up to 3 hours we're told for whole broiler-size birds—so the meat literally falls off the bones. Wright's Farm is popular with families, as kids are charged an even lower price, and whole Little League teams and the like come here for special occasions. Reservations are accepted for groups of 10 to 36—or for 2 to 22 on Easter, Mother's Day, and Father's Day. Although you might have to wait as long as 15 minutes without a reservation on other days, service is so quick that it probably makes fast-food places envious.

Armando & Sons Meat Market, 265 Pine St., Pawtucket, RI 02860; (401) 727-0707; armandosmarket.com. We love this shop because it embraces the culinary traditions of all the Spanish-speaking immigrant populations of the Blackstone Valley. The produce cases have all the various forms of starchy root vegetables (yuca, batata, etc.), fresh chile peppers, nopal cactus leaves, and chayote squash. The cold cases contain all sorts of corn tortillas, arepas, and other corn-flour products beloved from Mexico to Colombia. Dried chiles include many varieties from Mexico but also dried *aji* peppers from northern South America. Armando's biggest draw, however, is its incredible selection of fresh meat. This is the place where you come to have T-bone steaks cut to order and roasts expertly fashioned from prime cuts. It's also where you come for pig parts (snouts, ears, trotters) that you won't find at Stop & Shop, or for goat meat, mutton, and lamb. The fresh fish selection is more limited, but many tropical and subtropical species are available in the freezer cases.

Brown & Hopkins Country Store, 1179 Putnam Pike, Chepachet, RI 02814; (401) 568-4830; brownandhopkins.com. This 1799 building in Chepachet's tiny business district has housed a country store since 1809—generally considered to be the oldest country store in the United States in continuous operation. Much of the merchandise leans toward country decor, but you will find a wide selection of Stonewall Kitchen jams, jellies, salsas, mustards, and the like, along with Brown & Hopkins own line of dip mixes, including spinach, dill, sun-dried tomato and basil, and bacon with horseradish. But it's most worth stopping in for the old-fashioned candy counter, where some sweet treats are even still a penny!

Crugnale Bakery, 1764 Mendon Rd., Cumberland, RI 02864; (401) 721-5377 and 1342 Douglas Ave., North Providence, RI 02904; (401) 353-7166; crugnalebakery.com. The baking facility at Crugnale's home base in the Valley section of Providence (see p. 60) supplies the fresh baked goods for these shops, including the signature bite-size nuggets and party-size rings.

D. Palmieri's Bakery, 624 Killingly St., Johnston, RI 02919; (401) 621-9357; dpalmierisbakery.com. Like most Rhode Island Italian bakeries, D. Palmieri's has a great array of pizza strips, calzones, spinach pies, pastries, and breads. But it sets itself apart with an equally comprehensive selection of prepared foods such as meat-balls, sausage and peppers, or veal with peppers and mushrooms, and with a good menu of sandwiches including salami and cheese, eggplant, or Italian tuna. Palmieri's also sells jars of its own sauces (tomato basil, clam, roasted garlic, marinara, and fra diavolo) and bags of their popular pepper or wine biscuits, which do, in fact, make nice nibbles with a glass of wine.

DePetrillo's Pizza & Bakery, 105 Pleasant View Ave., Smithfield, RI 02917; (401) 231-4600; and 1153 Putnam Pike, Chepachet, RI 02814; (401) 568-4700; depetrillos.com. We have come to appreciate the genius of the Rhode Island pizza strip as a perfect small bite and have been amazed by the number of toppings that the small piece of dough can accommodate. But DePetrillo's emphasizes simplicity and is particularly known for its "red" pizza strips (no cheese) that are sold by the slice or cut into squares and packed into a box to take home. In fact, DePetrillo's calls itself the "home of the original pizza party tray." The shops, of course, also offer a variety of calzones and rolls, along with breads and cookies, and round thin-crust pizzas cooked to order. For the Warwick location, see p. 133.

Gem Ravioli, 39 Greenville Ave., Johnston, RI 02919; (401) 274-0800; and 981 Mineral Spring Ave., North Providence, RI 02904; (401) 475-2200; gemravioli.com. Gem has been making ravioli since 1955. For a quick and easy dinner you can't go wrong with their fresh raviolis filled with a blend of three cheeses or with Black Angus ground beef, spices, and bread crumbs. For a fancy meal, you might want to select some of the large round "gourmet" raviolis, such as wild mushroom in a sherry wine reduction, broccoli rabe and cheese, crabmeat and dill, or artichoke and mascarpone. You'll also find homemade fresh pastas and noodles as well as sauces, including a pink sauce of tomato puree, heavy cream, cheeses, and spices.

Hartley's Pork Pies of Rhode Island, 871 Smithfield Ave., Lincoln, RI 02865; (401) 726-1295. You don't have to be a Simple Simon to appreciate a pie man. Hartley's has been in business since 1902, and Dan Doire's family has owned the operation since the 1990s. The menu couldn't be simpler: individual-sized, English-style crown-rimmed pies of the type that gave the porkpie hat its name. Hartley's sells pork, beef, meat and potato, and chicken pies Wednesday through Saturday. On Friday (or by special order), you can also get salmon pies. They're all pre-baked, and when they come out of the oven, Doire ladles gravy over the tops (it seeps into the pies through steam slits). When he sells the pies, he ladles in some more. The back of the shop's business card advises heating in a microwave for 1 minute, or in a preheated 275-degree oven for 15 minutes. "A lot of people just eat them from the palm of their hands," says Doire. "It's kind of messy, but it's the thing to do." The shop opens weekdays at 7 a.m., Saturday at 8, and closes when all the pies are gone—usually between 1 and 2 p.m.

Ice Cream Machine, 4288 Diamond Hill Rd., Cumberland, RI 02864; (401) 333-5053; icecreampie.com. The Ice Cream Machine sells ice cream pies and other goodies wholesale, but you can also pick out a Grasshopper or a Raspberry Truffle ice cream pie to take home. For more immediate gratification, select from an almost overwhelming variety of flavors of ice cream, yogurt, and sorbet

PUTTING THE COFFEE IN COFFEE MILK

Every Rhode Islander is familiar with Autocrat coffee syrup—
the de rigueur ingredient for transforming plain cow's milk into
the magic elixir of the smallest state, coffee milk. The Autocrat
company began roasting coffee in Lincoln in 1895, and under the
fourth generation owners, it continues as one of the state's largest
coffee roasters and purveyors of coffee and tea extracts. In addition
to the syrup, Autocrat sells coffee and tea as well as instant coffee,
freeze-dried coffee, iced cappuccino bases, and liquid coffee
concentrates like those used in coffee vending machines. But for
generations of Rhode Islanders, Autocrat will forever conjure up
the familiar brown bottles of coffee syrup with the bright yellow
and red labels, available in grocery stores throughout the state. For
more about the company, see autocrat.com.

for a homemade jumble waffle cone or even a waffle bowl sundae.
Special seasonal flavors include apple, blueberry, caramel apple, key
lime pie, and pumpkin.

Krakow Deli Bakery Smokehouse, 855 Social St., Woonsocket,
RI 02895; (401) 765-4600. Marta Samek and her brother Krystian
Przybylko believe in doing things the old-fashioned way. "We
make our own breads, smoke our own meats, and make our own
pierogi," she says. Krystian is in charge of the brick-lined, wood-
fired smoke closets, where he hot smokes kielbasa for 4 to 5 hours

and also smokes bacon and pork loin. The double-smoked kielbasa with garlic is the most popular. "It's the most traditional," says Marta, noting that they also carry fresh kielbasa. "Most people make it once or twice a year," she says. "We make it year round." Krystian also handles the breads, including a slightly sour Polish style rye, Russian, and multigrain—all of which develop complex flavors in the slow rise in woven wooden baskets. Marta makes the soups, salads, delicious potato pancakes, and an array of pierogi including potato and onion, mushroom, cabbage, and strawberry. For a taste of Polish home cooking, order a combination plate at lunch and then pick up some potato pancakes and kielbasa to take home for dinner. Marta suggests making a cut down the length of the kielbasa, pressing it open, filling the cavity with sautéed onions, topping with cheese, and baking in the oven. "I love it. It's delicious," she says. For Marta Samek's recipe for **Latkes (Polish Potato Pancakes),** see p. 269.

La Sorpresa, 498 Broad St., Central Falls, RI 02863; (401) 475-0032. Don't worry if you're not familiar with Colombian food. The friendly counter staff and the enthusiastic regular customers will help you make your choices. If you're looking for a small bite with a cup of Colombian coffee, they'll probably suggest a small round cheese bread (*pan de queso*) or a golf-ball-sized fried *buñuelo* with cheese in the filling. A hot buffet table includes chicken, pork belly, *morcilla, chorizo,* fried yuca, and plantains. But best bets for lunch are the chicken or beef soup with rice, excellent beef or chicken empanadas, or an *arepa,* a cornmeal cake topped with melted cheese. Ask for a loaf of *pan de guayaba* (guava bread) to take home and toast for breakfast.

Mapleville Farm, 544 Victory Hwy., Mapleville, RI 02839; (401) 567-0232; maplevillefarm.com. This artisan bakery is a bit off the beaten path, but bright green signs point the way. The Ryan family built an addition to their farmhouse for a baking facility and a small shop. "We do all our baking here," says Mike Ryan, "and we use as many local products as possible." That could include the fruits for the blueberry bread or the apple cinnamon bread, which is very popular for french toast. Other breads include a beautiful braided white Italian loaf, a white bread with garlic and rosemary, and Tuscan Raider with sun-dried tomatoes and basil. The Ryans also make their own jams and jellies and sell honey "made right down the road by the town historian." They also sell Providence-made **Black Bear Peanut Butter** (see p. 72), which they use in their peanut butter cookies.

New Harvest Coffee Roasters, 999 Main St., Ste. 108, Pawtucket, RI 02860; (401) 438-1999; newharvestcoffee.com. Located in the Hope Artiste Village (a redeveloped mill complex), New Harvest is Rhode Island's leading specialty coffee roaster. The company sources most of its beans directly by meeting with growers in Central and South America, and it develops a very specific roast profile for each crop from each area. The company makes a lot of special blends for bakeries and restaurants (**Seven Stars,** see p. 69 and p. 158, uses New Harvest coffee), and sells in specialty shops and by mail order as well as at the roastery coffee shop.

The Original Palmieri's Bakery, 1933 Mineral Spring Ave., North Providence, RI 02904; (401) 228-7473; palmierisbakery.com. From its base on Federal Hill (see p. 66), Palmieri's supplies all the breads, calzones, pizza strips, biscotti, and beautiful baked goods for this North Providence offshoot.

Powder Mill Creamery, 777 Putnam Pike, Smithfield, RI 02828; (401) 949-3040; powdermillcreamery.webs.com. William Abramek loves to come up with elaborate flavor combinations for his ice cream and frozen yogurt. "They just come naturally," he says, of such pairings as mint chocolate yogurt with chocolate chips and Oreos ("like a Girl Scout cookie on steroids") or banana ice cream with walnuts and chocolate chips ("a banana split all in one"). One of our favorite retro flavors mixes orange sherbet and vanilla ice cream ("just like you got on a stick as a kid"), while one of the most elegant flavors for adults is Abramek's mix of lemon coconut cookie ice cream with white chocolate chips. Alas, he only makes ice cream from late April through Thanksgiving. The rest of the year, customers stop in for the shop's muffins and cider donuts with a cup of coffee.

Tacos Don Nacho, 234 Barton St., Pawtucket, RI 02860; (401) 688-2932. We literally did a double take the first time we spotted Don Nacho. The small dining car has been made to look like an Old West chuck wagon, complete with a mannequin cowboy holding the reins of a life-size brown fiberglass horse. (They're decorated as Santa and Rudolph at Christmas.) Don Nacho does a big take-out business, but there are also picnic tables for those who want to eat their food immediately. Truth is, the place is such kitschy fun that we would probably eat here anyway—but the food is delicious. It's worth stopping just for some *tacos al pastor* and a couple of tamales. On weekends Mexican specials such as *menudo* (tripe) and barbecued pork are a big draw. Many patrons call their orders in to pick up, but Don Nacho also does a booming business in the evening as the little wagon stays open every day until midnight.

Tedesco's Sausage Shop and Fine Cold Cuts, 56 Greenville Ave., Johnston, RI 02919; (401) 274-9356. Tedesco's is particularly busy in the summer when customers stop in for some sausage to toss on the grill. There are so many different choices (including tomato basil, garlic and cheese, rabe and cheese, or roasted pepper, sun-dried tomato, and sharp provolone) that they probably can try something different every weekend. The shop also has its own hot and sweet breakfast sausage and a good selection of cold cuts, hot dogs, and fresh chicken and beef.

Wild Flour Bakery, 727 East Ave., Pawtucket, RI 02860; (401) 475-4718; wildflourveganbakerycafe.com. Vegans get to snack, too—especially if they shop at this bakery where no animal products go into the muffins, scones, cookies, bars, tarts, and pizza sticks. The baked goods are certified kosher except for Passover, and the bakery even has a "raw cheese" cheesecake that is gluten-free. The pastries are not for every taste, but many omnivores also shop here.

Yacht Club Bottling Works, 2239 Mineral Spring Ave., North Providence, RI 02911; (401) 231-9290; yachtclubsoda.com. Yacht Club, the Official Soda and Water Company of Rhode Island, opened in 1915 and still makes its beverages with mineral water from an artesian well drilled under the building in 1923. "All our syrups are made on site with extra fine granular pure cane sugar," says Mike Sgambato, whose family has owned the company since 1961. "It's more expensive than high fructose corn syrup, but better." The local food movement has even led to a resurgence of interest in Yacht Club sodas and flavored seltzers. "People want glass bottles, cane sugar, and old-fashioned flavors," says Sgambato. Those old-fashioned flavors include sarsaparilla, birch beer, ginger beer, strawberry, grape, pineapple, and lime, along with such standards as cola, cherry cola, and pale dry and golden ginger ale. The bottles, by the way, carry a deposit and are reused. The company claims that each one saves enough energy to power a standard light bulb for 100 hours.

Appleland Orchard, 135 Smith Ave., Rte. 116, Smithfield, RI 02828; (401) 949-3690; Farmstand. Mary Lou and Joe D'Andrea are bringing a modern touch to the apple business that Joe's parents launched in the 1960s. In addition to growing apples, peaches, pears, plums, and pumpkins, the couple makes cider, apple wine, cider vinegar, and baked goods such as apple turnovers and dumplings. But they are probably best known for what they call their "gourmet chocolate apples." They dip large, crisp Mutsu apples in caramel, then "double-dip" them in dark or milk chocolate and finally add a drizzle of white chocolate. "There must be a pound of chocolate and a half pound of caramel on each one," says Mary Lou with only slight exaggeration. She advises slicing the apple into wedges for serving. Open late Aug through mid-May (closed in Jan).

Barden Family Orchard, 56 Elmdale Rd., North Scituate, RI 02857; (401) 934-1413; bardenfamilyorchard.com; Farmstand/PYO. For people who really like to see where their food comes from, this farmstand at the Barden family farm has a very personal feel. The family grows everything they sell, including corn, tomatoes, summer and winter squash, zucchini, eggplant, and cucumbers. Most visitors purchase a few vegetables after picking their own blueberries, blackberries, raspberries, apples, and, in some seasons, peaches. The orchard includes both easy-reach semi-dwarf trees as well as some of the original trees planted by John Barden in the

1930s and later grafted so that two apple varieties would grow on a single tree. Open mid-July through Oct.

Blanchard Farm, 225 W. Greenville Rd., North Scituate, RI 02857; (401) 934-0040; Farmstand. Sonny Blanchard says he's probably the last generation of his family to run this farmstand that sells the peaches, pears, plums, apples, and corn he grows on the eight remaining acres of the 1870 family farm. The stand is open from May through early January. "We have late storage apples to sell, even after Christmas," Blanchard says. He brings in some other local produce during the height of the summer season and also sells meat and fish cut to order.

Dame Farm & Orchards, 94 Brown Ave., Johnston, RI 02919; (401) 949-3657; damefarmandorchards.com; Farmstand/PYO. The Dame family began farming in the 1890s and has learned to adapt over the years. Originally focused on dairy cattle and apples, the farm now offers PYO blueberries, peaches, and apples in an idyllic spot set back from the road. The farm also grows other produce to sell at the modest stand set between blueberry bushes and peach trees. Look for cucumbers, squash, pumpkins, and gourds in season. Open July through Oct.

Diamond Hill Vineyards, 3145 Diamond Hill Rd., Cumberland, RI 02864; (401) 333-2751; favorlabel.com; Winery. "We see the same faces every weekend," says Claire Berntson of the visitors to the winery that she and husband Peter started in 1976. "We don't get too complicated here," she says. "We want people to have a good time." The tasting room, in fact, is on the first floor of the family's 1780 home and visitors are encouraged to take a glass of wine out to enjoy on the big front porch. The couple started by planting Pinot Noir and currently has 4½ acres under cultivation. (They also purchase Chardonnay grapes.) "Since the Pinot has to age, we also decided to make fruit wines," says Claire. "We try to balance the sugar level and acidity so that they are sweet, but with a tang." The fruit wines are the best sellers, including Cranberry Apple, which, says Claire's daughter Chantelle Rogers, "makes an awesome sangria when mixed with orange juice and triple sec." Diamond Hill's Blueberry wine is made with organic Maine blueberries grown on peat bogs, which gives the fruit a slightly smoky flavor. "It's great with sharp cheese," says Chantelle. Introduced in summer 2012, Crush—a blend of blueberries, black-berries, and raspberries—gained instant popularity. But in the fall, regulars gravitate to the spiced apple wine, which is blended with cinnamon, nutmeg, and clove. Serving it heated with a bit of light brown sugar has become a holiday tradition in many local homes.

Elwood Orchard, 58 Snake Hill Rd., North Scituate, RI 02857; (401) 949-0390; elwoodorchard.com; Farmstand/PYO. Just by chance we stopped at Elwood Orchard on the day that they opened for the season and found a steady stream of neighbors stopping by to eagerly purchase Jean and Alfred Fuoroli's nectarines. "There's not a lot of orchards that grow them," Alfred told us, noting that nectarines are more susceptible to frost than peaches. "But we have the perfect location. The frost just flows down off the hillside orchard into the swamp." The Fuorolis have made a commitment to organic farming and currently grow certified organic apples, raspberries, garlic, shallots, tomatoes, and winter squash. They offer PYO apples, nectarines, and peaches. The farm is also unusual in growing about a half-dozen different varieties of garlic. "They are all hard-neck garlic," says Alfred, "and they do have different flavor profiles." He clearly likes to experiment and even grows his own shiitake mushrooms. "We grow 6 to 12 logs a week," he says. Open mid-Aug through late Oct.

Goodwin Brothers, 458 Greenville Rd., Jct. Rtes. 5 and 104, North Smithfield, RI 02876; (401) 765-0368; goodwinsfarm.com; Farmstand/PYO. Robert Goodwin grows strawberries, blueberries, and raspberries, and you should call ahead to see if you can pick your own. Otherwise they are available at the farmstand along with Goodwin's own tomatoes, cucumbers, squash, eggplant, peppers, radishes, corn, cantaloupe, apples, and pumpkins. He supplements his own harvest with lettuce, beets, beans, peaches, and nectarines from other local farms. Open June through Oct.

Henry Steere Orchard, 150 Austin Ave., Greenville, RI 02828; (401) 949-1456; steereorchard.com; Farmstand/PYO. Established in 1930 and still in the Steere family, the orchard claims to be the largest in Rhode Island. The Steeres grow about a dozen varieties of apples including Macoun, Cortland, Macintosh, and the Rhode Island Greening, an heirloom apple favored for pies. In addition to apples, the farm grows peaches that are available in the farmstand along with apple butter and apple cider, local honey, jams and jellies, and some produce. Open late Aug through Jan.

Jaswell's Farm, 50 Swan Rd., Smithfield, RI 02917; (401) 231-9043; jaswellsfarm.com; Farmstand/PYO. "What I don't grow, I buy as local as I can," says Chris Jaswell. He and his sister Allison are the fourth generation of the family to operate the farm that was started by Italian immigrant Nicola Gesualdi in 1899. It's the oldest operating apple orchard in Smithfield, and Chris grows a number of varieties including Macintosh, Cortland, Empire, Macoun, and Red and Golden Delicious. Vegetables offerings follow the harvest, and you'll also find the farm's own preserves and other products including apple salsa, Dutch apple jam, apple butter, and apple butter BBQ sauce. The bakery's hand-size apple, blueberry, and raspberry pie pockets are a perfect small treat, as are the local favorite chocolate chunk cookies. PYO strawberries, raspberries, blueberries, and apples in season. Open May to Dec.

Knight Farm Cafe, 1 Snake Hill Rd., North Scituate, RI 02857; (401) 349-4408; PYO. This year-round country cafe makes a great stop for a hearty breakfast of pancakes, french toast, or an omelet before heading out into the orchard for a hayride and to pick your own apples. PYO open Sept and Oct.

Phantom Farms, 2920 Diamond Hill Rd., Cumberland, RI 02864; (401) 333-2240; phantomfarms.com; Farmstand/PYO. By growing more than 15 varieties of apples, Phantom Farms stretches its harvest season from mid-August into November. Varieties include Early Mac, Paula Red, Honey Crisp, Empire, Spencer, Northern Spy, and Rhode Island Greening, a 17th-century variety that is favored for cooking. The farmstand also carries fruits and vegetables from its own and other local fields and features a bakery with fruit pies, apple turnovers, cookies, and a variety of flavors of biscotti.

Salisbury Farm, 11 Peck Hill Rd., Johnston, RI 02919; (401) 942-9741; salisburyfarm.com; Farmstand/PYO. The Salisbury family plants about 12,000 strawberry plants every year, so there are plenty of berries for folks who want to pick their own. They can return later in the season to pick raspberries and then pumpkins and also select fresh sweet corn and other produce in the farmstand. Open June and July and Sept and Oct.

Sunset Orchards, 244 Gleaner Chapel Rd., North Scituate, RI 02857; (401) 934-1900; sunsetorchards.freeservers.com; Farmstand. Gloria McConville and her late husband Daniel Polseno started the orchard in 1964. The operation concentrates on apples, peaches, and nectarines, along with pears and a few blueberry bushes. Over the years, she has gotten to know her fruit. "The Macoun is the Cadillac of apples," she says. "It's crisp and juicy." Of the peaches, she considers Loring to be the best yellow. "It's freestone and easy to cut up," she says, noting that White Lady is her favorite of the candy-sweet white peaches. The farmstand opens in mid-July and stays open until Thanksgiving, but McConville's daughter Gail Chatfield doesn't start baking pies until around Labor Day. In addition to peach, apple, and blueberry, she turns out pumpkin and coconut custard pies, and even a sweet potato crumb pie.

Verde Vineyards, 50 Hopkins Ave., Johnston, RI 02919; (401) 934-2317; verdevineyardsri.com; Winery. "It's a hobby gone berserk," says Giacomo (Jim) Verde of his winery that started in 2002 when he planted his first vines on land that his father had purchased in 1960. "I'm a farm winery which means that I must make wine with grapes grown here," he says. He is concentrating primarily on the Saint Croix grape, which is resistant to both disease and cold weather. The grape originated in Wisconsin and was bred to ripen early. To give them more backbone (Saint Croix is low in tannins), Verde ages his wines for 18 to 24 months in American and French oak barrels. Open in summer; call ahead.

Wright's Dairy Farm, 200 Woonsocket Hill Rd., North Smithfield, RI 02896; (401) 767-3014; wrightsdairyfarm.com; Farmstand/ Bakery. Stop in between 3 and 5 p.m. and you can watch through big windows as the cows are milked at this family-owned dairy farm that has been in operation for more than 100 years. The milk from the 130-head herd is processed right at the farm and much of it goes directly into the farm store. Most of it is homogenized, but some "cream-on-top" non-homogenized milk is also available. Look for the milk and cream in the refrigerator cases on the left as you enter what appears to be a giant bakery. From a small pie opera-tion in the 1970s, the bakery has branched out into cookies, bars, cakes, éclairs and other fancy pastries, and scones. One display case behind the counter holds nothing but muffins—in flavors such as pumpkin raisin, apple spice, lemon poppy, and butter pecan. Apple dumplings are available in season, but we're particularly fond of the chocolate cow cakes and cupcakes, with white frosting accented with chocolate in a Holstein-like pattern.

Farmers' Markets

Blackstone River Visitors Center Farmers' Market, Rte. 295 N., Lincoln. Tues from 2 to 6 p.m., July through Oct.

Burrillville Farmers' Market, Austin Levy School, 135 Harrisville Main St., Harrisville. Sat from 9 a.m. to noon, June through Oct.

Governor Notte Park Farmers' Market, Governor Notte Park, North Providence. Fri from 3:30 to 6:30 p.m., June through Oct.

Johnston Farmers' Market, Johnston Memorial Park, Hartford Ave., Johnston. Mon from 2 to 6 p.m., July through Oct.

North Scituate Farmers' Market, Village Green, Rte. 116, North Scituate. Sat from 9 a.m. to noon, May through Sept.

Northwest Farmers' Market, 451 Putnam Pike, Glocester. Sun from 10 a.m. to 2 p.m., May through Oct.

Pawtucket Farmers' Market, Slater Park, Pawtucket. Sun from noon to 3 p.m., June through Oct.

Pawtucket Wintertime Farmers' Market, 1005 Main St., Pawtucket. Sat from 11 a.m. to 2 p.m., Nov through May.

Woonsocket Farmers' Market, Thundermist Health Center, 450 Clinton St., Woonsocket. Tues from 3:30 to 6:30 p.m., July through Oct.

Cranston & Warwick

The second and third largest cities in Rhode Island, Warwick and Cranston lie just south of Providence along Narragansett Bay. Both communities are fragmented into dozens of villages and neighborhoods connected (some might say divided) by highways lined with strip malls. It is a region with a strong Italian-American flavor, as roughly a third of the residents identify themselves as having Italian heritage. It is the home of specifically Rhode Island adaptations of Italian cooking, including the bakery pizza strip. It is a rare restaurant that does not serve chicken, veal, or eggplant parmesan, yet the area also boasts some of the state's most accomplished Italian-American eateries. As elsewhere in Rhode Island, fried seafood (especially calamari) is popular. Good dining is not limited to cute, closely knit neighborhoods like Knightsville or harbor villages like Apponaug—sometimes the best place to eat may be located in an otherwise undistinguished strip mall. Rolling farmland on the

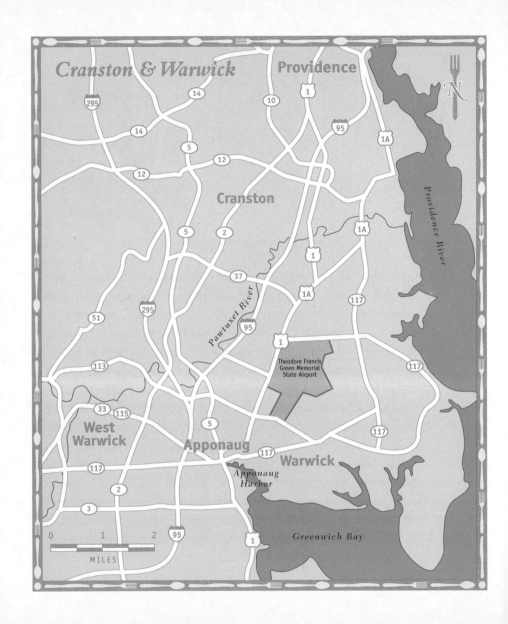

Cranston & Warwick

Providence

Cranston

West Warwick

Apponaug

Warwick

Theodore Francis Green Memorial State Airport

Pawtuxet River

Apponaug Harbor

Providence River

Greenwich Bay

N

0   1   2
MILES

western edges of the two communities yields bounteous harvests of fresh summer vegetables and fruits.

Foodie Faves

Chapel Grille, 3000 Chapel View Blvd., Cranston, RI 02920; (401) 944-4900; chapelgrilleri.com; New American; $$–$$$. How times change! The Cathedral Bar at this grand restaurant was once the chapel of a boys' reform school and the surrounding lands were farmland rather than a giant mall. Now the glamorous bar is jammed with people waiting for a table (they didn't call for reservations), and the dining room is serving steaks, chops, and grilled seafood rather than reform school mystery meat and mashed potatoes. Chapel Grille is a place to come for a big night out, complete with elaborate table service and an air of pomp and circumstance. (There's no dress code, but you'll rightly feel like a schmuck in a T-shirt and flip-flops.) And the food? Flawless steaks, excellent pizzas, and melt-in-your-mouth baby lamb chops served with an olive tapenade.

County Cork Irish Pub, 50 Waterfront Dr., Warwick RI 02889; (401) 732-2675; Casual American/Irish; $. Location, location, location. A few pub standards from the old sod are offered, most notably a Guinness Irish stew, cottage pie, and fish-and-chips. They are stick-to-your-ribs dishes well matched to an afternoon of lazily drinking drafts on the patio overlooking Narragansett Bay. For dining minus the Dublin lilt, the kitchen also grills burgers and makes a mean rib eye steak sandwich.

Crow's Nest, 288 Arnolds Neck Dr., Warwick, RI 02886; (401) 732-6575; crowsnestri.com; Seafood; $–$$. Nestled near the head of Apponaug Harbor, the Crow's Nest is just across the street from the village's main wharf and boat launch. The large menu includes many Italian-American classics (chicken parm and the like) and unadorned meat plates but stick to local scallops, haddock, lobster, clams, and flounder to get delicious fish well prepared. The restaurant is popular with early-bird diners, perhaps because they're trying to avoid the lines that form most evenings. The Crow's Nest does not take reservations.

Edgewood Cafe, 1864 Broad St., Cranston, RI 02905; (401) 383-5550; edgewoodcafe.com; Traditional American/Italian; $–$$. Chef-Owner John Walsh has created a dilemma in his corner of the residential Edgewood neighborhood. The cafe is so reasonably priced and the food is so good that regulars are torn between telling the world and keeping the secret to themselves. Walsh's garlic fries come with aioli dipping sauce, and the crisply fried calamari are tossed with tomatoes and hot peppers and served in a balsamic vinaigrette. Entrees range from a lemon-marinated chicken breast to spaghetti and meatballs to *steak-frites*—all handled with the finesse you'd expect from a Johnson & Wales culinary school grad who loves to cook for the neighbors. BYOB.

Elizabeth's of Portofino, 897 Post Rd., Warwick, RI 02888; (401) 461-8920; elizabethportofino.com; Italian; $$. The brown tufted-vinyl upholstery at this small restaurant in a strip mall may scream late-20th-century Warwick, but the low prices on good food also echo that era. Chef Joe Zacovic presents an appetizing menu of Italian-American dishes (lasagna, chicken and veal parm, grilled steaks and chops, and a handful of terrific fish dishes like rosemary-skewered scallops.

Ferrucci's Original New York System, 1246 Main St., West Warwick, RI 02893; (401) 821-9849; Casual American; $. This family-owned and operated casual joint has all the grill standards, from breakfast eggs and pancakes to luncheon burgers and sandwiches, but the wieners are the major attraction, and when a crowd comes in, the grill man pulls the old trick of lining up the hot dog buns in the crook of his arm and slathering each with condiments. These are individual wieners rather than the long rolls that the restaurant has to cut, so they tend to be a bit on the small side. The meat sauce is plain and simple. Unlike many wiener places, Ferrucci's stays open into the early evening except on Sunday.

Iggy's Doughboys & Chowderhouse, 889 Oakland Beach Ave., Warwick, RI 02889; (401) 737-9459; iggysdoughboys.com; Seafood; $. Open year-round, this original Iggy's (there's a seasonal stand in Narragansett, see p. 170) reigns over the ever-popular sands of Oakland Beach on Greenwich Bay. The eponymous doughboys are big gobs of deep-fried batter, and they're usually consumed doused with cinnamon and/or powdered sugar. If the batter contains finely chopped clams, they are Rhode Island clamcakes, to be eaten with ketchup or tartar sauce. "Fried" is the operative word at Iggy's, where many regulars rave about the calamari and the fried whole-belly clams. (You can also order fried clam strips, but most aficionados prefer whole-belly clams.) To complete the cholesterol count, get your potatoes as curly fries smothered with melted cheese.

The Iron Works Tavern, 697 Jefferson Blvd., Warwick, RI 02886; (401) 739-5111; theironworkstavern.com; New American; $$. Set in the landmark red-brick Rhode Island Malleable Iron Works building, this handsome tavern plays up its history with a mural sequence of photos of the iron workers displayed on the red-brick walls of the massive open space. A large bar stands in the middle and seating alternates between four-top tables and banquettes along some walls. The menu is a gastropub version of New American cooking with a Rhody accent—that is, great fried Point Judith calamari, rolled eggplant stuffed with melted cheeses and sopressata and topped with marinara sauce, and (at dinner) clear clam chowder, fried smelts, and littleneck clams simmered in *zuppa*. Iron Works also maintains a great raw bar (mostly from **Twin Shellfish,** see p. 137) and makes a terrific Caprese salad during local tomato season.

JP Spoonem's, 1678 Broad St., Cranston, RI 02905; (401) 941-3550; Casual American; $. Hard-core traditionalists insist that jonnycakes can only be made with finely ground white cornmeal and nothing else except water and the grease to fry them. JP Spoonem's adds a touch of sugar and uses yellow cornmeal, but their jonnycakes are still a true corncake (the New England tortilla), rather than a fancy pancake, and taste a bit like fried polenta. Principally a breakfast diner, JP Spoonem's serves large portions. Order a New Englander breakfast to taste all the house specialties on one plate: Johnny Cakes (as they call them), fluffy scrambled eggs, sausage, and nicely seasoned home fries. JP Spoonem's also makes that old standby of the '80s, the Bull's Eye (grilled Texas toast with fried sunny-side up eggs replacing the center of the bread). The kitchen also makes corned beef hash from scratch.

King's Garden, 90 Rolfe St., Cranston, RI 02910; (401) 476-8916; kingsgardenrestaurant.com; Chinese; $. Like many Chinese restaurants, King's Garden has a huge array of dishes from all over China (and many highly Americanized plates like chow mein and chop suey), but the house specialties are Sichuan dishes like eggplant in garlic sauce, or soft tofu stir-fried with pickle and minced pork.

Many diners prefer to make a meal of small dim sum plates, which are ordered by writing the number of servings of each plate on a checklist menu. Don't expect the rolling carts of the giant dim sum palaces in New York, San Francisco, or Boston, but do expect surprisingly good small plates, including hand-shaped shrimp dumplings.

L'Osteria, 1703 Cranston St., Cranston, RI 02920; (401) 943-3140; losteriari.com; Italian; $$. Mario Macera's handsome little restaurant has been the prize of Knightsville's Italian community since 1993. Don't expect any of the Italian-American standards here— even the Bolognese sauce is made the old-country way with veal and milk. And Macera is as finely attuned to seasonality as the best little *osteria* in Italy. His mother grows the tomatoes and basil that the restaurant uses. In midsummer, fried squash blossoms are a feature. "My mother grows the zucchini," Macera says. "My chefs stuff them." The house specialties are multiple preparations of veal or chicken (with artichokes and mushrooms, for example) and dishes like seared sea scallops with fennel risotto, but L'Osteria also offers some pasta plates uncommon in Rhode Island—dishes like orecchiette with broccoli rabe, tomatoes, roasted peppers, and olives.

Mike's Kitchen, 170 Randall St., Cranston, RI 02920; (401) 946-5320; Italian; $–$$. This Knightsville institution is poorly signed but it's inside VFW Post 2396 (which is well-marked) and is closed on Tuesday and Saturday evenings for VFW meetings. It's also closed Sunday just because it's Sunday. But the rest of the time you can eat a generous Italian-American lunch or dinner that should hold you for days. Rhode Island specialties abound, including stuffed quahogs, fried smelts, snail salad, and fried calamari with hot peppers. But Chef-Owner Mike Lepizzera also makes some old-time Italian-American favorites like veal with peas and eggplant parm, as well as all manner of fresh fish and veal dishes. Many regulars come specifically for his polenta. It is a smooth blend of cornmeal with chicken stock, olive oil, and pecorino Romano cheese, finished with a dab of butter. Lepizzera serves it with a rich tomato sauce and meatballs or sausage—or both. As one of the waitresses says, "It's wicked creamy." Cash only.

Newport Creamery, Garden City Shopping Center, 100 Hillside Rd., Cranston, RI 02920; (401) 944-3397; 400 Bald Hill Rd., Warwick, RI 02886; (401) 737-4309; and Warwick Mall, 1256 Warwick Ave., Warwick, RI 02888; (401) 463-8317; newportcreamery.com; Casual American; $. For shoppers who need a quick lunch or ice cream break, two of these three outposts of Newport Creamery are located in shopping malls and all offer the same menu of breakfast foods, salads, soups, sandwiches, dinners, and ice cream treats as the Middletown original (see p. 236).

Olneyville New York System, 1012 Reservoir Ave., Cranston, RI 02910; (401) 275-6031; Casual American; $. Home base is the

LEARNING ITALIAN FROM A MASTER CHEF

Chef Walter Potenza of Potenza Ristorante & Bar in Providence (see p. 47) loves to spread the gospel of Italian cuisine, and his cooking classes grew so popular that he moved all but the occasional team-building course from the Federal Hill restaurant to a dedicated facility in Cranston. The compact structure is just right for the small groups—rarely more than 12. Tuesday night classes tend to focus on specific regions, holiday feast dishes, and other themes. These 3-hour classes are split more or less equally between hands-on cooking instruction and family-style dining. On Thursday, chef Potenza runs 4-hour classes for the Italian Culinary Experience immersion cooking course. The classes in the 40-hour package focus on techniques, handling of ingredients, and making basic dishes (stocks, sauces, pastas, pastry) from which more elaborate dishes are built. The school also offers special courses for children, and during school vacations, courses for parents and children cooking together. Lest the facility sit idle, the cooking school also operates a cafe midday during the work week that serves flatbreads, panini, antipasto platters, individual pizzas, and signature salads.

Chef Walter's Cooking School, 162 Mayfield Ave., Cranston, RI 02920; (401) 490-0999; chefwalter.com.

Olneyville section of Providence (see p. 44), but these oil-grilled natural casing wieners with a spicy meat sauce have started appearing in suburban locations like this one and another in North Providence (see p. 90).

Peter's Coney Island System, 2298 W. Shore Rd., Warwick, RI 02889; (401) 732-6499; Casual American; $. We always like to see the triumph of the little guy. Principally a breakfast place with all the egg and pancake classics, Peter's thrives in a spot where a fast-food drive-through eatery couldn't cut it. The decor may still recall the world of corporate fast food, but the egg plates and the system hot dogs are pure down-home Rhode Island.

Poco Loco Tacos, 2005 Broad St., Cranston, RI 02905; (401) 461-2640; pocolocotacos.com; Mexican; $. Diners can add bacon to any menu item at Poco Loco, but the fillings for tacos or burritos are so well conceived (pork, black beans, jalapeños, cheese, and sweet chile barbecue sauce, for example, or chorizo, potato, corn salsa, sour cream, red onion, and Monterey jack) that further embellishment hardly seems necessary. This brightly decorated spot is a good place to relax with some of the favorites from the Poco Loco taco truck—and to enjoy other offerings such as avocado fritters or sheet pan nachos that may be less suited to peripatetic dining.

Remington House Inn, 3376 Post Rd., Warwick, RI 02886; (401) 736-8388; theremingtonhouseinn.com; Traditional American/ Italian; $$. The front door of this circa-1801 property opens on the main drag of Apponaug village, while the back deck overlooks the idyllic little harbor frequented by herons, swans, egrets, and the occasional bald eagle. In between lies a warren of dining rooms where locals love to chow down on fish-and-chips; reasonably priced filet mignon; veal braciole stuffed with mozzarella, sausage, and ham; and giant baked stuffed shrimp filled with scallops. When weather permits, the deck is almost irresistible, although the menu is a more casual selection of fried and grilled sandwiches, grilled pizza, antipasti, and chicken salad, lobster salad, or smoked salmon salad platters.

Seven Seas Chowder House, 26 Palmer Ave., Warwick, RI 02889; (401) 737-8368; Seafood; $. When this tiny and rather run-down clam shack opens for the season, the folks of Warwick know summer is on the way. Seven Seas makes a classic Rhode Island chowder and fried clamcakes that are studded with fresh clams. The doughboys are a signature item—known here as doughgirls if they are sprinkled with both cinnamon and sugar.

Spike's Junkyard Dogs, 640 Reservoir Ave., Cranston, RI 02910; (401) 781-7556; and 1623 Warwick Ave., Warwick, RI 02889; (401) 732-5858; spikesjunkyarddogs.com; Casual American; $. Dave Drake started Spike's some years ago, naming it after his bulldog. In a state already crazed about hot dogs, Drake's jumbo dogs with all manner of toppings were such a hit that he began to franchise the shops. To complete the all-American fast-food trinity, he added Lulu's Burgers & Fries to some of them, including the Cranston shop.

Stykee's New York System, 1617 Elmwood Ave., Cranston, RI 02910; (401) 461-9208; Casual American; $. For the uninitiated, Constantine Scapinakis's breakfast and lunch spot is one of the best places to learn the ins and outs of a New York System wiener, and definitely worth the trip to this strip on the Cranston-Warwick border. "I buy natural casing wieners in 10-pound rolls and then cut them to length," he says. "It's more money, but they're worth it." He cooks the wieners slowly on his grill and tops them with meat sauce made from his father's recipe, along with the traditional mustard, chopped onion, and celery salt. "The grill is always by the window, but the steam table is turned so that you can face the customer," he says. "That's the real New York System."

T's Restaurant, 1059 Park Ave., Cranston, RI 02910; (401) 846-5900; tsrestaurantri.com; Casual American; $. From a variety store selling some spinach pies, pizza strips, and calzones, Tony and Tina Tomaselli created a good-value casual restaurant so successful that this Cranston location has expanded a couple of times and additional outlets are in East Greenwich and Narragansett (p. 182). They all serve the same menu of eggs, pancakes, Benedict variations, and casual salads and sandwiches. Giant club sandwiches are

THE SIP OF SUMMER

Del's Lemonade may not be Rhode Island's "State Drink" (that honor goes to coffee milk), but it would be impossible to imagine the Ocean State without the little stands with their green roofs—not to mention the mobile trucks and carts that appear at most fairs and food truck gatherings. The first shop was opened in Cranston in 1948 by Angelo DeLucia, who based his icy treat of water, sugar, and chopped lemons on a recipe first made by his family members in Naples. The company claims to be the oldest producers of frozen lemonade in America. More than 2 million lemons go into Del's Lemonade each year, but the company offers other thirst-quenching flavors including watermelon, cherry, grapefruit, and blueberry.

Del's Lemonade & Refreshments, 1260 Oaklawn Ave., Cranston, RI 02920; (401) 463-6850; dels.com.

a signature of lunch offerings, but you can also go smaller and get a half sandwich with either a soup or salad.

Twin Oaks Restaurant, 100 Sabra St., Cranston, RI 02910; (401) 781-6677; twinoaksrest.com; Traditional American/Italian; $–$$. With six dining rooms seating 650 customers and three separate bars, Twin Oaks claims to be the largest single independent restaurant operation in Rhode Island (though **Wright's Farm**

Restaurant in Harrisville, see p. 97, can seat 1,400). For many Rhode Islanders, it is an institution—the restaurant for rites of passage like engagements, christenings, graduations, and other events that bring the whole extended family together. While seafood dishes can get a little pricey since they're market priced, the classic Italian-American fare like veal parm or macaroni with peppers, meatballs, and sausage barely breaks into two figures. Portions are usually gigantic, but the senior citizen menu (65-plus) scales back both the size and the price.

Wein-O-Rama, 1009 Oaklawn Ave., Cranston, RI 02920; (401) 943-4990; Casual American; $. With 13 stools along the counter and nine booths, Wein-O-Rama is fairly large for a hot dog joint. And the menu is more varied as well, with burgers, club sandwiches, fish-and-chips, and full dinners such as baked ham, veal cutlets, or spaghetti and meatballs. But most people stop by for a New York System wiener with Wein-O-Rama's somewhat spicy sauce. If you're really hungry, order the plate of two wieners with baked beans. Cash only.

Specialty Stores, Markets & Producers

Calvitto's Pizza & Bakery, 1401 Park Ave., Cranston, RI 02920; (401) 464-4200; and 285 Park Ave., Cranston, RI 02905; (401) 941-8863. Calvitto's opened its original bakery on 1401 Park

Avenue in 1985, but you can get the full range of products at both locations. As if the choices of pizza squares (pepperoni, olive, tomato, chicken), calzones (chicken parm, meatball with ricotta and pepperoni), and loaves (Italian cold cuts, eggplant) weren't already enough to make your head spin, Calvitto's also offers a variety of specialty loaves, such as the BLT (with bacon, lettuce, tomato, mozzarella cheese, and ranch dressing) or the chicken supreme (with grilled chicken, spinach, roasted peppers, black olives, and mozzarella). The same combinations can also top a whole pizza if you're in need of more than a few squares. Sometimes, it's easiest to stick with one of the "secret recipe" spinach pies and save room for a lovely glazed fruit tart.

Crugnale Bakery, 567 Reservoir Ave., Cranston, RI 02910; (401) 781-8800; crugnalebakery.com. This Cranston outpost of the Providence institution (see p. 60) carries a full assortment of pizza strips, calzones, fresh breads, and other specialties.

The Cupcakerie, 1860 Broad St., Cranston, RI 02905; (401) 467-2601; thecupcakerie.net. Baker Kristin Brennan has a knack for flavor combinations that range from subtle (lavender cake with vanilla buttercream) to spicy (chile chocolate cake with Mexican vanilla buttercream). Her Farmer's Pride cupcake changes with the harvest; in late summer, it might be a blueberry cake with honey buttercream.

DePetrillo's Pizza & Bakery, 1727 Warwick Ave., Warwick, RI 02889; (401) 732-3331; depetrillos.com. Like most of Rhode Island's Italian bakeries, DePetrillo's has a tempting array of pizza strips, calzones, and rolls (filled with spinach, cheese, and pepperoni or with ham, cheese, salami, and pepperoni). They also bake whole pizzas to order. But they set themselves apart as the "home of the original pizza party tray," a box containing sheet pizza cut into easily held squares. For other locations, see p. 100 and p. 133.

Dockside Seafood Marketplace, 2275 Warwick Ave., Warwick, RI 02889; (401) 921-5005; docksideseafoodri.com. We guess the name is supposed to suggest the freshness of the fish, even though Dockside is located on a main highway far from the water.

Indeed, the fish is very fresh, and Dockside carries a wide variety of the catch from Maine, Massachusetts, and Rhode Island boats, along with farmed salmon and tilapia. The shop has an even larger array of meats.

European Food Market, 102 Rolfe St., Cranston, RI 02910; (401) 461-1097. Lena Bondarenko and her daughter Natasha came to the United States from Russia and opened this specialty market about 20 years ago. They stock the shelves with foodstuffs from throughout Eastern Europe and many of their customers are right at home deciphering the Cyrillic lettering on the packaging. But for the rest of us, Natasha patiently explains the particulars of the brightly wrapped candies, the myriad jars of pickles and preserves, and tins of caviar. "With all the food and travel channels, ethnic shops are in vogue now," she says. Because of strict regulations on importing meat, the European stocks sausages, salami, hams, bacon, and other deli meats from US and Canadian companies started by earlier generations of immigrants from Poland, Russia, and Germany. She is happy to offer samples. "It's the only way to find the sausage that tastes like the one your grandmother used to make," Natasha says.

Freedom Seafood, 840 Park Ave., Cranston, RI 02910; (401) 223-1010. One of the stranger combination stores in the Rolfe Square neighborhood, Freedom is both a Chinese take-out restaurant with lots of stir-fries and a range of rib-sticking variations on congee, and a fresh fish market selling mostly local catch like smelt, cod, squid, and scallops. Lobster, rock crabs, and eels are all available live, while Dungeness crab from western Canada is sold precooked from the freezer.

Refai Pastry, 1486 Park Ave., Cranston, RI 02920. Owner Victor Refai is from Syria and his welcoming shop in a little strip mall features a few Syrian specialties such as cheese and meat pies with the fillings nestled like a precious cargo in boat-shaped pieces of dough. You'll also find familiar Middle Eastern dishes—baba ghanoush, falafel, stuffed grape leaves—to eat at one of a few tables or to take out. Chicken, beef, or lamb kebabs with vegetables—or gyros of the same meats—make good lunchtime sandwiches. Refai makes two delicious variations of baklava: one with pistachios, the other with walnuts.

Sandy Lane Meat Market, 459 Sandy Lane, Warwick, RI 02889; (401) 737-4246. Sandy Lane carries a full line of meats, but the house specialty is Angus beef. If you want prime cuts like those usually sold in restaurants, order ahead. The shop carries a whole line of groceries, but the butchers and their personalized service are the main reason to come here. It's a good place to get large cuts (frequently on sale) trimmed and prepared the way you like them.

Solitro's Bakery, 1594 Cranston St., Cranston, RI 02920; (401) 942-9840. The main bakery of Cranston's Italian-American Knightsville neighborhood, Solitro's is beloved by its customers for its fresh spinach pies, for the simple bakery-style pizza strips, and for the fresh Italian breads and ciabatta.

Sonia's Near East Market & Deli, 816 Park Ave., Cranston, RI 02910; (401) 941-9300; soniasdeli.com. Sonia's specializes in the foods of Armenia, Greece, Turkey, Syria, and Lebanon. One of the best ways to get a taste of this eastern rim of the Mediterranean is to order one of the sampler plates for lunch or dinner. Sampler Heaven, for example, includes hummus, tabouli, stuffed grape leaves, Kalamata olives, feta cheese, marinated eggplant, and falafel with sesame tahini dressing. For a lighter meal, try a *lamejun,* or "Armenian pizza" of thin dough topped with seasoned ground meat. Once your appetite is satisfied, you can peruse the shelves and cold cases for Turkish butter, Greek-style caviar spread, pomegranate soup, and a full array of lentils, grains, nuts, and dried fruits.

Superior Bakery, 1234 Oaklawn Ave., Cranston, RI 02920; (401) 463-6659; superiorbakery.com. Baker Maria Dercole favors a pizza strip topped with everything, but she also exercises restraint in turning out pies with red sauce only or with classic pairings such as pepperoni and mushroom, hot peppers and pepperoni, garlic and mozzarella, or spinach with roasted red peppers (a favorite of adherents to the Weight Watchers diet). In addition to pizza strips that are baked in a rectangular pan to create a thick but still-tender crust, Superior also offers round thin-crust pizzas cooked on a stone. The shop's spinach and olive calzone is also a favorite with customers, along with the Italian cold cut stromboli, a rolled, baked sandwich stuffed with sausages, cheeses, and roasted peppers and onions. The shop's ciabatta bread is baked without preservatives— and is so good that it probably never lasts long enough to go stale.

Sweenor's Chocolates, 43 Hillside Rd., Cranston, RI 02920; (401) 942-2720; sweenorschocolates.com. Walter Sweenor opened his first candy store in the Garden City neighborhood in 1955 so it seems only fitting that this modern shop is a fixture in the massive Garden City Shopping Center. The location may have changed, but the Sweenor family is still in charge and turns out an array of bars, truffles, and filled chocolates, including a delicious vanilla caramel enrobed in dark or milk chocolate and sprinkled with sea salt. Customers particularly favor anything with nuts, including the almond butter crunch (in milk or dark chocolate), the almond bark (in milk, dark, or white chocolate), and the peanut, pecan, or hazelnut clusters.

Twin Shellfish, L.L.C., 5 Harrop Ave., Warwick, RI 02886; (401) 737-1575; twinshellfish.com. Marty McGiveney buys his clams directly from the diggers and when you step into his tiny facility you might find him or one of his staff operating the ingenious machine that sorts the harvest by size. They will even pull bags of quahogs out of the big refrigerator to show you the difference between the littlenecks, cherrystones, and "chowders" that they carry. The chowders are the biggest, and many people use them for just that purpose. For a simple treat, McGiveney suggests putting littlenecks in a pot with basil, crushed red pepper, and garlic. Then pour in enough beer to fill the bottom inch of the pot, put on the lid, and steam for a couple of minutes until the clams open. Twin Shellfish also carries farm-raised Hope Island oysters and lobster. In the fall and spring, they have "snails" in the shell—which are "not the little squiggly ones," as one of the staff puts it, but a type of conch.

Whole Foods Market, 151 Sockanosset Cross Rd., Cranston, RI 02920; (401) 942-7600; wholefoodsmarket.com. Located in the Garden City Center, this is a full-size outpost of the Texas-based natural food market chain.

Farmstands & PYOs

Confreda Greenhouses & Farms, 2150 Scituate Ave., Western Cranston, RI 02831; (401) 827-5000; confredas.com; Farmstand. With 400 acres, Confreda is one of the largest vegetable growers in our country's littlest state. You can follow the harvest season with fresh fruit and vegetables from their own fields as well as from other local farmers. You can also order local grass-fed beef and select from a range of other local products, including honey and maple syrup, pancake mixes from **Kenyon's Grist Mill** (see p. 190), and pasta from **Venda Ravioli** (see p. 59). The farmstand cafe offers soups, salads, sandwiches, and a few light dishes. A lot of customers leave with a whole pie (apple, peach, strawberry-rhubarb). Join the Frequent PIE-er Club and the sixth one is free.

Morris Farm, 2779 Warwick Ave., Warwick, RI 02889; (401) 738-1036; Farmstand. This third generation farm was founded in 1915 and its 43 acres yield a bounty of vegetables across the growing season. Locals particularly prize the fresh sweet corn and a sign behind the counter gives precise instructions for cooking it: 1) BOIL WATER, 2) HUSK CORN, 3) PUT CORN IN BOILING WATER, 4) BRING TO BOIL, 5) COOK 3 MINUTES, 6) REMOVE TO PLATE, 7) COVER WITH TOWEL. To which we would only add: 8) slather with butter and sprinkle with salt! Open Apr through Dec.

Rocky Point Farm, 130 Rocky Point Ave., Warwick, RI 02889; (401) 738-8100; rockypointblueberries.com; PYO. Rhonda Shumaker and Joe Gouveia often advise pickers to toss a few barely ripe berries into their buckets to add a tart accent to the sweetness of the fully ripe fruit. They also welcome children to pick, as long as they are accompanied by an adult. Short, young bushes are kid height, while some of the older bushes tower six feet or more. If you don't have time to pick, you might find Rocky Point's berries at **Morris Farm** (see above). The season typically runs from late June or early July into August. For the Rocky Point Farm recipe for **Blueberry Cream Cheese Pie,** see p. 272.

Farmers' Markets

Goddard Park Farmers' Market, Goddard State Park, Warwick. Fri from 9 a.m. to 1 p.m., May through Oct.

Pastore Complex Farmers' Market, Pastore Complex Department of Labor & Training, 1511 Pontiac Ave., Cranston. Fri from 11 a.m. to 2 p.m., July through Oct.

Pawtuxet Village Farmers' Market, Rhodes on the Pawtuxet Parking Lot, Pawtuxet. Sat from 9 a.m. to noon, May through Nov.

Thundermist Winter Indoor Market, 186 Providence St., West Warwick. Sat from 9 a.m. to 1 p.m., Nov through Apr.

West Warwick/Thundermist Farmers' Market, 186 Providence St., West Warwick. Thurs from 3 to 6 p.m., July through Oct.

Whole Foods Farmers' Market, 151 Sockanosset Cross Rd., Cranston. Tues from 3 p.m. to dusk, June through Oct.

East Bay

The narrow strip of land between Narragansett Bay and the Massachusetts border contains some of Rhode Island's most picturesque maritime villages. East Providence, of course, contains the population spillover (and some of the Italian flavor) from Providence and retains vestiges of an industrial past. But start moving south, and the Riverside section of town is full of green open spaces. Keep going south to Barrington and Warren, and the landscape begins to take a backseat to the seascape. By the time land runs out in Bristol, the maritime character of East Bay fully reveals itself. These villages were shipbuilding and shipping centers even before the American Revolution. In more recent years, they have become recreational boating communities. All the little harbors of East Bay are dotted with sailboats, and some feature elegant motor yachts as well as sleek racing hulls. Even though East Bay is not Rhode Island's main fishing region, seafood tends to dominate the menus, and Bristol contains the preponderance of fine-dining restaurants.

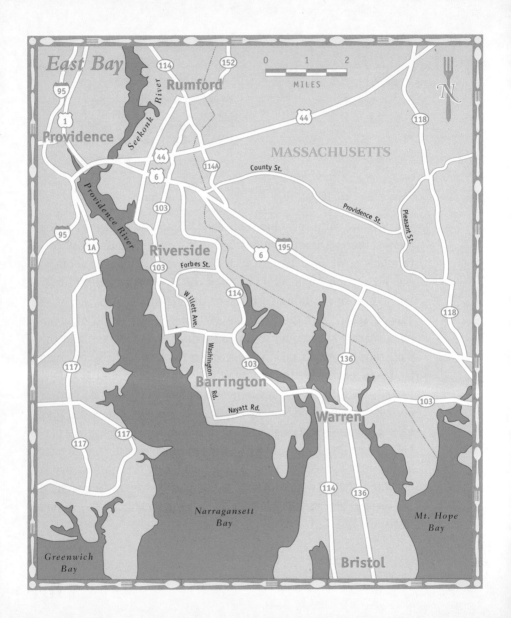

Amaral's Fish & Chips, 4 Redmond St., Warren, RI 02885; (401) 247-0675; amaralsfishandchips.com; Portuguese/Seafood; $. Rhode Island seafood gets a Portuguese twist at this local favorite set among auto garages on the industrial east side of town. Regulars swear by the fried fish (perfectly moist and greaseless haddock in a light batter shell) with a plate of chunky fries and a generous side of coleslaw. You can also get fried smelts, either marinated or plain—both rarities even in Rhode Island. The kitchen also makes hot and cold grinders, including a scallop grinder and, for customers tired of fish, a *chouriço* grinder.

Avenue N American Kitchen, 20 Newman Ave., East Providence, RI 02916; (401) 270-2836; avenuenamericankitchen.com; New American; $$. This neighborhood favorite certainly earned its industrial chic look—it occupies the former Rumford Chemical Company building where Rumford Baking Powder was manufactured for more than a century. Rumford's powder, in fact, shows up in the baking powder biscuits that top the chicken dumpling soup. That kind of attention to locale carries through the menu in straightforward presentations of local sirloin steak, free-range chicken (prepared with hen of the woods mushrooms!), and roasted Block Island cod served with pickled ramps, tomato salsa, and bits of country ham. Three pizza options are also available—best for splitting as an appetizer. Note that because Avenue N lacks a high-temp pizza oven, the pies are on the soft and tender side.

B. Pinelli's Simply Italian, 736 N. Broadway, East Providence, RI 02914; (401) 270-7111; bpinellis.com; Italian; $$. Once upon a time Nonna cooked for the whole family and everyone gathered around a big table and ate pasta and eggplant parm and meatballs and gravy and braciole and . . . B. Pinelli's raises the ante with large tables set with fine linens and glassware, but it's still a place where everybody gathers around big plates of Italian-American classics and no one goes home hungry. Nonna never made espresso or ice cream–filled *bombas,* but B. Pinelli's does. Sundays are family days, when kids under 12 eat free from the children's menu.

Blount Clam Shack, 684 Bullocks Point Ave., East Providence, RI 02915; (401) 628-0485; and 335 Water St., Warren, RI 02885; (401) 245-3210; blountretail.com; Seafood; $. The Blount family has been in the shellfish business since the late 19th century and has concentrated on clams since the 1940s. In fact, one of its two seasonal clam shacks is located on the water behind the company's clam processing facility in Warren. The other is in Crescent Park next to the 1895 Charles Looff carousel. The 66-figure carousel is a National Historic Landmark. The Blounts may not be able to claim landmark status, but they certainly loom large in Rhode Island's shellfish industry. At either location, you can grab a picnic table under a big tent and get a taste of the Blount family's way with clams by sampling clamcakes with chowder, a whole-belly clam roll or a clam-strip platter with coleslaw and fries. Both locations open

Memorial Day through Labor Day. For Blount's year-round location, see p. 23; for market, see below.

The Cheese Plate, 54 State St., Warren, RI 02885; (401) 245-3932; thecheeseplateri.com; Eclectic; $–$$. We've never before encountered a place quite like this cross between a cheesemonger and a wine bar. True to its name, the Cheese Plate offers a variety of themed pairings of four cheeses to be enjoyed with a glass of wine. The plates can be made for a couple or a group of four and might feature an assortment of goat- or sheep-milk cheeses or a range of cheeses from a single country such as France, Italy, or Spain. The cheese plates can be supplemented with a short list of charcuterie and other cheeses available a la carte. If you want to make a meal of it, the even shorter list of desserts features a pear and almond tart with crumbled blue cheese, a New York–style cheesecake with strawberries, and a cheese-free flourless chocolate torte.

DeWolf Tavern, 259 Thames St., Bristol, RI 02809; (401) 254-2005; dewolftavern.com; New American; $$–$$$. Chef Sai Viswanath brings some of the techniques and dishes of his native India to this rather elegant waterfront tavern in a historic stone warehouse at Bristol's Thames Street Landing, adjacent to the Bristol Harbor Inn. The kitchen makes especially good use of the tandoor oven for roasting chicken, fish, pork, and even lamb at very high temperatures. During the summer, the cooks even roast lobster in the tandoor. The "Philadelphia cheesesteak" (available at lunch) is served on naan. But besides the occasional curried dish and the samosas on the appetizer menu, most of the plates celebrate local Rhode Island seafood and farm produce. Viswanath does a marvelous fusion cod dish of chorizo-crusted fish served with roasted native corn, fenugreek, and tomato cream.

Horton's Seafood, 809 Broadway, East Providence, RI 02914; (401) 434-3116; hortonsseafood.com; Seafood; $. **Born in 1945 as a seafood market, Horton's has been cooking food to take out since 1963, and has had a small dining room since 1988. Still in the same family, this "clam shack" nowhere near the water is a magnet for lovers of Rhode Island fried fish—despite the difficult location due to one-way streets. The whole-belly fried clams are sweet and juicy and many fans rave about the fluffy stuffies with clams minced so fine that you can taste them but never bite down on a rubbery neck. Lobster for the lobster rolls is cooked on premises and the rolls are stuffed with meat.**

Hourglass Brasserie, 382 Thames St., Bristol, RI 02809; (401) 396-9811; hourglassbrasserie.com; French; $$$. **Chef-Owner Rizwan Ahmed studied marine biology at the University of Maine before he switched gears and studied culinary arts at the Cordon Bleu in London. That means he knows North Atlantic seafood and French cooking alike. Lightly hay-smoked local scallops with a garlic and anchovy relish, for example, make an inventive appetizer. Ahmed**

thinks outside the box with lobster, poaching it in butter and serving it with red-wine-braised baby octopus, chorizo, and smoked paprika risotto. The bistro atmosphere calls for dressing up a little, but not a lot. The idea is to relax and enjoy masterfully prepared cuisine. The wine list is less steadfastly French, dipping into California, Australia, and even South Africa to keep the prices affordable.

Jacky's Galaxie, 383 Metacom Ave., Bristol, RI 02809; (401) 253-8818; jackysgalaxie.com; Asian; $–$$. Jacky Ko is a believer in going big or going home. Not as glam as his Providence location, **Jacky's Waterplace** (see p. 37), this spot combines the appeal of a good sushi bar with Asian-themed banquet rooms perfect for business or family celebrations. (A separate American kitchen also caters events on premises.) Almost every Japanese, Thai, Vietnamese, or Chinese dish you have ever encountered in a restaurant is on the menu here, but some of the best dishes are those that cut across cuisines, like a steamed whole striped bass with ginger.

Le Central, 483 Hope St., Bristol, RI 02809; (401) 396-9965; lecentralbristol.net; French; $$. The motto of this friendly and casual bistro is "where the East Bay meets the Left Bank." Fortunately, the food is more like southern France than Paris, with homey dishes like hanger steak, coq au vin, and grilled lamb and lamb sausage with ratatouille and scalloped potatoes. French posters on the walls and a soundtrack strong on Edith Piaf help establish the mood. Le

Central also serves a popular Sunday brunch that includes roasted local oysters with horseradish cream, bacon, and scallions, as well as ethereal lemon-ricotta crepes with the fruit of the season.

Leo's Ristorante, 365 Hope St., Bristol, RI 02809; (401) 253-9300; leosristoranteri.com; Italian; $. Originally known as Leo's Pizzeria when it opened in 1948, this Italian-American standby is now in its third generation of management. It's the place you bring the family for littlenecks and flakes of red pepper on spaghetti, super-thick and cheese-oozing lasagna, and—yes—pizza with a long list of potential toppings. Leo's serves breakfast on the weekends and does a bustling business in sandwiches (including veal parm or classic Italian cold cuts on "torpedo" rolls) at lunch.

Nacho Mamma's, 76 State St., Bristol, RI 02809; (401) 396-9588; nachomammasri.com; Mexican; $. This small spot in a corner of the County Cleaners Building does not take a casual approach to preparing its menu of "casual Mexican" food. The guacamole is made fresh every morning and served with homemade chips. Fish tacos are made with fresh cod served with cabbage slaw and mango pineapple salsa, and diners can upgrade from ground beef to flank steak for a burrito served with black or refried beans, Spanish rice, and the spicy chopped salsa called *pico de gallo*. Try Mamma's signature chili served in a bowl with cheese, sour cream, and chips or used as a topping for nachos or chili cheese dogs.

Newport Creamery, 296 County Rd., Barrington, RI 02806; (401) 245-2212; newportcreamery.com; Casual American; $. **From its modest beginnings in Middletown (see p. 236), Newport Creamery has taken its menu of family-pleasing soups, salads, sandwiches—and great ice cream—across the state. Even in this small strip mall in Barrington, trying to drink an entire Awful Awful is a daunting pleasure.**

Persimmon, 31 State St., Bristol, RI 02809; (401) 254-7474; persimmonbristol.com; New American; $$$. **Plan to make an evening of it when you go to dine at Persimmon, where Chef-Owner Champe Speidel makes some of the prettiest food in Rhode Island while staying true to the pure flavors of great fish, produce, and meat. Speaking of meat—he also owns a butcher shop, Persimmon Provisions (see p. 157), which supplies the meat for the restaurant. Speidel tends to source his pork in New Hampshire, his lamb in Vermont, and as much fish as possible in Rhode Island. He can take a modest fish like tautog and dress it up for a magazine cover by pan-searing and serving it with littleneck clams and small shrimp, braised local chard and endive, and a butter sauce with fresh tarragon and oregano. In addition to the a la carte menu, Persimmon offers very reasonable 5- and 7-course tasting menus.**

Quito's Seafood Restaurant, 411 Thames St., Bristol, RI 02809; quitosrestaurant.com; Seafood; $$. **There's no denying the appeal of the waterfront in Bristol, and Quito's takes full advantage with its location at the south edge of Independence Park. Many diners don't**

get past the "appetizers" because they fill up on fried calamari, steamed clams, great fried clamcakes, and stuffed quahogs. Those who do usually opt for seafood (shrimp, littlenecks, lobster, mussels, or calamari) on pasta with a choice of "scampi" sauce (garlic, butter, olive oil, and white wine) or *zuppa* sauce (red sauce with extra-extra garlic). All three versions of clam chowder are available, as are burgers, steaks, and grilled chicken for the landlubbers. If you have the patience to wait (and who doesn't when you can sip wine and beer by the water), you can also get baked casseroles of shrimp, scallops, or lobster—or a combo of all three.

Redlefsen's Rotisserie & Grill, 444 Thames St., Bristol, RI 02809; (401) 254-1188; redlefsens.com; Continental; $$–$$$. Jeff Guertler used his business meals in Europe to good advantage when he finally retired from his business. He opened this restaurant across from Independence Park to replicate the experiences he and his wife had enjoyed at small-town restaurants all over Europe. The atmosphere is certainly relaxed. "We assume you'll be at your table for two hours or so," Gertler says. Many customers, he notes, start with appetizers and drinks in the bar, move to the dining room for dinner, and return to the bar for after-dinner coffee. The menu is filled with the Gertlers' favorite dishes from around the continent, and their personal taste seems to have struck a chord. The top sellers are chicken Provence (boneless breast with black olives, arugula, artichoke hearts, sun-dried tomatoes, and chèvre over eggplant ravioli) and wiener schnitzel (breaded veal cutlet with lemon, capers, and anchovies). The German dishes get special emphasis throughout October, when there's even Bavarian oompah music a couple of nights a week.

Rod's Grille, 6 Washington St., Warren, RI 02885; (401) 245-9405; Casual American; $. Like lots of casual eateries in Rhode Island, Rod's includes a "New York System Wiener" on its menu, and many locals consider it to be the best in the East Bay. But this lunch counter has lots of other tempting dishes, including the bacon cheeseburger with lettuce, tomato, onion, and hot peppers on a Portuguese muffin. Rod's was opened by Mariano and Margaret Rodrigues in 1955 and several dishes reflect their Portuguese heritage, including the *chouriço* and pepper sandwiches and the homemade Portuguese soup on Wednesday. If you visit on a Friday, don't miss the special of baked or fried fish-and-chips.

Siam Square, 1050 Willett Ave., East Providence 02915; (401) 433-0123; siamsquareriverside.com; Thai; $. Fans of pad thai and red curry flock to this Riverside strip mall restaurant—as much for the takeout as for dining in. Portions tend to be generous but not overwhelming, and hot dishes are toned down a bit for American palates. Freshness is everything in Thai cuisine, and Siam Square's veggies are always crunchy while the noodles are never overcooked or gummy.

The Sunnyside, sunnysideri.com; New American; $–$$. We have to confess that we've been big fans of Chef-Owner Joe Simone since his early days in Boston. Simone has always had an unerring palate for delicious food simply presented as well as for food combos so good that you wonder why no one ever thought of them before. (His bacon, baby arugula, and tomato sandwich with aioli on Seven Stars multigrain toast is a case in point.) This little restaurant along the riverfront in Warren feels a bit like a converted boathouse, and in warm weather, most diners prefer sitting on the patio closest to the water. Simone has specialized in breakfast and lunch (and weekend brunch) since he opened, extolling the virtues of "daytime dining" where the earlier meals get the same fine-dining attention as dinner at other restaurants. Get the crockpot grits with wood-grilled ham and eggs or the buttermilk soufflé pancakes at breakfast, or brine-cured and grilled boneless chicken thighs at lunch. As this book went to press, The Sunnyside went on hiatus. See website for new location and hours.

Tong-D, 156 Rear County Rd., Barrington, RI 02806; (401) 289-2998; tongdrestaurant.com; Thai; $. East Bay fans of Thai endlessly debate the merits of Tong-D versus **Siam Square** (see p. 151). A more formal restaurant, Tong-D also serves fresh, carefully crafted Thai food. In a departure from the luncheon buffet formula, Tong-D offers a prix-fixe menu at midday with a broad choice of entrees, including the signature mango curry with shrimp, chicken, and zucchini. To appreciate the kitchen's finesse at dinner, try the *koong ob woonsen:* a sautéed large shrimp seasoned with a sesame-ginger sauce and served with clear rice noodles and herbs.

Trafford Restaurant, 285 Water St., Warren, RI 02885; (401) 289-2265; traffordrestaurant.com; New American; $$–$$$. Located just downstream from **The Sunnyside** (see p. 152), Trafford also has a waterfront sundeck for alfresco dining. And if it's chilly or wet, there's always the airy upstairs dining room with window views of the boats bobbing along Warren's shore. (The restaurant even has two slips, should you decide to arrive by boat.) Although Trafford is only open for dinner, you can order off the sandwich and appetizer menu for a light meal (lobster and corn fritters, for example, or pan-fried haddock dusted with Parmesan and served on brioche), or opt for heartier fare like wood-grilled swordfish, seared duck breast with a port and blood orange reduction, or a wood-grilled tenderloin steak served with truffled whipped potatoes and fried onion strings. The wine list is long on good sippers, including some choices among sparkling wines to accompany the local oysters.

Tyler Point Grille, 32 Barton Ave., Barrington, RI 02806; (401) 247-0017; tylerpointgrille.com; Seafood/Italian; $$. This longtime local favorite tucked in behind the Barrington Yacht Club may lack direct water views, but Chef-Owner Brian Thimme knows his way around the local catch. Among his finest dishes is the plate of seared sea scallops with a roasted yellow pepper risotto drizzled with basil oil. There's bargain family dining on Sunday, when children can order off the kids' menu for free (one child's meal per adult meal). When it comes to dessert, remember that Thimme makes his own cannoli, which are filled just before serving.

Specialty Stores, Markets & Producers

Blount Market, 406 Water St., Warren, RI 02885; (401) 245-1800; blountretail.com. Blount's full line of soups is available at this market across the street from the clam shack (see p. 144), along with some of the soups that the company produces for other restaurants, including Massachusetts-based Legal Sea Foods. You'll also find live lobster and a variety of fresh fish—including, of course, clams. The store also stocks pasta from **Venda Ravioli** (see p. 59), a range of stuffed clams (with *chouriço* or bacon, or with a combination of scallops, lobster, and shrimp), and prepared dishes such as seafood or snail salad, shrimp with dill and orzo, or paella. Be sure to check the bargain case for good deals on soups manufactured under various labels including Panera Bread, Publix, Shaw's, and Captain Parker's.

Crugnale Bakery, 237 Newman Ave., East Providence, RI 02916; (401) 435-3037; crugnalebakery.com. A central baking facility

The Way We Were

Coggeshall Farm, a coastal farm on the edge of Bristol's Colt Park, occupies such a lovely setting that it's almost easy to forget the hard work that went into farming at the end of the 18th century. As a reminder, the farm operates as a living history museum, and its costumed interpreters work year-round tending to crops and animals and bringing in and preserving the harvest. Visitors can observe their efforts and also take part in a number of special programs including open-hearth cooking workshops featuring meat and produce raised on the farm. In this exercise in truly local eating, participants "follow a meal from field to washtub." **Coggeshall Farm Museum,** Coggeshall Farm Rd., Bristol, RI 02809; (401) 253-9062; coggeshallfarm.org.

,maintains the quality and consistency of the large variety of products made by this bakery that originated in Providence's Valley neighborhood (see p. 60). Chilled cases hold a variety of Crugnale's pizza strips and calzones—all perfect for a quick lunch on the go.

The Daily Scoop, 230 County Rd., Barrington, RI 02806; (401) 245-0100; and 446B Thames St., Bristol, RI 02809; (401) 254-2223; dailyscoopicecream.com. Some of us might get our ice cream fix by going to the supermarket and picking up a pint of Ben and Jerry's.

Not Deb and Bob Saunders. Craving premium ice cream in their home town of Barrington, they took courses at Penn State University and at the University of Maryland and opened the first Daily Scoop in 2000. The Saunders, of course, have their own versions of such classics as chocolate, chocolate chip, coffee, and vanilla. But they pride themselves on their unusual flavors, including banana chip, banana peanut butter cup, and coconut almond chip with chunks of fresh coconut. They even turn carrot cake into ice cream—an improbable treat that is quickly scooped up whenever it makes an appearance.

Delekta Pharmacy, 496 Main St., Warren, RI 02885; (401) 245-6767. "We opened in 1858 and have been here ever since," says Eric Delekta, the third generation of his family to run this establishment that he calls "a pharmacy with a soda fountain." And a great soda fountain it is. "We make our own coffee syrup with water, coffee, and a lot of sugar," he says. It's the basis for a quintessential coffee cabinet. For full strength, order it with milk, coffee syrup, and coffee ice cream. For more of a mocha flavor, ask for coffee syrup with chocolate ice cream, or for chocolate syrup with coffee ice cream. Delekta also makes his own vanilla syrup but has not revived the practice of making the chocolate syrup that his grandfather made until World War II. For a lighter treat, order a milk shake made with milk and syrup—and a dash of seltzer water on request. Soda fountain staff are also schooled in the dying art of making a proper ice cream soda.

Gray's Ice Cream, 259 Thames St., Bristol, RI 02809; (401) 624-4500; graysicecream.com. Nothing beats sitting on the dock, looking out at Bristol harbor, and licking a strawberry cheesecake ice cream cone. This seasonal ice cream stand of Tiverton-based Gray's (see p. 240) is open April through September.

Italian Corner, 10 Boyd Ave., East Providence, RI 02914; (401) 431-1737; italiancornerri.com. This market makes good use of its cold case for lunchtime sandwiches such as imported prosciutto with arugula and Parmigiano cheese or imported air-dried beef (*bresaola*) with truffle-flavored olive oil and arugula. But look carefully on the shelves of canned goods for some unusual sauces to use with pastas. We're particularly fond of the canned sardines with fennel, black currants, and onions; the Sicilian pesto with basil, tomatoes, and almonds; and the blends of white truffles with porcini mushrooms or artichokes. Add some of the shop's dried or fresh pasta and you've got the makings for a simple, delicious meal.

Persimmon Provisions, 338 County Rd., Barrington, RI 02806; (401) 337-5885; persimmonprovisions.com. Chef Champe Speidel of **Persimmon Restaurant** (see p. 149) refers to this butcher shop with a few gourmet provisions as his "pantry." Like Speidel's dishes at the restaurant, the cuts of meat in the cases are displayed with food-magazine perfection. Even the ground meat is presented with the grain of the grind in a straight line, while the big chicken and herb sausages are so lusciously plump that they could convert a vegan into a carnivore.

Seven Stars Bakery, Rumford Center, 20 Newman Ave., East Providence, RI 02916; (401) 521-2200; sevenstarsbakery.com. It's such a nice bit of serendipity that this offshoot of the **Providence Seven Stars** (see p. 69) is located in a former industrial complex that manufactured Rumford Baking Powder. We always get a kick out of the wall-size mural of the "Championship Contest for the title of Rumford Biscuit Baking Champion of 1945." Made with or without baking powder, Seven Stars' breads, pastries, cookies, and muffins could certainly hold their own in any contemporary competition.

Farmers' Markets

Bristol Farmers' Market, 461 County Rd., Bristol. Sat from 9 a.m. to noon, June through Oct.

Colt Park Farmers' Market, Colt State Park, Bristol. Fri from 2 to 6 p.m., May through Oct.

Haines Park Farmers' Market, Haines Memorial State Park, Metropolitan Park Dr., East Providence. Wed from 2 to 6 p.m., May through Oct.

Mount Hope Winter Farmers' Market, 250 Metacom Ave., Bristol. Sat from 9 a.m. to noon, Nov through May.

Rumford Farmers' Market, 20 Newman Ave., East Providence. Tue from 3 to 6:30 p.m., May through Oct.

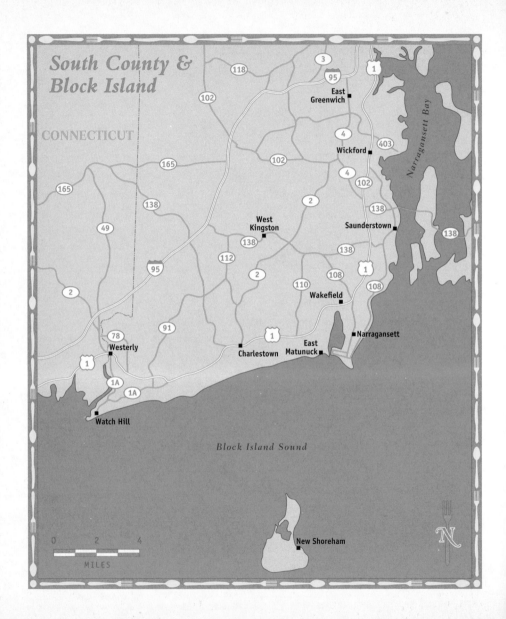

South County &
Block Island

CONNECTICUT

Narragansett Bay

East
Greenwich

Wickford

Saunderstown

West
Kingston

Wakefield

Narragansett

Westerly

Charlestown

East
Matunuck

Watch Hill

Block Island Sound

New Shoreham

0   2   4
MILES

N

South County
& Block Island

Technically known as Washington County, South County is not just the southwest quadrant of Rhode Island. To Ocean Staters, it is also a state of mind—a near-mythical land of endless sand beaches where quahogs practically jump out of the sand and into your collecting bucket, and battered and fried calamari grows on seaside bushes along with hot pepper rings.

It is the part of Rhode Island where land and sea fade gently, one into the other. There's some justification in seeing them as interchangeable. The nearly continuous barrier beach that stretches from the Narragansett Bay at Point Judith west to the Pawtuxet River dividing Watch Hill from the state of Connecticut is really a thin lacework of sand. Barely inland are hundreds of saltwater ponds cut off from the ocean by the barrier beaches. These ponds host eight oyster farms at this writing—probably more as the industry expands.

The east end of the barrier system contains the state's chief fishing ports at the Biblical-sounding Galilee and its counterpoint across a narrow strait, Jerusalem. The squid catch in these parts is gigantic, leading to the ubiquitous "Point Judith calamari" on restaurant menus. South County also harvests most of Rhode Island's clams. It should go without saying that South County is a great place to shop for fish—and to dine on fish at beachside fry joints, lively bistros, and even the dining room of an elegant resort.

Much of coastal South County is also a summer playground, from bustling, and vaguely honkytonk Misquamicut Beach to the pristine, nearly unspoiled beauty of East Beach in Charlestown and the rugged surfcasting shore of the Charlestown Breachway. The ferry docks at Point Judith in Narragansett are the gateway to tiny Block Island, a sandy hill in the sea that marks the southern boundary of the Gulf of Maine and the Atlantic entrance to Long Island Sound.

The proximity to the ocean tempers the climate of South County, even far inland, so expect to find a number of small farms that sell their produce directly at farmstands and help to supply local restaurants. Even apart from the beach communities, South County is rich with towns and villages steeped in history and character—the pocket harbor village of Wickford, handsome East Greenwich, and even little Wakefield, where the nearby University of Rhode Island imbues the village with a cosmopolitan air.

Foodie Faves

Aunt Carrie's Restaurant, 1240 Ocean Rd., Narragansett, RI 02882; (401) 783-7930; auntcarriesri.com; Seafood; $. Carrie Cooper was a practical cook. Camping on the beach with her husband, Ulysses, and their children, she tossed clams into her corn fritter recipe and created the clamcake that launched a restaurant. It opened in 1920 and "we really don't change too much," says Elsie Foy, whose late husband Bill was the grandson of the founders. The menu includes chowders (great for dunking the clamcakes), clam rolls, fried clam dinners, steamed clams, and stuffed clams. But Aunt Carrie's (the only establishment in Rhode Island to be named one of the "America's Classics" by the James Beard Foundation) is not a funky, take-out-only clam shack. The dining room features buttercup yellow walls and the windows are dressed with lace valances. Foy does occasionally introduce new menu items, such as a lobster BLT suggested by her son-in-law. "He's from Vermont," she says, "and he puts bacon on everything." But she also knows not to mess with success. Some of the homemade pies are from Carrie's original recipes. Open Apr through Sept. BYOB. For the restaurant's recipe for **Banana Cream Pie,** see p. 270.

Besos Kitchen & Cocktails, 378 Main St., East Greenwich, RI 02818; (401) 398-8855; besoskitchenandcocktails.com; Eclectic; $$. This stylish and polished room used to be known as Besos Tea Room but the name misled diners. Although Besos (Spanish for "kisses") does serve an afternoon tea of sweets, breads, and small sandwiches, it shines at regular mealtimes with Spanish and Italian-tinged menus of wraps and grilled fish and meat at lunch, and somewhat more elaborate entrees at dinner—blackened Chilean sea bass with mango salsa, for example, or grilled steak with black beans, rice, and sweet plantains. Brunch, available daily, is more Mexican in accent, with dishes like scrambled eggs in green chile sauce, or huevos rancheros (scrambled eggs in tomato-chile sauce). A wide selection of tapas ranging from Spanish-sounding bites like chorizo *bocadillos* (mini-sandwiches) on toasted garlic cheese bread to Maryland crabmeat crostini are available before or in lieu of dinner, and some can be ordered in the afternoon when you might like to sit on the gorgeous outdoor porch with a nibble and a glass of wine.

Cafe Fresco, 301 Main St., East Greenwich, RI 02818; (401) 398-0027; cafefrescori.com; Italian; $$. This wood-grill northern Italian spot features generously sized pasta dishes, grilled pizzas, and smoky grill treatments for fish and meat. Mind you, the wood grill does not translate into a wood-fired oven, so dishes like lasagna are assembled just before serving rather than baked. Warm and welcoming, Cafe Fresco is a couple of steps up from traditional Rhode Island Italian-American restaurants, providing just a little more finesse in each dish and offering a wine selection that, while slanted toward the US west coast, offers some surprising selections of food-friendly pours at good prices.

Catarina's Italian Village Restaurant, 945 Boston Neck Rd., Narragansett, RI 02882; (401) 789-1725; catarinas.italianvillage-ri .com; Italian; $–$$. The Mollo family hails from halfway between Rome and Naples in Italy's Lazio region, and the extensive menu of their Italian restaurant (incongruously located in a log building on a highway) represents a little bit of the best of both Roman and Neapolitan culinary traditions. Pizzas are prepared Naples-style in a hearth oven, and if you look carefully, you'll find some Lazian specialties like the sole fillet on a bed of sautéed spinach, topped with herbed bread crumbs and a wine sauce, and served with a side of penne.

Centro Martini, 149 Main St., East Greenwich, RI 02818; (401) 885-8580; centromartini.com; New American/Casual American; $$. We've never thought of the martini as a particularly food-friendly cocktail, but this martini bar also has some tasty white and red wines to complement the list of mostly sweet variants on the martini. Drinkers can keep their bar legs by eating the burgers, wraps, and quesadillas, while diners for whom the food comes first can skip farther down the menu to the *steak-frites,* ginger-seared salmon, or roasted chicken roulade stuffed with prosciutto, fresh mozzarella, fire-roasted red peppers, and spinach.

Champlin's Seafood Deck, 256 Great Island Rd., Galilee, Narragansett, RI 02882; (401) 783-3152; champlins.com; Seafood; $. Talk about going to the source. The Seafood Deck sits above a fish market. Step up to the window and place your order for fish-and-chips, a lobster salad roll, or charbroiled swordfish and then grab a table on the deck for a bird's-eye view of the fishing boats as they enter and leave the harbor.

The Coast Guard House, 40 Ocean Ave., Narragansett, RI 02882; (401) 789-0700; thecoastguardhouse.com; Seafood/Traditional American; $$. Perched on the south side of Narragansett Town Beach, the Coast Guard House occupies a grand building constructed as a US Life-Saving Service station (later incorporated into the Coast Guard). It is a dramatic spot, with surf breaking on the rocks out front and great views from the wraparound deck on the second level. A limited menu is served on the deck (burgers, lobster salad roll, stuffies), but that's all anyone needs on a sunny day between April and October. The indoor menus are somewhat more extensive and rely on fresh seafood landed just a few miles away at the Port of Galilee. Sunday brunch buffet is extremely popular.

Crazy Burger Cafe and Juice Bar, 144 Boon St., Narragansett, RI 02882; (401) 783-1810; crazyburger.com; Casual American; $–$$. Not only is Crazy Burger a BYOB place, it's "BYOB all day, in case you want a mimosa," as one of the staff told us when we stopped in at breakfast. If you like well-prepared and nicely priced casual fare, Crazy Burger has you covered for all three squares. Eggs and bacon/sausage/ham, latkes, homemade hash, crepes, and omelets only scratch the surface of breakfast. You can also get pancakes, waffles, and all manner of scrambles, including several variants of scrambled tofu. Several vegan variations of burgers are offered the rest of the day, as are several burgers of chicken, beef, salmon, mahi-mahi, and turkey. Only dinner crosses over into the $15-plus range, with entrees like a vegan pumpkin-sage risotto, mahi-mahi with Thai peanut sauce, and braised short ribs. Crazy, man. Crazy like a fox. BYOB.

DiMare Seafood Marketplace Restaurant & Bar, 2706 S. County Trail, East Greenwich, RI 02818; (401) 885-8100; ridimare .com; Seafood; $$. When she was growing up, Kate LeBore planned on opening a seafood restaurant with her older brother Danny, who operated a small seafood market in North Kingstown. When her brother perished in a boating accident, she fulfilled their dream and opened this modest fish market (with perfectly cut and iced fish from local boats and a few imports for variety) and the adjoining restaurant in 2008. The terrific seafood is prepared simply but with care, whether it's the clams steamed in a beer broth; the fried calamari tossed with peppers, sliced olives, tomatoes, and baby greens; or the grilled local swordfish. We're particularly fond of DiMare's clear clam chowder, a family recipe developed by Kate's father Wayne, a retired US Navy commander. DiMare also prepares a number of pasta dishes, including homemade lobster ravioli. The ravioli—along with stuffed scallops and quahogs—are available from a freezer case for cooking at home. From the refrigerator case, you can get chopped clams, whole quahogs, and buckets of chowder. For DiMare's recipe for **Rhode Island Clam Chowder,** see p. 251.

Georges of Galilee, 250 Sand Hill Cove Rd., Galilee, Narragansett, RI 02882; (401) 783-2306; georgesofgalilee.com; Seafood; $. Over the years Georges has grown from a modest restaurant into a sprawling complex with five dining rooms on two floors. It's still a great place for a comprehensive taste of the Rhode Island shore, though it's worth paying attention to where the fish comes from. Georges Bank scallops, for example, are likely a day or two fresher than Digby scallops from Nova Scotia, and Alaskan king crab legs have to be flown nearly halfway around the world. Lobster is a big deal at Georges, and the Point Judith Combo of steamed lobster, mussels, corn on the cob, fries, and coleslaw makes a perfect shore dinner. On Friday afternoon (3 to 5 p.m.), you can order all the fish you can eat— either a combo of clamcakes, chowder, and fish-and-chips, or (for a few dollars more) roasted cod or baked stuffed flounder. Georges is agnostic on the subject of chowder, serving Manhattan, New England, and Rhode Island styles.

Greenwich Bay Oyster Bar, 250 Main St., East Greenwich, RI 02818; (401) 398-2462; greenwichbayoysterbar.com; Seafood; $$. This friendly bar is a labor of love for Chef-Owner Dave Spaziano, who counts among his friends many of the fishermen who supply the seafood. The raw bar of local oysters, littlenecks, and cherrystones is augmented by some chilled Gulf shrimp. The entire appetizer menu fairly bristles with local shellfish—stuffies, steamers, clams *zuppa,* fried calamari with a honey-balsamic glaze. . . . Spaziano offers a choice of New England or Manhattan chowders as well as a silken lobster bisque. Entrees all depend on the catch, but you can pretty much count on pan-seared scallops, steamed lobster, and a fried seafood platter. A few grilled pizzas and a filet mignon also cut the non–fish-eaters some slack.

The Grille on Main, 50 Main St., East Greenwich, RI 02818; (401) 885-2200; marrarestaurantgroup.com; Eclectic; $$. **Although** the Grille on Main offers almost every appetizer you'd find on a bar menu (wings, spring rolls, spinach and artichoke dip, phyllo-encrusted brie, nachos, tacos . . .), some of the best and most popular items on the menu are the grilled pizzas available in two sizes. Wraps and sandwiches are big at lunch (pressed Cubano, grilled chicken, open-faced meat loaf) but dinner is a feast of comfort food that can range from the grilled sirloin to baked cod,

from pork chops brined in Sam Adams beer to hickory-smoked baby back ribs. Vegetarian choices are slim, but the black bean and quinoa cakes are good enough that even non-vegans order them.

Iggy's Doughboys & Chowderhouse, 1157 Point Judith Rd., Narragansett, RI 02882; (401) 783-5608; iggysdoughboys.com; Seafood; $. In warm weather, the grassy lawn with picnic tables is the perfect place to enjoy Iggy's signature fried doughboys and seafood specialties. For the original, year-round location in Warwick, see p. 122. Open March through Columbus Day.

Jim's Dock, 1213 Succotash Rd., East Matunuck, RI 02879; (401) 783-2050; Seafood/Casual American; $–$$. Whoever Jim is, he's managed to dominate the waterfront in East Matunuck. This restaurant, which is sort of an extension of Jim's Marina, sprawls over the wooden docks with indoor dining rooms and indoor and outdoor decks furnished with varnished wooden picnic tables. Outside, beach pails on each table hold paper towels and condiments. The menu is rudimentary: burgers and basic sandwiches, most kinds of fried seafood, and the Rhode Island waterfront classics of clamcakes, stuffed quahogs, steamed clams, and spicy fried calamari. The location can't be beat: Sit outside and watch the ferries and large fishing vessels come and go from Galilee across the narrow channel while you guard your meal zealously from the predatory gaze of herring gulls. BYOB. Open mid-May through mid-Oct.

Nautical Suds

Jen Brinton isn't a typical stay-at-home mom. When she was considering re-entering the work force as her youngest was about to enter school, she opted instead to launch a home-based brewery. The name "Grey Sail" was inspired by a visit to Misquamicut Beach, where on a hazy day the sails all look gray. Fittingly enough, Grey Sail was conceived as a beer to quaff at the beach or on a boat. The company makes bright, light beers and sells the Flagship Ale (an American-style pale ale) and the Flying Jenny Extra Pale Ale in cans rather than bottles. Cans are just as recyclable as bottles and a whole lot safer in places where people go barefoot. Those two ales are augmented by Hazy Day Belgian Wit for cask distribution to bars and restaurants throughout Rhode Island and Connecticut. The brewery is open for tours on Saturday.

Grey Sail Brewing Company, 63 Canal St., Westerly, RI 02891; (401) 212-7592; greysailbrewing.com; Brewery.

Jigger's Hill and Harbour Diner, 145 Main St., East Greenwich, RI 02818; (401) 884-6060; jiggersdiner.com; Casual American; $. A classic piece of Americana, Jigger's Diner actually dates from 1917, although this particular dining car (Worcester Lunch Car Co. #826) has been on the spot only since June 21, 1950. The diner underwent one restoration in 1992 and another extensive restoration over the summer of 2012 before Karie and Steve Head reopened it with the new name as a nod to its location in the Hill and Harbour District of East Greenwich. The Heads have given the menu a locavore bent, using all-natural local eggs, Autocraft coffee, and **Yacht Club** sodas (see p. 107). The Rhode Island Johnny Cakes (as the menu deems them) are made with Kenyon's cornmeal (see p. 190). Hamburger comes from local farms, and the fish for fish-and-chips comes out of Rhode Island waters. Jigger's also makes classic Rhode Island ice cream cabinets as well as ice cream floats.

La Masseria, 223 Main St., East Greenwich, RI 02818; (401) 398-0727; lamasserianyc.com; Italian; $–$$. This authentically Puglian restaurant is a real standout in the sea of Rhode Island Italian-American eateries. Moreover, it's the only branch of a very successful Manhattan Italian restaurant by the same name. Chef Giuseppe "Pino" Coladonato hails from Puglia and that region's cuisine informs the menu. For example, Coladonato cooks *granotto* (a Puglian grain from the wheat family) like risotto and pairs it with white beans and seafood. His love of evanescent fresh vegetables might lead him to toss zucchini blossoms into the seafood *frito misto.* The chef's two business partners grew up together on Capri, so some great Caprese dishes also star on the menu, including the *torta di mamma paola,* a flourless chocolate and ground almond cake.

The Malted Barley, 42 High St., Westerly, RI 02891; (401) 315-2184; themaltedbarleyri.com; Casual American; $. Truly a beer-lover's bar, TMB promotes upcoming beers the way some bars list upcoming live bands. (Musicians *do* play here on weekends.) There are always two dozen ales and beers on tap, most of them local or at least regional, and there's always a cask-conditioned ale in the mix. (Hint: The cask is tapped on Wednesday, so don't delay or you could miss out.) Normally that great beer selection wouldn't be quite enough to get them listed here, but the owners came up with a clever bar cuisine that complements the brews—snacks and sandwiches built around big pretzels made fresh every day. So you can get an Asiago and Parmesan pretzel with a blue cheese dip, a turkey and Havarti sandwich on a pretzel, or even a waffle pretzel with Nutella for a sweet bite. We'll drink to that.

Matunuck Oyster Farm, 629 Succotash Rd., East Matunuck, RI 02879; (401) 783-4202; rhodyoysters.com; Seafood; $–$$. This is our idea of farm-to-table cuisine: sitting outside in the sun as the waitstaff bring plate after plate of Rhode Island farm-raised oysters to enjoy with a bottle of Bastianich "Adriatico" Friulano. Matunuck Oyster Farm raises its bivalves on Potter Pond and grows much of the produce used in the restaurant on a patch of land on the north end of the pond. The restaurant stocks oysters from up to eight other oyster farms along the south coast, and carries the whole range of Rhode Island seafood. You can order a plate of seared scallops, grilled yellowfin tuna, a lobster salad roll, and (of course) Point Judith calamari. Oysters attach themselves to a single spot where the feeding is good and never move for the rest of their lives. We begin to understand. Inquire about occasional tours of the oyster farm.

Narragansett Grill, 1200 Ocean Rd., Narragansett, RI 02882; (401) 789-6171; narragansettgrill.com; Seafood/Italian; $$. Steps from the shore but removed from the main parking area, Narragansett Grill goes the extra mile to make it worth searching out. Fried calamari, for example, come tossed in a sauce of black olives, pepperoncini, and garlic butter—a vast improvement over tartar sauce or ketchup. If the calamari don't appeal, start the meal with grilled local oysters topped with bacon and bread crumbs. Then make your entree a plate of pasta—linguine with marinara and meatballs, or lobster ravioli in pink vodka sauce. During the winter, the grill offers bargain "hometown" entrees like fish-and-chips or half a roast chicken on Wednesday night.

Newport Creamery, 7679 Post Rd., North Kingstown, RI 02852; (401) 294-2087; and 781 Tiogue Ave., Coventry, RI 02816; (401) 821-2265; newportcreamery.com; Casual American; $. The original is in Middletown (see p. 236), but both of these outposts of Rhode Island's own chain of medium-fast food establishments built around good ice cream serve the system-wide menu of burgers, sandwiches, and salads as well as the "Awful Awful" thick ice cream shakes.

Oatley's Family Restaurant, 1717 Ten Rod Rd., North Kingstown, RI 02852; (401) 295-5126; Casual American; $. A breakfast and

lunch spot, Oatley's has a winning staff and a menu of lightly seasoned traditional fare. Egg dishes are handled well, though home
fries tend to be a bit bland (good for those on a limited-salt diet).
Oatley's is a favorite with many self-proclaimed New York System
wiener aficionados since it serves a spicy meat sauce full of big
pieces of onion. Cash only.

Ocean House, 1 Bluff Ave., Watch Hill, RI 02891; (401) 584-
7000; oceanhouseri.com; New American; Bistro $$–$$$, Seasons
$$$–$$$$. Moored like a big yellow ocean-liner version of Noah's
Ark on Mount Ararat, the looming Ocean House resort overlooks the
village and beaches of Watch Hill from the highest point around.
The dining program includes a light veranda menu in season, a
robust bistro menu for somewhat more casual dining, and the
Seasons dining room for elegant service that would do any of the
Swiss grand hotels proud. But while Seasons adheres to the kind of
organized perfection of a Swiss kitchen, the food is decidedly north-
eastern American—drawing on local fisheries and farms for every-
thing from the butter-poached lobster to the grilled Long Island
tuna with Hudson River *foie gras* to the natural grass-fed beef
from Pineland Farm in Maine. The ocean vistas are as striking
as on any real ocean liner. For a special experience, try to
arrange dinner at the Chef's Counter overlooking the open
kitchen and watch your meal as it's made. The dress code
at Seasons rules out jeans and shorts at dinner and
requires men to wear collared shirts and suggests
they add a jacket as well.

Olympia Tea Room, 74 Bay St., Watch Hill, RI 02891; (401) 348-8211; olympiatearoom.com; New American/Casual American; $$–$$$. Olympia Tea Room bills itself as "Famous Not Fancy Since 1916." Jack and Marcia Felber have operated the restaurant since 1980, and their daughter is in the business as well. That kind of close attention to detail makes the Olympia Tea Room a consistent winner. The menu ranges from casual fare like calamari (breaded and fried, sautéed in marinara, or grilled and chilled with chopped cucumber, tomato, red onion, garlic, and red pepper) to roasted whole flounder or bone-in rib eye steak. Seasonal specials take advantage of whatever fish are running in Long Island Sound and whatever is being picked on the local farms. (Like many Westerly/Watch Hill restaurants, Olympia gets its fish from nearby Stonington, Connecticut.) Open May through Nov.

Perks & Corks, 48 High St., Westerly, RI 02891; (401) 596-1260; perksandcorks.com; Casual American; $. Like its neighbor, **The Malted Barley** (see p. 172), Perks & Corks settled on doing one kind of food well. In this case, it's the grilled cheese sandwich, which comes in 11 variations named rather haphazardly for musicians, with another 24 potential add-ons that range from bacon to ricotta cheese. Daytime drinks of choice are usually coffee ("perks"), while the "corks" come out when the sun's over the yardarm. (The wines are augmented by beers and cocktails.) Musicians play live on the weekends, further enhancing the feel of a hippie-era coffee house.

Phil's Main Street Grille, 323 Main St., Wakefield, RI 02879; (401) 783-4073; philsmainstreetgrille.com; Casual American; $–$$. The original Phil's has been a breakfast and lunch stalwart of this end of South County since the 1940s. It's long been a favorite breakfast spot for URI students. The basic menu is available in the street-level "diner" room (complete with wooden booths). That might mean a kielbasa omelet at breakfast or a tuna melt at lunch. In 2010, Phil's opened an upstairs dining room ("the loft") and an outdoor deck ("the roof") where lunch and dinner are served. The dinner plates are a little more ambitious than the time-honored lunch menu, but they're still homey renditions of classics—baked scallops, meatballs or sausage in red sauce with pasta, fish-and-chips, and (on Friday and Saturday night) prime rib in 12-ounce and 16-ounce portions. You couldn't ask for a friendlier place, and the paper placemats at breakfast and lunch even have discount coupons for other local merchants.

Phil's of Bonnet, 909 Boston Neck Rd., Narragansett, RI 02882; (401) 789-1351; philsmainstreetgrille.com; Casual American; $. Open just for breakfast and lunch, this strip-mall offshoot of the original Phil's in Wakefield serves the same menu of eggs, pancakes, burgers, and sandwiches.

Plum Pt. Bistro, 1814 Boston Neck Rd., Saunderstown, RI 02874; (401) 667-4999; plumptbistro.com; New American/Italian; $$–$$$. Some people know how to throw a party, and some people know how to cook for a crowd. Ralph and Elisa Conte know how to do both: It's called running a bistro. They proved it in Providence with the late, lamented Raphael Bar-Risto, and they've made it happen again practically in the shadow of the Saunderstown-Jamestown bridge just up the road from historic Casey's Farm. This time around daughter Zoe manages the front of the classy-looking house and son Raffi tends bar. This being the Rhode Island coast, you can't go wrong with the local littlenecks, cherrystones, and oysters on the raw bar. Ralph's fabulous homemade pastas are still around, but in new permutations like pappardelle with hen-of-the-woods mushroom, fire-roasted tomatoes, vermouth, green peas, and just a dab of mascarpone. Conte has always shown a willingness to go big with a few simple flavors on a plate. That shows in a simple cornmeal-crusted local cod with slaw, espresso- and cocoa-braised short ribs, or even an appetizer of duck confit crepes with blueberry brown butter. During warm weather, there's lots of outdoor seating on a covered wooden deck adjacent to a marble bar, but reservations are taken only for the indoor tables. The wine list tends toward soft, off-dry California, French, and Italian sips, almost all of them nicely matched to the menu.

Shelter Harbor Inn, 10 Wagner Rd., Westerly, RI 02891; (401) 322-8883; shelterharborinn.com; Traditional American; $$–$$$.

This country inn serves three meals a day to guests and non-guests in its warren of small dining rooms (and, in season, on the sun porch) in a circa-1810 farmhouse. The dinner menu is rather classic (butter-poached lobster, grilled steak, cedar-plank salmon, grilled lamb chops) except for the inn's "classics," which include some old-fashioned dishes that we haven't seen in years—finnan haddie (smoked salmon, instead of the traditional haddock, poached in cream), hazelnut-crusted chicken, and sautéed calf's liver. The simple Sunday brunch menu consists of six to seven dishes ranging from the quiche of the day to banana-walnut french toast, but it may be the inn's most popular meal. Be sure to reserve ahead.

Siena Cucina-Enoteca, 5600 Post Rd., East Greenwich, RI 02818; (401) 885-8850; sienari.com; Italian; $$$. The Tarro brothers (Chris at the front of the house, Anthony as the chef) may have been born and raised in Warwick, but their hearts and tastebuds belong to Tuscany. This suburban sister to the **Federal Hill Siena** (see p. 51) finds room to stretch out a bit in its strip mall location, so the menu is a little broader, the wine list a little longer, and the vibe a little more laid back. The *enoteca's* signature tasting boards are a good way to assemble antipasti of meats, cheeses, and olives, and if you're really planning to spend an evening sipping good Italian wine and nibbling, you might make the next course a grilled pizza to share. But if you've come for a meal, look farther down the menu at the beef and fish dishes. Wines by the bottle are unusual bargains by restaurant standards.

Small Axe Cafe, The Fantastic Umbrella Factory, 4820 Old Post Rd., Charlestown, RI 02813; (401) 364-3638; New American; $$. You can be forgiven if you assume that Small Axe Cafe is a bean-sprout-and-avocado eatery, since it's located on the side of the Small Axe Productions crafts and imports store at the neo-hippie Umbrella Factory compound. But while you might find the occasional black bean burrito at lunch, this collaboration between Chef Mark Pendola and grower Gino Turano (whose father owns the property) is dead-serious contemporary farm-to-table cooking. Menus change frequently, based on available ingredients. Dinner might feature pan-seared yellowfin tuna with a marinated tomato and cucumber salad one week, and swordfish in a brown butter sauce the next as that big fish moves up the coast. Garden salads are celebrations of the land's bounty, and the countercultural compound vibe even pays off—the chickens that have free run of the property supply about half the restaurant's eggs. BYOB.

Snoopy's Diner, 4001 Quaker Ln., North Kingstown, RI 02852; (401) 295-1533; snoopysdiner.com; Casual American; $. This classic 1941 Silk City Diner, manufactured in Paterson, New Jersey, may be one of the best-preserved stainless steel diners of its kind in the country. Located in this rural spot since 1981, Snoopy's is open for breakfast and lunch, serving simple morning egg classics (including steak and eggs), New York System wieners, and lunchtime grinders and sandwiches. The "businessman luncheon special" consists of a cup of soup, a grilled cheese sandwich, coffee or tea, and pudding or Jell-O. Ward Cleaver would have approved.

Spain of Narragansett, 1144 Ocean Rd., Narragansett, RI 02882; (401) 783-9770; spainri.com; Spanish/Seafood; $$. This Galilee restaurant is a wonderful amalgam of a classy Spanish restaurant, an American grill, and a seafood emporium. All three come together in the paella Valenciana for two, which is so loaded with shrimp, sea scallops, clams, mussels, chicken, chorizo, and calamari that the saffron rice barely gets to play a supporting role. (In Spain, it would be the other way around.) A sprinkling of other traditional Spanish dishes (spinach sauteed in olive oil with garlic, golden raisins, and pine nuts, for example) justify the restaurant's name, but the owners long ago opted for pleasing their customers over maintaining some sort of misguided authenticity. During the summer, Spain is full every night, in part because it offers some of the most glamorous dining and finest service in South County.

Station House Restaurant, 3711 Kingstown Rd., South Kingstown, RI 02892; (401) 783-0800; stationhouseri.com; Casual American; $. Chef-Owner Michael LaBonte caters to folks who like their breakfast late and lunch early. The Station House (so-called for its proximity to the South Kingstown Amtrak station) serves breakfast all day and usually starts lunch service around 10:30 a.m. LaBonte whips up a lot of hollandaise sauce for the weekends to top eggs Benedict or Florentine as well as crabcakes. During the week, the "Johnny Combo" is a good bet: two jonnycakes, two eggs, and a half order of breakfast meat. Cash only.

T's Restaurant, 5600 Post Rd., East Greenwich, RI 02818; (401) 398-7877; and 91 Point Judith Rd., Salt Pond Plaza, Narragansett, RI 02882; (401) 284-3981; tsrestaurantri.com; Casual American; $.

 These two outlets of the Cranston original (see p. 129) serve the same menu of eggs, pancakes, Benedict variations, and casual salads and sandwiches. And they are just as packed because the food is simple fare, well made, at great prices.

Tara's Tipperary Tavern, 907 Matunuck Beach Rd., Matunuck RI 02879; (401) 284-1901; tarasfamilypub.com; Irish/Seafood; $. When you belly up to the bar for a pint at Tara's (formerly the Joyce Family Pub), you'll likely hear a tale or two of how the taps kept pouring here right through Prohibition. Who doesn't love a good story, even when its veracity could be in question? The staff and owners claim Tara's as Rhode Island's oldest Irish pub, and we're happy to grant that distinction. Tara's certainly has a time-worn authenticity and the beachy setting means a clientele that ranges from lobstermen to yachtsmen thirsty for a pint to seaside artists with paint-smeared smocks. The pub fare has a bit of an Irish accent and ranges from a solid Irish breakfast (eggs, bangers, rashers of bacon, hash, baked beans, fried tomato, home fries, and toast) to fish-and-chips to a mile-high corned beef sandwich and burgers. Drafts include the usual Irish suspects as well as Newport Storm.

Tavern by the Sea, 16 W. Main St., Wickford Village, RI 02852; (401) 294-5771; tavernbytheseari.com; Traditional American; $$. Location, location, location. On a sunny afternoon or clear summer evening, there's hardly a more idyllic spot than the outdoor tables of this fixture located on one bank of the tidal inlet that flows through the village. Ducks and swans cruise past as diners enjoy grilled pizzas, Italian-American pastas, steaks, and oven-roasted fish. Even more casual fare—burgers, wraps—is available at lunch and dinner alike.

Wickford Diner, 64 Brown St., Wickford Village, RI 02852; (401) 295-5477; Casual American, $. Originally broadside to Brown Street on the opposite side, this Tierney Dining Car has undergone many modifications over the years, including the grafting of a much larger dining room onto what was once the back of the diner. The original diner section still has striking wood paneling and a wooden counter that serves as a lively bar. The menu is a fairly standard mix of eggs and pancakes at breakfast, and burgers and sandwiches the rest of the day—with a couple of surprises. One such surprise is a terrific flounder wrap. We've never seen a place that rolls up the thin deep-fried fillets to make a sandwich, but it's the easiest-to-eat fish sandwich we've ever encountered. It also tastes terrific.

Block Island: Dining Out (at Sea)

Ten-square-mile, pear-shaped Block Island lies about 13 miles south of the Rhode Island coast and about 14 miles east of Montauk, New York. The only vehicle ferry to the island operates from Point Judith all year. As the island is principally a summer vacation retreat, dining generally falls into two categories: fine restaurants patronized largely by guests at the larger hotels, and extremely casual spots for catching a meal going to or from the beach or your boat. Most establishments are open from early May through October.

Aldo's Bakery, Weldon's Way, New Shoreham, RI 02807; (401) 466-2198; aldosbakery.com; Bakery Cafe. Stop at the bakery or call for delivery of scones and breakfast sandwiches, lunchtime stuffies, an "Italian Taco," as well as baked goods and fresh breads. Aldo's pastry boat delivers to boaters at anchor.

Aldo's Pizzeria & Italian Restaurant, Weldon's Way, New Shoreham, RI 02807; (401) 466-5871; aldosrestaurantblockisland.com; Italian; $$. Originally just a pizza and sub shop, Aldo's has evolved into a full-scale Rhode Island Italian restaurant, complete with fried calamari, eggplant parm, and a clam chowder that often wins island chowder competitions.

Atlantic Inn Restaurant, High Street, New Shoreham, RI 02807; (401) 466-5883; atlanticinn.com; New American; $$$–$$$$. Start with small plates (glazed pork belly, truffled fries) and a cocktail on the veranda or the lawn before settling in for a romantic evening in the dining room where the menu features dinner entrees such as grilled pork tenderloin with pickled cherries.

Ballard's Inn, 42 Water St., New Shoreham, RI 02807; (401) 466-2231; ballardsinn.com; Seafood/Casual American; $$–$$$$. The oceanfront restaurant of this sun-and-fun resort hotel offers a wide range of seafood dishes, lots of steak and chops, and no fewer than 12 different preparations of lobster.

Finn's Seafood Restaurant, 212 Water St., New Shoreham, RI 02807; (401) 466-2473; finnsseafood.com; Seafood; $–$$. Right across from the Old Harbor ferry landing, Finn's has the largest fish market on the island and also operates this casual restaurant that makes everything from stuffies and fried fish sandwiches to boiled lobster and grilled swordfish. Carnivores can order burgers and steaks, but it's really all about the fish.

Hotel Manisses, Spring Street, New Shoreham, RI 02807; (401) 466-2836; blockislandresorts.com; New American; $$$. The main dining room at the Manisses is a throwback to Victorian pomp, but the menu is surprisingly contemporary. Fish dishes lean toward Asian spicing (cod with miso or ginger-turmeric crusted scallops), but there are many meat dishes to satisfy the carnivores. Signature desserts are flaming coffees, served in the upstairs parlor.

Spring House Hotel, Spring Street, New Shoreham, RI 02807; (800) 234-9263, (401) 466-5844; springhousehotel.com; New American; $$$–$$$$. Immense steaks and chops as well as oversized lobsters make dining at the Spring House an exercise in living large. The hotel grows most of its own salad and summer vegetables. A more modest bistro menu strong on pastas is also offered on the Veranda and in Victoria's Parlor.

Winfield's Restaurant, Corn Neck Road, New Shoreham, RI 02807; (401) 466-5856; winfieldsrestaurant.net; New American; $$$. Next to the island's main "nightclub," Yellow Kittens, Winfield's offers fine dining with French and Italian accents in a casual setting. Start with a roasted tomato crab bisque or a duck confit potato salad, then proceed to a spring pea risotto or grilled local swordfish.

Specialty Stores, Markets & Producers

Allie's Donuts, 3661 Quaker Ln., Rte. 2, North Kingstown, RI 02852; (401) 295-8036. We wonder how many people arrive at work with a dusting of white sugar on their clothes from the Allie's doughnut they ate in the car. For eating on the run, it's probably wiser to stick with a simple cake doughnut or honey-dipped or glazed cruller from this immensely popular shop. But a jelly stick with powdered sugar is mighty hard to resist.

Brickley's Homemade Ice Cream, 921 Boston Neck Rd., Narragansett, RI 02882; (401) 789-1784 and 322 Main St., South Kingstown, RI 02879; (401) 782-8864; brickleys.com. Brickley's makes all the ice cream for both locations at the Narragansett facility. That includes seasonal specialties such as blueberry, peach, apple pie, and pumpkin and old favorites such as sweet cream, coffee Oreo, ginger, and "Butter Brickley" (a buttery ice cream with bits of hard caramel crackle). Open mid-March through mid-Oct.

Calvitto's Pizza & Bakery, 90 Point Judith Rd., Narragansett, RI 02882; (401) 783-8086; Bakery. This outpost of the Cranston-based bakery (see p. 131) carries the same range of choices for a quick lunch or snack, including pizza squares, calzones, specialty loaves, and "secret recipe" spinach pies.

Champlin's Seafood, 256 Great Island Rd., Galilee, Narragansett, RI 02882; (401) 783-3152; champlins.com. Although Champlin's stocks cod, haddock, mackerel, whiting, flounder, swordfish, tuna, conger eel, scup, and squid from its various suppliers, the seafood purveyor specializes in lobster, crabs, clams, mussels, and scallops.

Charlestown Wine and Spirits, 4625 Old Post Rd., Charlestown, RI 02813; (401) 364-6626; charlestownwineandspirits.com. Geothermally heated and cooled, this bright, open-beamed wine shop adds "green" to the usual wine-lover's palate of white, red, and rosé. This successor to the Charlestown Package Store is now under the third generation of family manage-ment, and the business has shifted decidedly toward small producer wines from around the world along with craft beers. Free tastings are held every Friday and Saturday, and wine-makers, importers, and other spe-cialists often present their wines at special events in the Tasting Loft.

Chocolate Delicacy, 219 Main St., East Greenwich, RI 02818; (401) 884-4949; chocolatedelicacy.com. You'll find nonpareils, chocolate-covered cherries, cashew and pecan turtles, barks, fudge, and all sorts of filled and molded chocolates at aptly named Chocolate Delicacy. But the shop is especially known for its hand-rolled truffles, including raspberry, rum, pistachio, amaretto, and dark chocolate. A White House chef from the Reagan years taught founder Dave Schaller how to make them. Son Alexander Schaller is also a chocolate enthusiast and is particularly excited about the Easter special "zombie" bunnies. "They're beautiful," he says. "A massive hit."

Co-Op Natural Food Market, 357 Main St., Wakefield, RI 02879; (401) 789-2240; alternativefoodcoop.com. Proximity to the University of Rhode Island makes a natural foods market a no-brainer. This one has been satisfying the organic interests of South County since 1970. There's nothing all that unusual about the goods—except that a small amount of the produce, eggs, and even meat comes from local organic farms. It's also more than a half-hour drive to the nearest **Whole Foods** in Cranston (see p. 138).

DePetrillo's Pizza & Bakery, 797 Tiogue Ave., Coventry, RI 02816; (401) 828-4300; depetrillos.com. DePetrillo's bills itself as the "home of the original pizza party tray," a box containing sheet pizza cut into small squares, that is, in fact, perfect for a party. For a quick snack, stick to a couple of pizza strips or a calzone. For other locations in Smithfield and Warwick, see p. 100 and p. 133.

Ferry Wharf Fish Market, 296 Great Island Rd., Galilee, Narragansett, RI 02882; (401) 782-8088. **Champlin's** (see p. 187) may have the broadest line of seafood among the Galilee fishmongers, but Ferry Wharf has what we think of as a boutique line of fish—just a few species, but the true top of the catch on any given day. If you're planning on cutting your own sashimi or making a tuna carpaccio, come to Ferry Wharf for the fish. Open Apr through Dec.

Hauser Chocolatier, 59 Tom Harvey Rd., Westerly, RI 02891; (401) 596-8866; hauserchocolates.com. For proof perfect that the Swiss are geniuses with chocolate, stop at this retail shop at the factory of Hauser Chocolatier. The company was founded by Swiss-born Reudi Hauser Sr. in 1983 and is best known for its hand-finished truffles. They are made with fresh cream and butter and feature a variety of flavors that enhance the rich chocolate, such as blueberry port, pomegranate, black vinegar, and caramel with sea salt. The company also makes delicate chocolate lace. This unusual confection features lacy patterns of crisp caramel covered in dark chocolate, dark chocolate with mint, or milk chocolate with almonds. We're particularly fond of the beautifully packaged 1-ounce bars. With

flavors such as dark chocolate ginger or milk chocolate pecan, they make a great small treat or gift. A short self-guided tour features views of the factory through a big window and displays of vintage chocolate-making equipment, including elegant hand-dipping forks and decorating tools.

Kenyon's Grist Mill, 21 Glen Rock Rd., West Kingston (Usquepaugh), RI 02892; (401) 783-4054; kenyonsgristmill.com. The folks at Kenyon are almost apologetic when they explain that their current building on the banks of the Queen's River only dates from 1886. The site's history as a grist mill dates back to 1696 and Kenyon still grinds meal and flour using granite millstones quarried in nearby Westerly. Products available in the mill store include, of course, stone-ground white cornmeal for jonnycakes. But you'll also find other stone-ground flours such as whole wheat, rye, and buckwheat, along with mixes for pancakes, cornbread, clamcakes, and clam fritters. Kenyon's invites a lot of other food producers to its **Johnny Cake Festival** in October (see p. 297). Staff also travel to other fairs during the late summer and fall, so call ahead to make sure the mill is up and running if you plan to make a special trip.

Kitchen & Table of Wickford, 68 Brown St., Wickford Village, RI 02852; (401) 295-1105; kitchenandtableofwickford.com. This well-stocked kitchenware store has an excellent selection of hand-made ceramics, including berry bowls from Emerson Creek Pottery in Virginia, "handwarmer" mugs from Clay in Motion in Washington

State, and braided handle bowls from Harry Spring Pottery, made right in Wickford Village. Casting farther afield, the shop also stocks beautifully glazed pottery from Colm De Ris in Ireland and colorful handpainted pitchers and olive servers from Spain.

Michael Gelina's Ice Cream, 975 Tiogue Ave., Coventry, RI 02816; (401) 826-7374. There are lots and lots of choices of hard ice cream, hard yogurt, soft-serve ice cream, and Italian ice at this establishment that recently celebrated 30 years in business. But Gelina's is known for its soft watermelon sherbet. For a refreshing treat, ask for it as a twist with vanilla soft-serve. Otherwise, try a triple-chocolate-dipped frozen banana. Open mid-Feb through late Nov.

The Savory Grape, 1000 Division Rd., Unit 120, East Greenwich, RI 02818; (401) 886-9463; thesavorygrape.com. Even with some of the least restrictive wine-importing regulations in the country, Rhode Island has a paucity of great wine shops—which makes the Savory Grape all the more significant. Wines are arranged not by country or grape, but by body and color, which might give you new ideas about pairing wine with food. That means you'll find a stainless steel Chardonnay in the same "Medium and Rounded" group with a Vermentino or a Viognier, and a fruity Oregon Pinot Noir in the "Light & Juicy" category with a Gattinara. The shop also has a selection of "under $11" finds and a good range of certified organic wines.

Getting into the Spirit

In another age, Michael Reppucci might have been branded a troublemaker or a rabble-rouser. One thing's for sure: He's a revolutionary. Extensive personal market research while pursuing a master's degree in London convinced him that there's no finer libation than a single-malt whiskey, and that America was long overdue for such a drink, even if it couldn't be called scotch. Since malt whiskey is distilled from beer, Reppucci starts with a full-bodied, dark-roasted base beer that has the depth and flavor of a stout. He and master distiller David Pickerel age their product in oak barrels and release it to the Rhode Island market as Uprising Single-Malt Whiskey. As a service to the segment of drinkers that prefers more neutral spirits, Sons of Liberty Spirits also produces Loyal 9 Vodka and Loyal 9 Mint Cucumber Flavored Vodka. Distillery tours are offered on Saturday.

Sons of Liberty Spirits Co., 1425 Kingstown Rd., Peace Dale, South Kingstown, RI 02879; (401) 284-4006; solspirits.com.

Scrumptions, 5600 Post Rd., East Greenwich, RI 02818; (401) 884-0844; scrumptions.com. Scrumptions specializes in wedding cakes but also has an assortment of 6-inch cakes on hand (vanilla with lemon filling, for example, or chocolate with vanilla butter cream) that are perfect for a smaller celebration. Even tinier treats include peanut butter swirl brownies, mini carrot cakes, white chocolate lemon mousse tartlets, cupcakes, and linzer cookies.

Sweenor's Chocolates, 21 Charles St., Wakefield, RI 02879; (401) 783-4433; sweenorschocolates.com. Founded and still based in Cranston (see p. 137), Sweenor's claims to be the largest chocolate manufacturer in Rhode Island. This shop also stocks the full assortment of bars, truffles, filled chocolates, and very popular nut barks and clusters.

Wickford Factory Outlet, 21 W. Main St., Wickford, RI 02852; (401) 294-8430. We're always pleased to find shops that carry commercial-grade cooking and serving pieces. This "outlet" stocks commercial-quality baking dishes, whisks, aluminum pans, and peppermills, along with hotel dinnerware, old-fashioned diner mugs, and lots of commercial barware and pub glasses. That's in addition to beautiful linens from France, wooden salad bowls and breadboxes, various sizes of stainless steel mixing bowls or glass canning jars, and great starter sets of four place settings of dinnerware. Oh, did we mention that everything is discounted at least 20 percent and often considerably more?

Carpenter's Farm, 522 Matunuck Beach Rd., Wakefield, RI 02879; (401) 783-7550; carpentersfarm.org; Farmstand. In addition to fresh-picked vegetables, this family farm, now in its fifth generation, also sells its own fresh beef and Thanksgiving turkeys. If you're planning a cookout, you can also pick up some of Carpenter's own barbecue and steak sauces, along with beautiful jars of corn, sweet pepper or zucchini relish or hot roasted garlic or apple cranberry salsa. If you're planning Thanksgiving dinner, you can select a pumpkin or apple walnut pie. Open Apr through Thanksgiving.

Delvecchio Farms, 302 Potter Rd., North Kingstown, RI 02852; (401) 884-9598; PYO. Once you've picked your fill of blueberries, you can select some tomatoes, squash, or peppers at the small honor-system farmstand—more a tented table—at this picturesque property with tall trees and stone walls. Open July through Sept; call first.

Langworthy Farm Winery, 308 Shore Rd., Westerly, RI 02891; (401) 322-7791; langworthyfarm.com/thewinery.html; Winery. Located only a half-mile from Misquamicut Beach, Langworthy takes advantage of the buffering effect of the ocean on the climate to grow Chardonnay, Pinot Blanc, and Riesling grapes, along with a little Merlot. The winery buys additional grapes from Long Island to extend the line of wines to include several Chardonnays with varying levels of oak, Cabernet Franc, Merlot, Pinot Noir, and a white blend.

The wines are made with a lot of restraint and elegance, making good expression of the varietals. The big surprise is a white Merlot, a blush wine with a strong Merlot character and substantial residual sugar. It's quite good with strong cheese and crackers.

Macomber's Blueberry Farm, Old Rice City Rd., Coventry, RI 02816; (401) 397-5079; macombersblueberryfarm.shutterfly.com; PYO. If you don't have time to pick your own blueberries, you can call ahead and ask if a member of the Macomber family can pick some for you. The carefully maintained 2-acre farm was founded in 1985. In addition to blueberries, the Macombers also grow vegetables, including German garlic, a hardneck variety with large cloves that is good for roasting. Open July and Aug; call ahead.

Manfredi Farms, 77 Dunn's Corner Rd., Westerly, RI 02891; (401) 322-0027; Farmstand/PYO. Even if your kids don't like vegetables, they will love Manfredi Farms with its pens of goats, sheep, and donkeys just waiting to be petted and fed. (Small bunches of carrots and single apples are sold for just that purpose.) But Manfredi is best known for its gourmet sweet corn and tomatoes and adults generally stop in for a few ears of bicolor, white, or triple-sweet yellow corn along with luscious ripe tomatoes (the names of which seem to be a closely guarded secret). In addition to the usual strawberries, raspberries, blueberries, and pumpkins, the farm's PYO offerings include lettuce, peas, green beans, and rhubarb. Open June through Oct.

Narrow Lane Farm, 213 Narrow Ave., North Kingstown, RI 02852; (401) 294-3584; Farmstand/PYO. **Narrow Lane is a perfect** name for this spot that is, in fact, tucked into the woods down a narrow road. As they ripen, blackberries, peaches, nectarines, and apples are available for picking. Dwarf stock makes it easy for the kids. You might want to pick up a jar of honey while you're at it. Open Aug through Oct.

Schartner Farms, Route 2 and 1 Arnold Place, Exeter, RI 02822; (401) 294-2044; schartnerfarms.com; Farmstand/PYO. **We like the** careful signage at this large farmstand. All Schartner Farms produce carries a "Schartner's Own" label, including several varieties of eggplant; hot or green peppers; green leaf, red leaf, and romaine lettuce; yellow, white, red, and cipollini onions; shallots; tomatoes; and Italian pole beans. Schartner supplements its harvest with other local crops, along with local honey and maple syrup, cheeses, and both Rhode Island– and Connecticut-made goat cheeses. For a quick meal, pick up Schartner's own eggplant parmesan made with fresh or smoked mozzarella and a peach or apple pie. Open Feb through Dec.

Sunset Farm, 505 Point Judith Rd., Narragansett, RI 02882; (401) 789-4070; Farmstand. We're hard-pressed to think of a more beautiful agricultural spot than Sunset Farm, with its historic buildings set far back from the road and surrounded by green pasture. You can purchase fresh vegetables, homemade jams, relishes, and pies, but Sunset is primarily a place to come for fresh, all-natural beef and pork. The animals are slaughtered and butchered in a USDA-inspected facility off-site, and return as tidy freezer packages of the usual cuts. Pork is also available as cured bacon and as breakfast and Italian sausages. Many restaurants feature Sunset Farm beef on their menus. Open July through Nov.

Farmers' Markets

Block Island Farmers' Market, Manisses Corner, Block Island. Wed from 9 to 11 a.m., June through Sept.

Block Island Farmers' Market, Negus Park, Block Island. Sat from 9 to 11 a.m., June through Oct.

Charlestown Farmers' Market, Crossmills Public Library, 4417 Old Post Rd., Charlestown. Fri from 9 a.m. to noon, June through Sept.

Coastal Growers Farmers' Market, Casey Farm, 2325 Boston Neck Rd., Saunderstown. Sat from 9 a.m. to noon, May through Oct.

Cross Mills Farmers' Market, 4219 Old Post Rd., Charlestown. Sat from 9 a.m. to 1 p.m., May through Oct.

East Greenwich Farmers' Market, Rector St. between Church and Spring streets, East Greenwich. Mon from 3 to 6 p.m., Sept and Oct.

Exeter Farmers' Market, Exeter Library, 773 Ten Rod Rd., Exeter. Wed from 3:30 to 6:30 p.m., July through Oct.

Fishermen's Memorial Park Farmers' Market, Fishermen's Memorial State Park, Narragansett. Sun from 9 a.m. to 1 p.m., May through Oct.

Richmond Farmers' Market, Richmond Town Hall, 5 Richmond Townhouse Rd., Richmond. Sat from 8:30 a.m. to noon, May through Oct.

South Kingstown Farmers' Market, University of Rhode Island East Farm, Kingston. Sat from 8:30 a.m. to noon, May through Oct.

South Kingstown Farmers' Market, Marina Park, Wakefield. Tues from 2 to 6 p.m., May through Oct.

South Kingstown Indoor Wintertime Market, Peacedale Mill Complex, 1425 Kingstown Rd., Peacedale. Sat from 10 a.m. to 2 p.m., Nov through May.

Weekapaug Farmers' Market, 4 Wawaloam Ave., Westerly. Fri from 8:30 to 11:30 a.m., June through Aug.

Westerly/Avondale Farmers' Market, 93 Watch Hill Rd., Westerly. Fri from 3 to 5:30 p.m., June through Sept.

Westerly/Pawcatuck Farmers' Market, 85 Main St., Westerly. Thurs from 10 a.m. to 2 p.m., June through Oct.

Wintertime Coastal Growers Market, Lafayette Mill, 640 Ten Rod Rd., North Kingstown. Sat from 10 a.m. to 1 p.m., Nov through May.

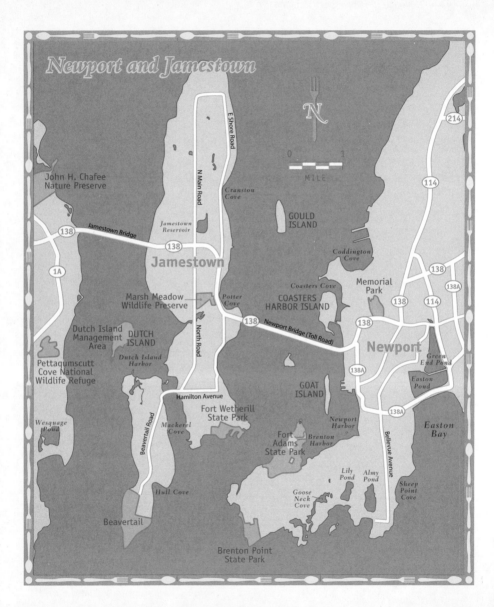

Newport and Jamestown

214

114

John H. Chafee
Nature Preserve

E Shore Road

N Main Road

Jamestown Bridge

138

138

1A

Jamestown

Jamestown
Reservoir

Cranston
Cove

GOULD
ISLAND

Coddington
Cove

138

138A

Marsh Meadow
Wildlife Preserve

Potter
Cove

Coasters Cove

COASTERS
HARBOR ISLAND

Memorial
Park

114

Dutch Island
Management
Area

DUTCH
ISLAND

North Road

138

Newport Bridge (Toll Road)

138

138

Newport

Dutch Island
Harbor

Pettaqumscutt
Cove National
Wildlife Refuge

138A

Green
End Pond

Hamilton Avenue

Easton
Pond

Beavertail Road

Wesquage
Pond

Mackerel
Cove

Fort Wetherill
State Park

GOAT
ISLAND

138A

Belleve Avenue

Easton
Bay

Fort
Adams
State Park

Brenton
Harbor

Newport
Harbor

Lily
Pond

Almy
Pond

Sheep
Point
Cove

Hull Cove

Goose
Neck
Cove

Beavertail

Brenton Point
State Park

N

0   1
MILE

Newport &
Jamestown

Newport is one of the great yacht harbors of the world. The yachty crowd that frequents the beautiful city would rather go out to dine than eat aboard and usually has the wherewithal to do so. Fortunately, while Newport's harbor bristles with the masts of pleasure vessels, the fishing ports of southern Rhode Island are not that far away. The best restaurants tend to emphasize the local catch. Menus lean extensively on seafood, from casual joints selling fried calamari and stuffed clams to day-tripping tourists to elegant white-tablecloth rooms serving delicate treatments of native swordfish or yellowfin tuna to those on a yachtsman's budget.

The greatest concentration of restaurants in Newport is along the harbor on Thames Street and on the various wharves that bristle along the shore. But you might find a greater sense of neighborhood by leaving the touristic side of Newport behind and investigating some of the youth-oriented establishments on Washington

Square and Broadway, or the ethnic (mostly Italian and Old WASP) restaurants of Memorial and Bellevue Avenues. For an altogether different kind of community, cross the Pell Bridge (or take the ferry) from Newport to funkier, more rustic Jamestown. A smattering of restaurants on Narragansett Avenue offer a good time with good fish and good company.

Foodie Faves

Aloha Cafe, Seamens Church Institute, 18 Market Sq., Newport, RI 02840; (401) 846-7038; Casual American; $. A striking mural of a Narragansett Bay nautical chart greets visitors in the foyer of the Seamen's Church Institute, which was founded in 1919 to "provide a safe haven for mariners." The Institute welcomes everyone to its Aloha Cafe, a good-value breakfast and lunch choice on Newport Harbor. Breakfast options include three-egg omelets, egg sandwiches, and pancakes. At lunch, Aloha Cafe's clam chowder is a local favorite to pair with a BLT, grilled cheese and tomato, or turkey club sandwich. Profits help support the work of the Institute, which has expanded its mission to serve a broader base of people in need.

Asterisk, 599 Thames St., Newport, RI 02840; (401) 841-8833; asterisknewport.com; Seafood/New American; $$–$$$. Since Asterisk rather resembles an auto service garage from the outside, the unknowing pass it by, while foodies who've listened to the local grapevine already have a reservation. Chef John Bach-Sorensen hails from Denmark, and the contemporary Scandinavian bent for clean, simple flavors is very much at the fore on his menus. Given his druthers, though, Bach-Sorensen is happy to throw fish on the grill and pair it with delicious sides. Grilled shrimp might be accompanied by a melange of Spanish paprika, Vidalia onions, and corn over grits. A summer ratatouille and tomato basil butter are more likely to go with grilled swordfish.

Barking Crab, 151 Swinburne Row, Newport, RI 02840; (401) 846-2722; barkingcrab.com; Seafood; $–$$$. A dry-land clone of the Boston waterfront original, this Barking Crab is a casual seafood joint located in the Brick Market Place II development off Lower Thames Street. Prices and clientele reflect the tourist location, but you can get all manner of traditional seafood, usually with a Boston accent (no doughball clamcakes, for example). The emphasis here is on deep-fried seafood, but you can order steamed lobster, crab, and clams, as well as baked scrod and grilled swordfish. Rib eye steak and barbecued St. Louis–style ribs satisfy the non-fish-eaters. Dining is on picnic tables under a yellow-and-red striped awning.

Bay Voyage Inn, Wyndham Bay Voyage Inn, 150 Conanicus Ave., Jamestown, RI 02835; wyndhambayvoyageinn.com; Traditional American; $$–$$$. Established in 1889, when New Yorkers of the Gilded Age still came to Newport on their steam yachts, the Bay Voyage Inn has a spectacular view of Newport harbor and the Pell Bridge. Although the traditional fare of the dinner menu has its adherents, the Sunday brunch is celebrated far and wide for its selection of egg dishes, its carving table, its smoked salmon display, and the dessert station with bananas Foster and hand-dipped chocolate strawberries.

Benjamin's Restaurant and Raw Bar, 254 Thames St., Newport, RI 02840; (401) 846-8768; benjaminsrawbar.com; Seafood/Traditional American; $$. Open from breakfast through late evening, Benjamin's aims to be everyone's all-purpose restaurant. Seafood gets top billing on the menu, with Long Island Sound bluepoints and Cape Cod oysters starring on the raw bar. The post-dinner evening bar scene can get hectic in the summer, making a late dinner inadvisable, but lunch can be a feast that you can spread out across the afternoon with raw bar goodies and drinks or make haste with a lobster salad roll or a Philly cheesesteak.

Bishop's 4th Street Diner, 184 Kalbfus Rd., Newport, RI 02840; (401) 847-2069; Casual American; $. This 1950s Jerry O'Mahony dining car was relocated from Swansea, Massachusetts, to Newport in 1967. The awkward traffic circle location does not deter diners looking for a friendly spot for a breakfast of "johnny cakes" (as they are spelled on the menu), biscuits and gravy, or Portuguese french toast. Lunch options include burgers, club sandwiches, and fresh sliced turkey or meat loaf sandwiches. The diner stays open on Friday night to serve fried scallop or clam strip plates, fish-and-chips, shepherd's pie, and other dinner specials. Cash only.

The Black Pearl, Bannister's Wharf, Newport, RI 02840; (401) 846-5264; blackpearlnewport.com; Seafood/Traditional American; $–$$$. The forest-green walls and polished black trim of the Commodore's Room recall the decorating style of the salons aboard late-19th-century yachts. Indeed, the Black Pearl was named for the brigantine rig owned by Barclay H. Warburton III, who transformed the former sail loft and machine shop into a formal dining room in 1967. Lobster, swordfish, steaks, and chops dominate the dinner menu, though you can order lighter sandwiches and burgers in the tavern, or go full-on casual and sit outside on the patio to sip cocktails and order plates of oysters and clams or shrimp cocktail. Closed Jan through mid-Feb.

Bouchard Restaurant, 505 Thames St., Newport, RI 02840; (401) 846-0123; bouchardnewport.com; French; $$$. There's a certain gastronomic poetry to reciting the classical French menu of Bouchard, beginning with the *pâté de foie gras* or the *assiette de saumon fumé* (smoked salmon) and moving on to the *sole de Douvre*

(Dover sole) and the *magret de canard* (duck breast). Chef-Owner Albert Bouchard handles the kitchen, wife Sarah the dining room. Surprisingly relaxed for a formal French restaurant, Bouchard excels at the classics. The Grand Marnier soufflé is inevitably a dessert that ends the meal (literally) on a high note.

Brick Alley Pub & Restaurant, 140 Thames St., Newport, RI 02840; (401) 849-6334; brickalley.com; Traditional American; $–$$. With its wood-paneled walls covered in Newport memorabilia, Brick Alley has been a hit with Newport visitors for decades. In addition to almost every burger and sandwich variation you can imagine, Brick Alley serves grilled steaks, baked pastas and seafood dishes, and the new standard for comfort food with attitude, the lobster mac and cheese. The bowl of Portuguese clams (steamed with crushed red pepper and *chouriço,* among many other ingredients) remains one of the restaurant's most popular dishes. All full dinners include the soup, salad, and bread buffet—which is available by itself at lunch.

Buskers Pub and Restaurant, 178 Thames St., Newport, RI 02840; (401) 846-5856; buskerspub.com; Irish/Casual American; $–$$. It's always great to see a bar upgrade its kitchen and reach for a little more glory with a true gastropub menu. Even the burgers are a little classier than you might expect, coming on a Kaiser roll. In fact, the "Gourmet" burger is an immense patty of ground beef, egg, Dijon mustard, red onion, Parmesan cheese, and herbs. An authentic lamb stew headlines the Irish corner of the menu. Buskers serves brunch dishes (including eggs Benedict variations) daily from 11 a.m. to 3 p.m., but you can order a traditional Irish breakfast of eggs, rashers (bacon), bangers, black and white pudding, Irish baked beans, homemade brown bread, and tomato at any hour. Beers are poured in imperial measure—a "pint" is 20 fluid ounces, a "glass" is 10.

Cafe Zelda, 528 Thames St., Newport, RI 02840; (401) 849-4002; cafezelda.com; New American; $$–$$$. Striking a pose as a casual, almost Caribbean restaurant, Zelda serves a number of Mediterranean seafood classics (such as bouillabaisse and scallops in Pernod cream sauce). But the beef and chicken dishes are no mere afterthoughts—they receive the same attention as the fish. Even the house burger comes with melted Vermont cheddar, sautéed mushrooms and onions, and can be ordered on a Portuguese bun. Best bets are the nightly specials, which tend to take good advantage of the local catch and the harvest of nearby farms.

Canfield House, 5 Memorial Blvd., Newport, RI 02840; (401) 847-0416; canfieldhousenewport.com; Continental; $$–$$$. In an age when every restaurant is striving to be youthful and trendy, Canfield House prizes its sense of decorum and its time-tested cuisine. The building was a small Edwardian-era casino (the card rooms are bedrooms in the B&B side) and boasts a large function room for weddings, anniversaries, and business events. A dependable spot to get grilled prime rib or lobster and scallop pie, Canfield House has a certain récherché appeal.

Castle Hill Inn, 590 Ocean Dr., Newport, RI 02840; (401) 849-3885; castlehillinn.com; New American; $$$$. The stunning views from the hilltop at the mouth of Newport Harbor combine with exquisitely prepared food, polished service, and a beautiful dining room to make a meal at Castle Hill Inn a repast to remember. If you charge it, you could be remembering it for months to come. But you get what you pay for—painstakingly crafted plates composed of the best possible ingredients. The scallops are not just pan-seared, they're accompanied by a disk of compressed melon, some chile peppers, and a curry emulsion. The applewood-smoked confit of wild boar appears with shaved radish and candied citrus. Even the grilled swordfish fillet comes with lemon salt and a smoked piperade emulsion. Dinner menus offer three options: a 3-course prix-fixe, a 5-course tasting menu, and an 8-course *dégustation* menu. You can enjoy some of the sense of privilege at a fraction of the price by opting for lunch on the lawn. The surf 'n' turf burger of local beef and Maine lobster pairs well with a light Burgundy.

Chopmist Charlie's, 40 Narragansett Ave., Jamestown, RI 02835; (401) 423-1020; chopmistcharlies.com; Seafood; $$. Despite the hokey nautical decor, many patrons consider Charlie's their favorite restaurant for Rhode Island seafood. Clams are minced very fine in both the chowders and clamcakes, leading the uninitiated to wonder if they were inadvertently left out. Nope—that's an old-time Rhody style. To really see the clams, order the fried whole-belly clams. Some of the best dishes come from beneath the broiler—broiled scrod with a butter crumb topping, broiled scrod with lobster cream sauce, broiled sea scallops, and two versions of steak.

Clarke Cooke House, 26 Bannister's Wharf, Newport, RI 02840; (401) 849-2900; clarkecooke.com; Continental; $$–$$$$. This circa-1780 building features a warren of rooms, including the more formal (and more expensive) Porch and Skybar, as well as the less formal (and less expensive) Candy Store and the Bistro. The bistro menu features a limited selection of three fish, three meats, and three pasta dishes, while the Porch menu features refined delicacies such as butter-poached Kobe beef sirloin, sautéed breast of squab with mission figs and *foie gras,* and a classic roast rack of lamb with minted tarragon glaze.

Corner Cafe, 110 Broadway, Newport, RI 02840; (401) 846-0606; cornercafenewport.com; Casual American; $. The Corner Cafe was originally intended as a breakfast and lunch hangout for folks who work in other restaurants. But the inventive menu that such a clientele expected has served to draw a much broader following. The choices can be a bit overwhelming. For simplicity's sake, stick with the burritos. Breakfast options include the West Coast with eggs, Canadian bacon, avocado and pepper jack cheese or the East Coast with eggs, *chouriço,* onion, mushrooms, and Gorgonzola. Among the lunchtime offerings are the Sea Side with grilled shrimp, sun-dried tomato, avocado, spinach, and pepper jack cheese, or the Avocado Chicken, which pairs its namesake ingredients with feta, lettuce, tomato, onion, and blue cheese dressing.

Fluke Wine, Bar & Kitchen, 41 Bowen's Wharf, Newport, RI 02840; (401) 849-7778; flukewinebar.com; New American; $$–$$$. Fluke proves the old adage that dining out should be fun. True to its name, this handsome little upstairs room at Bowen's Wharf features more than 20 wines by the glass in addition to a huge bottle list (most under $50). The food complements the wines—whether you order chicken empanadas or almond-filled, bacon-wrapped dates off the snacks list, crispy fried oysters with mango-pepper relish off the small plates, or rabbit orecchiette with fava beans and tomatoes off the large plates. Cleverly conceived, perfectly executed, and efficiently served food of this order makes for a memorable night out.

Gary's Handy Lunch, 462 Thames St., Newport, RI 02840; (401) 847-9480; Casual American; $. A true greasy spoon, Gary's is at its best for the first few hours after opening at 5 a.m. None of the grub breaks new gastronomic ground, and it sometimes backslides a bit from contemporary fresh-and-local standards. That said, keep your order simple—eggs, home fries, and toast, or, at your peril, pancakes—and the hash slingers at the grill will deliver classic American food that would have satisfied Edward Hopper's diner denizens. Popular with Salve Regina students who've pulled all-nighters, Gary's is probably the least expensive food in Newport.

Jamestown Fish, 14 Narragansett Ave., Jamestown, RI 02835; (401) 423-3474; jamestownfishri.com; Seafood; $$–$$$. This small spot a quick walk from the ferry landing offers casual fine dining on top-notch local fish. The de rigueur starter is the fish soup, made with the catch of the day, tomato, fennel, and hot peppers—no shellfish, and no milk or cream. If you opt instead for the roasted strips of eggplant with goat cheese or the mozzarella and roasted peppers, you can always return to the fish soup theme with the signature Jamestown Fish Cookpot, which includes lobster, clams, mussels, scallops, monk-fish, leeks, saffron, garlic, hot pepper, Pernod, fingerling potatoes, and *chouriço*. During warm weather, Jamestown Fish also serves a limited menu outside on the patio—a few fish dishes, a steak, a burger, and a slew of tasty pizzas.

Jamestown Oyster Bar, 22 Narragansett Ave., Jamestown, RI 02835; (401) 423-3380; Seafood; $–$$. Should your cravings for fish and shellfish in Jamestown take a more casual turn than

Jamestown Fish, the Oyster Bar fries up Point Judith calamari with hot peppers, olives, diced tomatoes, and garlic butter. It also sells fresh steamed clams by the pound, and even offers a couple of fancier dinner specials like flounder piccata or oven-roasted cod served with a pair of stuffed jumbo shrimp. Wine is available, but this fish mates better with beer.

The Landing, 30 Bowen's Wharf, Newport, RI 02840; (401) 847-4514; thelandingrestaurantnewport.com; Seafood/Traditional American; $$–$$$. Located at the end of Bowen's Wharf, The Landing has some of the city's best sunset harbor views. The high-ceiling, open rooms also give the space a casual, seasonal air, and there's additional dining on the outdoor patio and upstairs deck. Entrance is through **Aquidneck Lobster** (see p. 224), and the lobster tanks make it tempting to order the crustacean boiled, baked stuffed, or on a roll. Nothing wrong with that. Some old-fashioned 1950s flourishes haunt the menu, like the crab and artichoke dip and the offer to top an 8-ounce steak with fresh lobster meat and creamy sauce. As in all restaurants with menus so long they make your eyes hurt, the best bet is to stick with simple preparations that have to be made to order—grilled, broiled, or sautéed fish without the cover of cream sauce.

Malt on Broadway, 150 Broadway, Newport, RI 02840; (401) 619-1667; New American; $–$$. With a great beer list, a casual mismatched silverware/tableware aesthetic, and a smart small-plates menu at bargain prices, Malt launched as a gastropub from the ground up in 2012 with the challenge of succeeding another neighborhood favorite restaurant that had occupied the same space. Cheese plates are a perfect accompaniment to the malt beverages, and sizzling grilled steaks are a real bargain.

The Mooring, Sayer's Wharf, Newport, RI 02840; (401) 846-2260; mooringrestaurant.com; Seafood; $$–$$$. With a terrific waterfront dining room, the Mooring can't help but emphasize seafood on the menu. Signature sandwiches are available all day, which can keep costs down—a grilled swordfish wrap is roughly half the price of a grilled swordfish steak dinner, for example. It's tempting to simply make a meal of the appetizers—mussels in a broth of *chouriço*, fennel, and tomato; panfried lump crabcakes; flash-fried Galilee calamari with Kalamata olives, hot peppers, and toasted cumin tomato dip; or even a mound of tuna tartare with pickled red onions, carrots, and watermelon. The seafood pie is what we think of as an old yachtsman's comfort food: fish, scallops, shrimp, and lobster in a cognac shellfish cream sauce baked in a savory pastry crust.

Muse by Jonathan Cartwright, Vanderbilt Grace Hotel, 41 Mary St., Newport, RI 02840; (401) 846-6200; vanderbiltgrace.com; New American; $$$$. Dinner is an event at Muse. You make the reservation far in advance, you dress the part (jackets, at least, are recommended for men), and you let yourself be whisked away by the elegance of it all. The prix-fixe menu of appetizer, intermezzo, main course, and dessert is quite reasonably priced for food of this caliber. And the plates are not only lovely to behold and professionally served—they also taste terrific. Cartwright is the executive chef of all the Grace hotels, and he remains based at the White Barn Inn in Kennebunkport, Maine. But there's a synchrony of style with moneyed Newport. You might start with butter-poached smoked lobster with a sweet corn puree, take a break with a chilled cucumber soup with mint crème fraîche, and tuck into a pan-roasted halibut fillet. For dessert, you'll be torn between the chocolate cake with caramelized bananas and the lemon soufflé with vanilla bean ice cream and lavender custard sauce. After dinner, consider retiring to the rooftop bar for a drink and a kingly view over the glittering town.

Newport Creamery, 181 Bellevue Ave., Newport, RI 02840; (401) 846-6332; newportcreamery.com; Casual American; $. You'd think this location would be the original Newport Creamery, but you'll have to drive to Middletown (see p. 236) to see where the original milk bar opened in 1940. As at all the others, you can get a fast meal and a big sundae.

Perro Salado, 19 Charles St., Newport, RI 02840; (401) 619-4777; perrosalado.com; Mexican; $$. Newport is an unlikely place for a Mexican restaurant, but the Salty Dog is an unlikely Mexican-inspired restaurant. The decor is bright and whimsical, the live music is bluesy and rootsy, and the food draws on the flavor profiles

ANY STORM IN A PORT

Four friends at Colby College in Maine spent enough of their undergraduate years developing a taste for beer and getting educations in, among other things, biochemistry, that upon graduation they decided to start a brewery rather than face the "real" world. They're still product-testing, but Coastal Extreme Brewing launched its first Newport Storm beer in 1999, Hurricane Amber Ale. Thousands of bottles, cans, and kegs later, Newport Storm is the dominant "local" beer brand in this end of Rhode Island. The same folks also founded Newport Distilling Company to make Thomas Tew rum, a local spirit found in many a Newport mai tai. The beers and rum are carried by most Newport bars and restaurants with the appropriate license. You can also visit the facility for guided and self-guided tours and tastings Wednesday through Monday. Beer tastings include four beer samples and the sampling glass. Rum tours include tastings of three stages of the process and the tasting glass.

Coastal Extreme Brewing Co., 293 JT Connell Rd., Newport, RI 02840; (401) 849-5232; newportstorm.com.

of traditional Mexican cuisine without trying to be too "authentic." Make no mistake—this isn't one of those formulaic "south-of-the-border" chain restaurants. It's quirky and individualistic, and Chef

 Dan Hall has enough faith in his own palate and vision to make real food with chile flavors. That means dishes like beer-battered mahi-mahi fish tacos; chile-pepper-dusted scallops over a crunchy salad of arugula, jicama, cucumber, and mango; and a chicken tamal with the brick-colored *mole coloradito*. It's a smart and lively scene at night—eclipsed only by the bustle of midday Sunday brunch. Brunch-only dishes include lots of egg variations with salsas and an intriguing chorizo hash.

Pour Judgement Bar & Grill, 32 Broadway, Newport, RI 02871; (401) 619-2115; pourjudgement.com; Casual American; $. This friendly, youth-oriented beer bar features a monster list of ales and beers on tap, an equally good selection in bottles (including large format), and a food menu that matches the malt vibe to a T. Grilled burgers (beef, black bean, chicken, Boca) with a side of the house fries accompanied by smoked Gouda sauce are usually the repasts of choice. Have a Newport Storm Blueberry Ale for a taste of place.

Puerini's Kitchen, 24 Memorial Blvd. W., Newport, RI 02840; (401) 847-5506; puerinisrestaurant.com; Italian; $$. Puerini's has been quietly serving solid Italian-American fare for more than three decades, and every time a tourist ventures off Thames Street and discovers the place, it's celebrated as a "find." The menu is time-tested, and diners in the know order from the veal page—it's been Puerini's specialty from the outset. In fact, it's worth having *vitello* *parmigiano* (veal parm) here at least once to taste how the dish is supposed to be made.

The Red Parrot Restaurant, 348 Thames St., Newport, RI 02840; (401) 847-3800; redparrotrestaurant.com; Seafood/Casual American; $$. Located in a historic red-brick building that was built as a meatpacking house, the Red Parrot claims to be the busiest restaurant in Newport and boasts a 20-page menu of food and specialty frozen drinks. Honestly, it's the type of place that we might have dismissed if it hadn't been for a local couple who advised us to stick with the lobster nachos (with sun-dried tomato cream and cheese) on the appetizer menu and the Luca Bratsies Hot Seafood Pizza (with shrimp, scallops, and crabmeat) on the lunch menu.

Safari Room at OceanCliff, 65 Ridge Rd., Newport, RI 02840; (401) 841-8868; newportexperience.com; New American/Traditional American; $$–$$$. The OceanCliff Resort has some pretty spectacular views from its hillside location on Ocean Drive. The polished New American menu of the Safari Room offers some fancy views on the plate as well, in Italian-influenced dishes like orecchiette tossed with baby artichokes and curled shavings of prosciutto, or grilled wahoo on a bed of asparagus. The selection of prime chops and steaks climbs the size ladder from a delicate filet mignon (10 ounces) to a massive 40-ounce bone-in rib eye.

Salvation Restaurant & Bar, 140 Broadway, Newport, RI 02840; (401) 847-2620; salvation cafe.com; New American; $$. Over two decades, Susan Lamond has made Salvation a fixture among the year-round residents of Newport by serving comfort food for food lovers and running a tropical-themed bar that appeals to the inner Parrothead in us all. (Winter sangria, for example, has green apples, grapes, rosemary simple syrup, a touch of cinnamon, apple cider, and ginger beer.) There's definitely a seafood bias to the daily menu, which usually includes a catch of the day with chickpea fries, and Rhode Island littlenecks swimming in a smoked-tomato nage. Recent renovations of the ancient building created a "barn" area out back, and an outdoor deck and patio. All the better to party, my dears.

Sardella's Restaurant, 30 Memorial Blvd. West, Newport, RI 02840; (401) 849-6312; sardellas.com; Italian; $$. This old-school Italian-American alternative to **Puerini's** (see p. 216) has one leg up on its friendly competitor in that Sardella's has outdoor court-yard dining in warm weather as well as a warren of large and small rooms for parties and functions. Antipasti and salads are among the strengths of the menu, with little surprises like eggplant fries and a salad built around roasted fennel. The lasagna is a hefty, meat-filled entree.

Scales and Shells Restaurant, 527 Thames St., Newport, RI 02840; (401) 846-3474; scalesandshells.com; Seafood; $$–$$$. It's all about the fish in this loud, even raucous brasserie on Thames. The details of the menu are entirely dependent on the catch, as are the prices. But you can always count on local calamari (fried or stuffed), steamed littlenecks (with white wine sauce or spicy marinara), and a bevy of shellfish and pasta dishes. Wood-grilled fish is a bit pricier and varies from night to night. Many patrons come for beer and a clam pizza. And some more beer. The scene at "Upscales," which is located up a flight of stairs, is more sedate and, dare we say, even a little formal. The specific dishes are spelled out in more detail on the menu, but represent more refined versions of the blackboard dishes served downstairs. Although the bill can add up, the restaurant does not accept credit cards.

Smoke House, America's Cup Avenue, Newport, RI 02840; (401) 848-9800; smokehousecafe.com; Barbecue; $–$$. There's something incongruous about a restaurant serving Southern barbecue occupying such a prominent spot along the blue-blooded Yankee harbor of Newport, but the guys in Topsiders with cable-knit sweaters tied around their shoulders have a yen for a pork pig-out now and then too. Quite seriously, this family-friendly restaurant (with a kids' menu) offers some of the best-priced meat-intensive dining in town. This is barbecue for diners who like a heavy, very sweet barbecue sauce on everything. It goes very well with the extremely sweet cornbread.

The Spiced Pear Restaurant, The Chanler Hotel, 117 Memorial Blvd., Newport, RI 02840; (401) 847-2244; thechanler.com/dining; New American; $$$. With warm-weather service on the outdoor terrace high above Easton's Beach, the Spiced Pear has an ambience advantage over many of Newport's other posh dining rooms. Elegant 7- and 9-course tasting menus emphasizing New England fish and meat are offered nightly, while many of the same dishes are also available on the expanded a la carte menu. The Maine diver scallops demonstrate the kitchen's bold approach to classic dishes. They are broiled, but rather than sitting alone in a little casserole surrounded by some bread crumbs and melted butter, they are served with a potato latke, crispy pork belly, some vegetables, and a verjus sauce. Think of the dish as the apotheosis of scallops.

Tallulah on Thames, 464 Thames St., Newport, RI 02840; (401) 849-2433; tallulahonthames.com; New American; $$$. Chef and co-owner Jake Rojas may hail from El Paso, but he's embraced the farmers and fishermen of Rhode Island, Massachusetts, and Connecticut with open arms. Tallulah on Thames is about as locavore a restaurant as can be found in Newport, which means that the menu changes nightly during the growing season and that most of the major ingredients in a dish are credited to their growers/purveyors. Rojas may start with New England provender, but he's not afraid to interject spice profiles from around the globe. Grilled native swordfish, for example, might show up with a basil pesto couscous, a piece of juicy watermelon, segments of heirloom tomato, and a dusting of the Moroccan master spice blend, *ras* *el hanout*. Presentation is worthy of a food magazine, and diners are allowed (maybe even expected) to linger over their meals. That pacing, combined with limited seating, makes reservations essential.

Thames Street Kitchen (TSK), 677 Thames St., Newport, RI 02840; (401) 846-9100; thamesstreet kitchen.com; New American; $$$. Newport twins Julia and Anna Jenkins married a couple of chefs (Chad Hoffer and Tyler Burnley) who had met while working together in the kitchen of BLT Prime in New York. All four moved back to Newport and Chad and 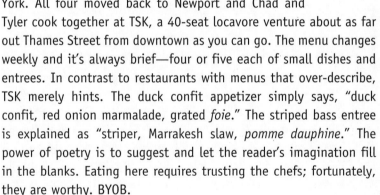 Tyler cook together at TSK, a 40-seat locavore venture about as far out Thames Street from downtown as you can go. The menu changes weekly and it's always brief—four or five each of small dishes and entrees. In contrast to restaurants with menus that over-describe, TSK merely hints. The duck confit appetizer simply says, "duck confit, red onion marmalade, grated *foie*." The striped bass entree is explained as "striper, Marrakesh slaw, *pomme dauphine*." The power of poetry is to suggest and let the reader's imagination fill in the blanks. Eating here requires trusting the chefs; fortunately, they are worthy. BYOB.

Trattoria Simpatico, 13 Narragansett Ave., Jamestown, RI 02835; (401) 423-3731; trattoriasimpatico.com; Italian/New American; $$–$$$. Trattoria Simpatico offers outdoor garden dining all year round, thanks to outdoor heaters. In summer, at least, this is where

Table on the Rails

It takes about 2½ hours for the Newport Dinner Train to make a 22-mile journey along scenic Narragansett Bay on the west coast of Aquidneck Island—plenty of time to enjoy a leisurely lunch or dinner. The tables in the vintage dining cars are dressed in white linen to evoke the storied elegance of rail travel and many diners opt for a simple journey with music and candlelight. But special family nights, a comedy murder mystery, and packages that combine dining with sightseeing are also available.

Newport Dinner Train, 19 America's Cup Ave., Newport, RI 02840; (401) 841-8700; newportdinnertrain.com.

the action is, as the indoor dining rooms seem close and a bit lonely after the expansiveness of the outdoor scene, which often features a live jazz band. Budget diners fare well with pasta dishes, including an excellent pasta Bolognese. The catch of the day fish plate is often the best dish in the house, but it's hard to go wrong with local clams, calamari, and mussels—all offered in a choice of preparations.

22 Bowen's, 22 Bowen's Wharf, Newport, RI 02840; (401) 841-8884; 22bowens.com; Traditional American/Seafood; $$$. We've enjoyed eating lunch here at the dockside tables where a lobster grilled cheese sandwich and a glass of Sancerre seem precisely the right way to while away part of the afternoon. Come evening, most diners prefer indoor tables and the choices shift toward the meals that go well with scotch and with big California reds: porterhouse, Delmonico, sirloin, filet mignon, veal chop. Mind you, some lighter options are available (roasted pork tenderloin, shrimp and linguini, roasted cod with shellfish), but the atmosphere fairly trembles with the smell of grilled beef.

White Horse Tavern, 26 Marlborough St., Newport, RI 02840; (401) 849-3600; whitehorsetavern.us; New American; $$–$$$. A tavern since 1673, White Horse certainly has ye olde atmosphere, although the colonial dining room is rather more formal than many 21st-century diners might expect a tavern to be. The kitchen stays abreast of contemporary tastes, serving a nice house charcuterie platter, salt-cod fritters with preserved lemon aioli, and pan-seared fluke with preserved orange and a spring vegetable succotash. There's a strong emphasis on using local ingredients when possible. Although the kitchen is forging no new frontiers in American dining, the combination of good taste and winning atmosphere makes the White Horse a favorite special-occasion spot for many Rhode Islanders.

Aquidneck Lobster Co., 31 Bowen's Wharf, Newport, RI 02840; (401) 846-0106. Sharing quarters with **The Landing** (see p. 212), this fishmonger is primarily a dealer in lobster. Big spenders like to consider buying some of the monsters swimming in its tanks, although crustaceans that size would be illegal to capture in some lobster-fishing regions. (Lobsters have to be the same size to breed, and the giant lobsters produce exponentially more eggs.) Still, as long as you do the ecologically right thing and stick to bugs under 3 pounds, this is a perfect place to buy live lobster to cook at home. Given a little notice, Aquidneck will even steam the critters for you at $5 per order. At any given time, the fishmonger will also have soft-shell clams, littlenecks, local oysters, sea scallops, and an array of finfish. Cash only.

Cold Fusion Gelato, 389 Thames St., Newport, RI 02840; (401) 849-6777; coldfusiongelato.com. Cold Fusion makes small batches of gelato in the traditional Italian style, but hints of American tastes have found their way into such flavors as sweet corn and blackberries, chipotle peanut butter, bourbon butter pecan, or root beer float. More subtle flavor pairings include blueberry lavender, honey vanilla, and pistachio and saffron. Fresh fruit sorbets might feature passion fruit and mango, dark cherries, or watermelon and mint.

Empire Tea & Coffee, 22 Broadway, Newport, RI 02840; (401) 619-1388; empireteaandcoffee.com. This shop does exactly what the sign says. It sells tea and coffee—either the supplies to make your own, or freshly brewed hot and cold beverages. If you're dragging, perk up with the ultimate caffeine experience called a Midnight Express. It's a shot of espresso and a melted bar of Ghirardelli chocolate topped up with hot coffee. Buzz on.

Jonathan's Cafe, 22 Washington Sq., Newport, RI 02840; (401) 846-6060. A licensee of pioneer micro-roaster Ocean State Coffee, Jonathan's serves a slew of breakfast pastries and egg dishes, but it is prized by locals for the wide variety of single-origin and blended coffees. The espresso roasts tend to be based on Nicaraguan beans.

Kilwins, 262 Thames St., Newport, RI 02840; (401) 619-3998; kilwins.com/newport. Newport is one of only two New England locations for this Michigan-based chocolatier that was founded in 1947 and still relies on many original recipes. Stop for a moment to watch through the window as staff turn out big rolls of fudge on marble slabs or dip apples into copper kettles filled with thick caramel and you will probably find it almost impossible not to enter the shop. Many Kilwins treats feature a combination of chocolate and caramel, such as the signature caramel, chocolate, and pecan turtle or the whole line of "tuttles"—nuggets of dark or milk chocolate and caramel with pecans or cashews. Look also for chocolate fudge with ribbons of caramel, sea-salt caramels enrobed in dark chocolate, and vanilla ice cream with chocolate chips and a caramel swirl.

La Maison de Coco, 28 Bellevue Ave., Newport, RI 02840; (401) 845-2626; lamaisondecoco.com. Michele De Luca-Verley fulfilled a 20-year dream when she opened her chocolate shop in December 2010. All her study and planning has certainly paid off. Her offerings include biscotti, scones, cookies, and tarts, but she has really made a name for herself with her bowls of rich hot chocolate and her tea-infused chocolate truffles. De Luca-Verley makes the truffles daily with fresh cream from **Arruda's Dairy** (see p. 243). In the fall and winter, she favors warming flavors such as ginger and Indian spices, while in the spring and summer she leans toward jasmine peach blossom, lavender, bergamot, and other herbal and floral infusions. "The combination of rose and mint was my biggest surprise," she says. "I thought it might be too perfumey." For those who can't live on chocolate alone, the shop serves crepes, soups, and quiche for lunch.

Long Wharf Seafood, 17 Connell Hwy., Newport, RI 02840; (401) 846-6379; longwharf.info. Just off the downtown Newport exit from the Pell Bridge, this modest little fishmonger almost always has a great selection of finfish and shellfish off local boats. Check the refrigerator and freezer cases for seafood casseroles, chowders, stuffies, and other ready-to-heat dishes.

Mad Hatter, 64 Broadway, Newport, RI 02840; (401) 847-0354; madhatterbakery.com. Baker Audra Lalli Richardson loves creating cakes and cupcakes for special occasions. But she's equally adept at breakfast pastries that can get any day off to a good start. Favorites include scones (apple cinnamon, cranberry, apricot), blueberry coffee cake, and banana bread, which several restaurants use to make french toast. She also turns out cupcakes, bars, cookies, and pies, along with take-out soups, sandwiches, and stuffed quahogs for lunch.

Newport Spice Company, 24 Franklin St., Newport, RI 02840; (401) 846-8400; newportspice .com. Spices run the gamut from adobo seasoning to zahtar, so you'll probably find the ingredient you need for any ethnic cuisine including Cajun seasoning, Indian curry powder, New Mexican chile powder, and sweet and smoked Spanish paprika. You'll also find a good assortment of peppercorns and salts along with flavoring extracts and teas.

Newport Wine Cellar & Le Petit Gourmet, 24 & 26 Bellevue Ave., Newport, RI 02840; (401) 619-3966 (wine) and (401) 619-3882 (cheese); newportwinecellar.com. Set in a small residential neighborhood just uphill from downtown Newport, this two-pronged answer to a refined appetite began as a wine shop selling selected (mostly imported) bottles that represented high quality for the price. The buyers have an uncanny ability to locate the less expensive wines in superb districts—the oenophile's equivalent of buying the most modest house in a great neighborhood. The owners asked the logical question—what's good wine without good bread and cheese?—and subsequently opened Le Petit Gourmet next door. You can even get lunch (a slice of quiche, a bowl of soup, bread and cheese) to eat at one of the tables in the window.

Pan Handlers, 35 Broadway, Newport, RI 02840; (401) 619-3780; panhandlersnewport.com. Small cookware shops often reflect the tastes of their owners. Pan Handlers co-owner Patti Kendall is particularly keen on a beautiful blue enamel Staub bouillabaisse pot with a fish-shaped handle. We like the sleek, modern design of the Breville line of small appliances, including toasters, blenders, coffeemakers, burr coffee grinders, and even a juice fountain. Kendall also stocks a good selection of knives and has an on-site knife-sharpening service. Our choice for most fun product is the battery-powered Kuhn-Rikon Frosting Deco Pen that puts a little oomph into cake decorating.

Slice of Heaven, 32 Narragansett Ave., Jamestown, RI 02835; (401) 423-9866; sliceofheavenri.com. Along with muffins, scones, cookies, and other baked goods, Slice of Heaven offers some interesting variations on classic dishes to enjoy at indoor or outdoor cafe tables. Breakfast options include Grand Marnier french toast made with a croissant or the "lumberjacques" special of french toast, eggs, and bacon. Slice of Heaven's lunchtime clam chowder is spiced with Italian pancetta, sweet corn, and dill, while the "chips" on the beer-battered fish-and-chips plate are actually spicy Cajun fries.

Virgin & Aged, 395 Thames St., Newport, RI 02840; (401) 849-3029; virginandaged.com. "Never forget your first crush" proclaims a T-shirt in this coyly named shop. But the crush in question is not a high school heartthrob. The shirt refers instead to the first crush of the olive harvest, which many consider to yield the finest oil. You can taste for yourself at Virgin & Aged, which imports oils from Europe, the Mediterranean, Australia, and South America to ensure a fresh product throughout the year. In addition to single varietal and blended oils, the shop carries flavored oils such as blood orange, garlic, or tarragon; balsamic vinegars; and a small selection of specialty oils such as white or black truffle or roasted French walnut.

Farmers' Markets

Aquidneck Growers & Artisans Market, 141 Pelham St., Newport. Tues from 2 to 6 p.m., June through Sept.

Aquidneck Growers Market II, Memorial Boulevard between Thames Street and Belleview Avenue, Newport. Wed from 2 to 6 p.m., June through Oct.

Pier 9 Farmers' Market, Pier 9, Newport. Fri from 2 to 6 p.m., July through Oct.

Newport County

Moving away from the city of Newport, the county's population center, this chapter rambles through the villages and along the byways of Aquidneck Island and the communities of Tiverton and Little Compton sandwiched between the Sakonnet River and the Massachusetts border. Millennia of river topsoil deposits over the glacial outwash plain have combined with a climate moderated by the nearby ocean to make these areas some of Rhode Island's most fecund and productive farmland. The state's best wineries are in Newport County, and so are some of the best fruit farms. Casual fish shacks dot the shores, and fine restaurants are also in good supply.

Foodie Faves

Atlantic Grille, 91 Aquidneck Ave., Middletown, RI 02842; (401) 849-4440; atlanticgrille.com; Casual American; $–$$. The Atlantic Grille is especially popular for breakfast and draws a big crowd

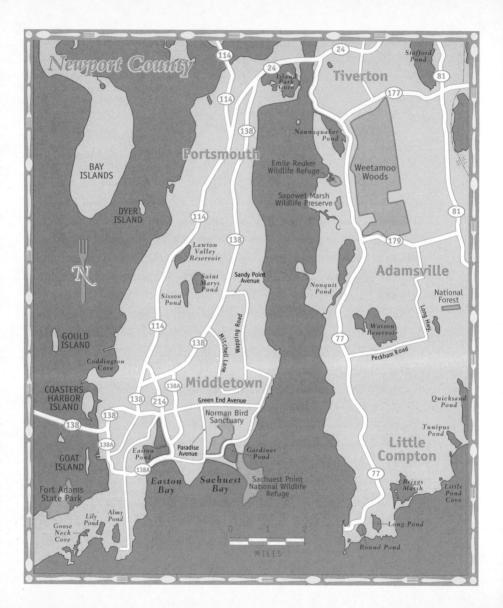

Newport County

Stafford Pond

114

24

Tiverton

24

114

81

Island Park Cove

177

138

Nannaquaker Pond

Portsmouth

BAY ISLANDS

Emile Reuker Wildlife Refuge

Weetamoo Woods

DYER ISLAND

Sapowet Marsh Wildlife Preserve

81

114

179

Lawton Valley Reservoir

138

Adamsville

N

Saint Marys Pond

Sandy Point Avenue

National Forest

Sisson Pond

Nonquit Pond

Long Hwy.

GOULD ISLAND

114

Watson Reservoir

Coddington Cove

138

Mitchell Lane

Wapping Road

77

COASTERS HARBOR ISLAND

138A

Middletown

Peckham Road

Quicksand Pond

138

214

Green End Avenue

138

Tunipus Pond

Norman Bird Sanctuary

Little Compton

138A

138

GOAT ISLAND

Easton Pond

Paradise Avenue

Gardiner Pond

77

Briggs Marsh

138A

Fort Adams State Park

Easton Bay

Sachuest Bay

Sachuest Point National Wildlife Refuge

Little Pond Cove

Goose Neck Cove

Lily Pond

Almy Pond

Long Pond

0   1   2

MILES

Round Pond

on the weekends for its imaginative variations on eggs Benedict, including the Atlantic Benedict with bacon on a grilled corn muffin, the Irish benny with corned beef hash on an English muffin, and the Florentine Benedict with Canadian bacon and spinach. During the week, diners can opt for omelets, egg sandwiches, pancakes, and french toast. For a light lunch or dinner starter, try the clam boil appetizer, which features littlenecks, *chouriço,* hot dog, sausage, potato, onion, and corn steamed in Narragansett beer. The Grille continues the beer theme with Sam Adams beer-battered fish-and-chips.

The Barn, 15 Main St., Little Compton, RI 02837; (401) 635-2985; Casual American; $. This breakfast place in a former barn is a good spot to try a plate of jonnycakes made with cornmeal from **Gray's Grist Mill** (see p. 239). The Barn is also known for its corned beef hash, eggs Benedict special with lobster, Portuguese omelet with *chouriço* and peppers, and for the "six gun on a bun"—eggs, hash, and cheese on a Portuguese sweet roll.

Boat House, 227 Schooner Dr., Tiverton, RI 02878; (401) 624-6300; boathousetiverton.com; Seafood/New American; $$–$$$. The Newport Restaurant Group took great advantage of the location in designing the Boat House. Walk to the door and you're tempted to continue around to the deck on the harbor. Walk *in* the door and you can't help but look toward the water. Of course, not everyone can get a harborfront table, but things are arranged so you know you're on the water. The menu speaks of the sea more than the land as well, offering predictable but excellent fish-and-chips, pan-roasted Georges Bank scallops, and grilled swordfish. The Portuguese-influenced dishes are among the best, though, and include a pork and clam appetizer and the "Hall of Fame" chowder with tiny Maine shrimp and *chouriço*. Be sure to check the catch of the day.

Coddington Brewing Co., 210 Coddington Hwy., Middletown, RI 02842; (401) 847-6690; coddbrew.com; Casual American/Seafood; $–$$. This family-style brewery might be faulted by malt heads for emphasizing food over suds, but that doesn't detract from the slightly heavy IPA and the nutty brown ale. Dining is mostly casual fare, including char-broiled burgers and a grilled tuna steak with wasabi mayo. As proof that Coddington lies within Rhode Island, you can also order pasta dishes (including a classic chicken parm) and scallops baked with *chouriço* and bread crumbs.

Evelyn's Drive-In, 2335 Main Rd., Tiverton, RI 02878; (401) 624-3100; evelynsdrivein.com; Seafood/Casual American; $–$$$. Certainly photogenic, Evelyn's *looks* the part of an iconic fish shack by the water, and it's been touted as such by several local and national TV shows. Best bets here are the Rhode Island classics—chowder, doughballs (aka clamcakes), and the fish sandwich—that you can enjoy at the picnic tables. Fancier fish dinner plates are mostly $20 and up, sometimes way up. Open April through Sept.

15 Point Road Restaurant, 15 Point Rd., Portsmouth, RI 02871; (401) 683-3138; 15pointroad.com; Seafood/Traditional American; $$. Set on a small cove at one end of the Cove Escape Bridge, 15 Point has a small deck and a dining room with large windows. Most seating is in booths, but most have a view of the Sakonnet River that is especially pleasant around sunset. The menu is traditional—so traditional that the New England Classics section includes a deconstructed Beef Wellington (grilled filet mignon layered with puff pastry, portobello mushrooms, and pâté) as well as stuffed scrod. Along with dishes labeled "native" (like the sole and all the shellfish), 15 Point also serves some farmed and South American fish.

Flo's Clam Shack, 4 Wave Ave., Middletown, RI 02842; (401) 847-8141; and Park Ave., Island Park, Portsmouth, RI 02871; (401) 847-8141; Seafood; $. Bracketing south and north ends of Aquidneck Island, Flo's is the quintessential clam shack. The larger Middletown location has a vaguely Polynesian feel to it, mostly as camouflage for the busy road that separates the restaurant from First Beach. While there are a few tables on the sparse grass surrounding the more modest Island Park location, most folks cross the street to eat their clamcakes, stuffies, fried clams (or strips), fish-and-chips, lobster roll, or box of fried oysters, calamari, or scallops seated on the sea wall of the beach. Open March to mid-Oct.

Newport Creamery, 208 West Rd., Middletown, RI 02842; (401) 846-2767; newportcreamery.com; Casual American; $. The menu may be the same at Newport Creamery locations throughout the state, but there is something a little bit more fun about eating here on the site where the original milk bar was opened in 1940 by the father and son team of Samuel and Mason Rector. The Rectors were in the milk business and at first focused solely on ice cream. When the company began to expand after World War II, they added casual food to the menu as well. Though no longer family owned, Newport Creamery remains a family-friendly eatery with choices to satisfy everyone who feels the need to have a meal before they dig into a hot fudge banana sundae or a simple dish of butter crunch ice cream.

The Stone House, 122 Sakonnet Point Rd., Little Compton, RI 02837; (401) 635-2222; stonehouse1854.com; New American; $–$$$. This 1854 Italianate manse turned country inn has sweeping lawns and great views down to the sea, which is probably why it's booked every summer weekend for weddings. The Tap Room is below ground, substituting a cozy camaraderie for the vistas but more than compensating with a well-conceived and beautifully executed contemporary menu. You can order a full-size entree like native cod wrapped in applewood-smoked bacon and accompanied by roasted littlenecks and fava beans—or go for a more casual sandwich. We're especially impressed with the tuna melt of grilled yellowfin, baby spinach, local tomatoes, and Bermuda onion on garlic crouton, all topped with melted local cheddar. Even the bar food (described as "tapas") is great: lobster sliders, Scotch egg, grilled pizzas. When wedding parties haven't claimed the upstairs, you can also order dinner at tables on the porch. Open May through Nov.

Specialty Stores, Markets & Producers

Anthony's Seafood, 963 Aquidneck Ave., Middletown, RI 02842; (401) 846-9620. For those in the mood to cook, Anthony's has all the local finfish and shellfish, as well as a few species brought in from Boston or by air, along with mixes for clamcakes or fish batter, fish stock, and even quahog juice. For those in the mood to eat well without all the bother, the attached restaurant serves all the fried and baked seafood classics of the Rhode Island coast, as well as lobster and steamed clam shore dinners. For those who want to impress their guests at their next dinner party, the take-out cases offer seafood-stuffed mushrooms, oysters Rockefeller, clams casino, stuffed sole, mild or hot stuffies, and other seafood classics.

Coastal Coffee Roasters, 1791 Main Rd., Tiverton, RI 02878; (401) 624-2343; coastalroasters.com. Tiverton and Little Compton comprise a world all their own, and every micro-world needs a micro-roaster. Coastal Coffee buys small lots of fair trade, specialty, and organic beans from around the world and roasts them just dark enough for the full flavor to explode in the cup. Even the espresso roasts are more Milanese than Neapolitan— full, rich coffee flavor without the burnt edges. The funky coffee shop carries all the choices *du moment,* and you'll find bags of beans at farm stands and stores along the peninsula. If you love coffee, you're nuts not to stop here, no matter how hard it is to park.

The Cottage, 3847 Main Rd., Tiverton, RI 02878; (401) 625-5814; thecottageri.com. This home furnishings shop doesn't neglect the small details such as fine linen dish towels, classic white porcelain serving pieces, glasses from Vermont's Simon Pearce or Finland's Iittala, and Sabre flatware from Paris with handles in a rainbow of colors. The shop's small selection of cookbooks seems particularly suited to entertaining.

Eva Ruth's, 796 Aquidneck Ave., Middletown, RI 02842; (401) 619-1924; evaruths.com. It's a bit difficult to find Eva Ruth's, which occupies a lower level space on the back of a small strip mall. But people with food allergies seek out this bakery where all breads, cookies, cakes and cupcakes, pies, scones, and quiches are gluten-free. Patient staff will further identify items that are also dairy-free, soy-free, corn-free, yeast-free, or vegan.

Fatulli's Gourmet Bakery & Deli, 909 East Main Rd., Middletown, RI 02842; (401) 847-5166; fatullis.com. According to the counter staff, chocolate treats such as brownies, whoopie pies, and Oreo bars are favorites from the bakery case. We're personally fond of the somewhat more elegant Italian truffle bar with a shortbread crust, chocolate cream cheese filling, and crumb top. But baked goods are only the tip of the iceberg at this establishment, which also offers several soups (such as split pea and ham or creamy tomato) and sandwiches (grilled chicken with pesto mayonnaise or Italian cold cuts and cheese on herbed focaccia bread) for lunch and a variety of salads and roasted vegetables to take home for dinner.

Gray's Grist Mill, Adamsville Mill Store, 638 Adamsville Rd., Westport, MA 02790 (mailing address PO Box 364, Adamsville, RI 02801); (508) 636-6075; graysgristmill .com. The state line between Massachusetts and Rhode Island runs right through the mill pond, and as a result Gray's Grist Mill has a physical address in Massachusetts and a mailing address in Rhode Island. But its heart belongs to the state of Rhode Island and its jonnycake devotees. One of the oldest continuously operating grist mills in New England, Gray's grinds dried Narragansett Indian Flint Corn using a 56-inch, 1½-ton granite millstone.

The resulting white cornmeal is the gold standard, so to speak, for Rhode Island jonnycakes. Miller Thornton Simmons often grinds between noon and 1 p.m. But even if the mill is not operating you can stop in to inspect the old apparatus and then purchase Jonnycake Corn Meal or Gray's Pancake & Waffle Mix at Gray's Daily Grind next door. In addition to the mill's products, the coffee shop also sells cast-iron skillets and griddles, cornbread pans, maple syrup, and the definitive Jonnycake cookbook commissioned by the Society for the Propagation of the Jonnycake Tradition. Open Mar through Dec; call for winter hours. For Simmons' recipe for **Miller's Jonnycakes,** see p. 253.

Gray's Ice Cream, 16 East Rd., Tiverton, RI 02878; (401) 624-4500; graysicecream.com. You could almost say that Mrs. Annie Gray set Tiverton Four Corners on its course as a foodie destination when she began selling ice cream (made elsewhere) out of a house in 1923. Sometime in the 1930s she began making 12 flavors of ice cream on site. When her daughter Florence "Flossie" Brow took over in 1938 she added more flavors including the well-received rum raisin and frozen pudding that are still on the menu. Of the 40 or so flavors made on the premises today, coffee, mocha chip, and black raspberry are among the most popular. The take-out window can turn out all the soda-fountain classics such as malts, cabinets, and ice cream sodas. This original Gray's is open 365 days a year. For a seasonal stand in Bristol, see p. 157.

Milk & Honey, 3838 Main Rd., Tiverton, RI 02878; (401) 624-1974; milkandhoneybazaar.com. This small shop carries a changing selection of more than 100 cheeses from France, Italy, Switzerland, Germany, Ireland, Holland, England, and the United States, including New England. Expect to find aged Goudas, English farmhouse cheeses, and most of the Vermont and New Hampshire artisanal cheeses aged and distributed by Jasper Hill (Bayley Hazen Blue, Landaff, etc.). Not surprisingly, they also stock beautiful wooden cutting boards, the Boksa line of elegant cheese slicers and spreaders from Holland, and all manner of crackers, nuts, mustards, cornichons, and fruit pastes that pair so well with cheese.

Provençal Bakery and Cafe, 750 Aquidneck Ave., Middletown, RI 02842; (401) 845-9313; provencalbakery.com. In 2005 Brenda Sabbag bought a bread bakery from a Frenchman who had baked in Marseilles for 18 years. "We haven't changed a thing," she says of the breads (including sourdough, whole wheat, rye, and traditional baguettes) that she sells to markets and restaurants around the state. In 2010, Sabbag opened her cafe and locals warmed immediately to the retro feel of its turquoise Formica counters and tabletops and to its sparkly gray vinyl chairs and stools. They are even more pleased with the breakfast and lunch fare turned out in the kitchen. They can start the day with blueberry cream cheese croissants or warm apple crepes, or enjoy such daily specials as Portuguese kale soup, a roast beef, avocado and brie panini, or a chicken potpie for lunch.

Who You Calling Chicken?

The Rhode Island Red, the official state bird of Rhode Island, is memorialized in a 1925 bronze bas-relief mounted in Adamsville (a village of Little Compton), where the chicken breed was created around 1850. The Rhode Island Red is a feisty, hardy chicken that handles outdoor winters with aplomb and will attack unfamiliar humans or other animals rather than run away. Their hard, strong feathers and substantial muscle mass (roosters often weigh in at more than 8 pounds) make the Rhode Island Red a chicken to be reckoned with. They are particularly popular among hobbyist poultry fanciers, as they can be trained to come when called and even sit on an owner's lap to be preened. They are raised commercially both for eggs (extra-large eggs with brown shells) as well as for roasting chickens.

Among the more unusual items are the "bombs"—an apple with cinnamon and sugar or a tomato with cheese, garlic, and basil baked in puff pastry. Of course, all the breads and other baked goods are also available.

Provender, 3883 Main Rd., Tiverton, RI 02878; (401) 624-8084; provenderfinefoods.com. Counter staff at Provender are fond of telling customers that everything is made from scratch—no "scoop and bake." That goes for the muffins, scones, lemon squares, chocolate or lemon buttermilk cakes, and the chocolate orange and gingersnap cookies. Lunchtime sandwiches range from the sophisticated (curried chicken salad, mango chutney, and lettuce) to the whimsical (peanut butter and jelly with a side of gummy bears). Soups and salads are also available. Located in an elegant Victorian building with big front porch, Provender sits across the street from **Gray's Ice Cream** (see p. 240) and is open Mar through Christmas.

Roseberry Winn, 3842 Main Rd., Tiverton, RI 02878; (401) 816-0010; roseberrywinn.com. Roseberry Winn's porcelain pieces meld delicately carved surfaces with richly colored glazes. They are so lovely and distinctive that it would be tempting to order a whole set of dinnerware. But even a teapot or a pitcher would add flair to the table.

Farmstands, PYOs & Wineries

Arruda Dairy Farm, 408 Stafford Rd., Tiverton, RI 02878; (401) 624-8898; Dairy. Founded in 1917, Arruda is one of the few remaining dairy farms in the area. Its milk is available in many markets throughout the state and it supplies coffee milk to numerous hot wiener shops. But it's still fun to stop at the bare bones store adjacent to the processing room to pick up some milk (including coffee, chocolate, and strawberry flavored) as well as some stew meat, patties, or steak from the Arruda's Red Barn brand of beef. Christmastime egg nog is immensely popular.

DeCastro Farms, 1780 E. Main Rd., Portsmouth, RI 02871; (401) 683-4688; Farmstand. This garden center also offers a wide variety of locally grown produce including corn, tomatoes, beans, carrots, squash, peaches, blueberries, and apples. They also have a nice selection of their own food products such as spiced peaches, Vidalia sweet onion relish, pumpkin butter, and strawberry-rhubarb preserves. Open Apr through Dec.

Greenvale Vineyards, 582 Wapping Rd., Portsmouth, RI 02871; (401) 847-3777; greenvale.com; Winery. Like many New England wineries, Greenvale started out with hybrid and native American *labrusca* grapes in the 1980s. Owners soon realized that the climate would support European wine grapes and began planting Chardonnay. Winemaker Richard Carmichael has been with Greenvale since 1997, and he's overseen the further introduction of Cabernet Franc, Pinot Gris, Merlot, Malbec, and even a few vines of Albariño, the sprightly white grape of Galicia and Portugal's *vinho verde* vineyards. Carmichael makes a smooth yet tangy Pinot Gris that is a terrific shellfish wine, as well as both French- and California-style chardonnays. The French version is light and fruity with just a touch of oak, while the California version is rich and buttery.

The friendly and knowledgeable tasting includes seven wines and a souvenir glass.

Helger's Turkey Farm, 2554 Main Rd., Tiverton, RI 02878; (401) 624-4087; Butcher. Founded in 1939, this family-run turkey ranch sells frozen birds all year and fresh turkeys in the fall. Thanksgiving orders can be placed anytime after October 1 for birds ranging from 14 to 30 pounds (assuming you have an oven big enough).

Newport Vineyards & Winery, 909 E. Main Rd., Middletown, RI 02842; (401) 848-5161; newportvineyards.com; Winery. Making 17 different varietals grown on 60 acres, Newport Vineyards was a pioneer winery on Aquidneck Island. It rents facilities to other winemakers in the region and does a big business providing its wines with custom labels. Among the most interesting of the products are the Vidal ice wine, the Vintner's Select Merlot, and the Rhody Coyote Hard Apple Cider. The tasting room in a small roadside mall also has many gift items.

Quonset View Farm, 895 Middle Rd., Portsmouth, RI 02871; (401) 683-1254; PYO. Quonset View Farm was established in 1915 as a dairy farm, but the soil on Aquidneck Island is particularly well-suited to growing potatoes, and the Cotta family planted their first potato crops in the 1940s. They also grow strawberries (PYO June to early July) and regular, sugar, and mini pumpkins (PYO October).

Rocky Brook Orchard, 997 Wapping Rd., Middletown, RI 02842; (401) 851-7989; rockybrookorchard.com; PYO. Greg and Katy Ostheimer grow about 60 varieties of apples. To help customers determine which are ripe for picking, they have labeled each tree by name and by approximate ripening period from early September to November. PYO peaches, pears, and quince are also available. Call ahead for availability and picking days starting in August.

Sakonnet Vineyards & Winery, 162 W. Main Rd., Little Compton, RI 02837; (401) 635-8486; sakonnetwine.com; Winery. If you're seeking the Napa/Sonoma wine lifestyle experience, complete with manicured grounds, picnic tables, and cafe food, then look no farther. Sakonnet Vineyards pioneered serious winemaking in southeastern New England in 1975, and blossomed as a destination winery at the turn of the century. Now with its third set of owners, Sakonnet has made the shift almost exclusively to vinifera grapes on the 169-acre estate, growing Chardonnay, Pinot Noir, Gewürztraminer, and Cabernet Franc as well as the French-American hybrid Vidal Blanc. The winery also buys additional varietals from nearby farms. Sakonnet wines tend to be food-friendly and light.

Sweet Berry Farm, 915 Mitchell's Lane, Middletown, RI 02842; (401) 847-3912; sweetberryfarmri.com; Farmstand/PYO. This hillside location is so idyllic that people must return again and again to follow the PYO season from its start with strawberries in June through raspberries, blueberries, peaches, blackberries, apples, and pumpkins. Even when PYO season ends in October, the handsome post-and-beam farmstand is a destination in itself for beautiful baked goods, artisan cheeses, smoked meats, and other products. The farm kitchen turns out soups and sandwiches for the self-serve cafe as well as a variety of dishes (such as Caribbean fried chicken, fishermen's stew, or ham, tomato, and broccoli quiche) to take home. The kitchen's own line of jams, salsas, and relishes is comple-mented by a range of gourmet items including French mustards and Indian curries. This busy spot is also home base for Susanna's Ice Cream and Sorbet, which celebrates local fruits in season with such treats as crème fraîche and fresh blueberry ice cream or strawberry daiquiri sorbet. Open mid-April through Dec.

Walker's Roadside Stand, 261 W. Main Rd., Little Compton, RI 02837; (401) 635-4719; Farmstand. There are usually a lot of cars parked at Walker's, but it's hard to tell if people are stopping for the fresh fruits and vegetables or for the baked goods at adjacent Wilma's at Walker's Bakery and Cafe. There's really no need to limit yourself. Have a lobster salad sandwich or mozzarella, tomato, and basil panini at Wilma's for lunch and grab a beau-tiful fruit pie to take home for dessert. You can easily plan the main course of your meal around the farmstand's sweet corn, tomatoes, beans, zucchini, and several varieties of squash, including Q Ball, 8 Ball, and flying saucer. Operation opens in June.

Wilma's closes after Labor Day, while the farmstand stays open through Oct.

Young Family Farm, 260 W. Main Rd., Little Compton, RI 02837; (401) 635-0110; youngfamilyfarm.com; Farmstand/PYO. **The Young** family celebrates the harvest with strawberry, corn, and apple festivals. But you can stop at the farmstand any time between mid-May and late November for fresh fruits and vegetables, milk and beef from **Arruda Dairy Farm** (see p. 243), and the Young family's own jars of barbecue sauce, hot chow chow, pickled garlic, watermelon pickles, and sweet and hot pepper relish. PYO apples in season.

Farmers' Markets

Aquidneck Growers' Market, 909 E. Main Rd., Rte. 138, Middletown. Sat from 9 a.m. to 1 p.m., June through Oct.

Island Market at Aquidneck Grange, 499 E. Main Rd., Middletown. Thurs from 2 to 6 p.m., June through Oct.

Sakonnet Growers' Market, Pardon Gray Preserve, Main Rd., Tiverton. Sat from 9 a.m. to 1 p.m., July through Sept.

Recipes

We always find that re-creating recipes in our own kitchen is a good way to bring the taste of travel back home. So we are grateful to the chefs and growers who provided these recipes that highlight local flavors and reflect Rhode Island food traditions. We have adapted the recipes for home kitchens and standardized their presentation. Any errors are our inadvertent introductions rather than the fault of our sources.

Rhode Island Clam Chowder

DiMare Seafood Marketplace, Restaurant & Bar makes this chowder fresh daily from scratch. It's the recipe of owner Kate LaBore's father Wayne A. LaBore Sr., a retired US Navy commander, who made it in this volume for parties. This classic Rhode Island clear chowder can be used as the base to make Manhattan red chowder or creamy New England chowder. Kate notes that a food processor is useful for dicing the clams and also advises that the parboiled red bliss potatoes should always be added right before the chowder is served so that they will not become too soft. The base chowder (without potatoes) also freezes well.

Makes 3 gallons

- **25 pounds chowder quahogs (live in the shell)**
- **1 cup salted water**
- **4 stalks celery, cut in small dice**
- **2 yellow or Spanish onions, cut in medium dice**
- **1 tablespoon minced garlic**
- **½ cup bacon fat (rendered from 2 pounds bacon)**
- **½ stick (4 tablespoons) unsalted butter**
- **5 pounds red bliss potatoes, diced with skin on**
- **2 bay leaves**
- **1 gallon tap water**
- **½ tablespoon ground black pepper**
- **6 basil leaves, finely chopped**
- **Salt to taste**

Scrub the chowder quahogs. Place in large steamer pot and add salted water. Cover and steam until clams open, about 3 to 6 minutes. As clams open, remove with tongs until all clams are cooked. Reserve the cooking liquid. Remove clams from shells and dice in large chunks.

Sweat the celery, onions, and garlic in the bacon fat and butter until half cooked. Set aside.

Boil the diced potatoes until half cooked, about 5 minutes. Set aside.

Strain reserved broth to eliminate pieces of shell, sand, or foreign objects. Add the strained broth to the mix of celery, onion, and garlic. Add the bay leaves, 1 gallon of tap water, black pepper, chopped basil, and chopped clam meats.

Simmer for 10 minutes. If serving all the chowder at once, add the parboiled potatoes and serve. Otherwise, cool the chowder. When ready to serve a smaller portion, heat and add potatoes before serving.

Adapted recipe courtesy of Kate LeBore of
DiMare Seafood Marketplace, Restaurant & Bar in East Greenwich (p. 167).

Miller's Jonnycakes

Some Rhode Islanders prefer their jonnycakes thick, while others like them thin. This recipe from miller Thornton Simmons at Gray's Grist Mill is the perfect compromise—neither too thick nor too thin. The sugar is optional, since some people prefer jonnycakes as a morning substitute for pancakes, served with syrup, while others prefer them as a savory complement to meat like roast pork. The recipe, of course, calls for white cornmeal ground at Gray's. Mind you, Gray's meal is bolted whole-grain cornmeal with the germ intact, and it's ground from a Rhode Island–specific strain of flint corn, so there really is no mass-market substitute. If you can't make it to Gray's (they also sell online), use a good commercial white cornmeal for an approximation of the flavor.

Makes 16–20 jonnycakes

1 cup white cornmeal

1 teaspoon salt

2 teaspoons sugar (optional)

1 cup water

4 tablespoons to ½ cup milk

Mix the dry ingredients in a bowl. Add water. To thin batter to desired consistency, add milk one tablespoon at a time.

Drop batter by tablespoon onto a well-greased and hot (375°F) griddle. Cook 5 to 6 minutes on each side until brown.

Adapted recipe courtesy of Gray's Grist Mill in Adamsville (p. 239).

Blueberry Turnovers

Seven Stars Bakery makes these turnovers when berries are available from local farms. Jim Williams uses a 6-inch round piece of dough which he notes is "about right for a single turnover per person." The details in this recipe will give you a feel for the extra care and attention that goes into artisanal baking. Making pie dough is easy with the right technique, Williams notes. "Just don't overmix the dough or let it warm up." Your reward for the effort is a turnover fresh from the oven. "There is definitely something about these piping hot from the oven dripping all over the place with pie crust flaking on your clothes that makes them taste better," he says.

Serves 10

Pie dough

.3½ cups pastry flour

2 tablespoons sugar

1½ teaspoons salt

1⅓ cups butter

5 tablespoons ice water

Combine flour, sugar, and salt. If possible, do this the day before and freeze.

Cut butter into ½- to ¼-inch cubes. Keep cold in the refrigerator.

Put cold, dry mixture into food processor fitted with blade and pulse to combine. Add cold butter in stages, pulsing between each addition. Once all the butter is added, pulse machine until mixture is chunky and butter is completely broken down into small pea-sized chunks. Do not overpulse! When it is perfect, the mixture will be dry to the touch, but will clump together if pressed in your hand.

Add water slowly, pulsing between additions. Dough will just barely come together. Do not overmix! Depending on flour, you may need more or less ice water.

Put pie dough into large ziplock bag and form into square or rectangle. Store in refrigerator until ready to roll out—at least 1 hour, preferably 2 to 4 hours.

Take cold pie dough out of refrigerator and roll out about ⅛-inch thick and cut into circles. If dough warms up, put circles back into fridge. Always work with cold pie dough.

Filling

¼ cup plus 3 tablespoons sugar	2 cups blueberries
3 tablespoons cornstarch	1 tablespoon lemon juice

Make filling just before assembling turnovers, otherwise it will get too juicy and will leak out during the bake.

Combine sugar and cornstarch, then toss mixture with the berries. Once berries are coated, add lemon juice.

Assembly

Lay out cold pie dough rounds on a lightly floured surface. Scoop 2 tablespoons blueberry filling into the center of each round. Fold dough over to create half-moon shape. Crimp edges with fork and poke holes in top to allow steam to escape.

Place assembled turnovers on sheet pan and put back into fridge to rest. If they don't get 30 minutes or so of chilling after shaping, they will taste great, but will shrink and look funky. Let them rest! COLD!

Baking

All ovens are different. Pie dough needs to be baked hot for the best texture.

Preheat oven to 400°F, but be prepared to possibly turn it down or cover the turnovers if they color too fast.

Bake for 20 to 25 minutes. Keep in mind that the turnovers need a good solid bake. Cooling is optional.

Adapted recipe courtesy of Jim Williams
of Seven Stars Bakery in Providence (p. 69) and East Providence (p. 158).

Spaghetti alle Vongole

A photo of this dish graces the cover of this book because it is one of the classics of Italian food throughout New England and especially in Rhode Island. It's also a kind of magic—one of those dishes made with simple techniques from simple materials that turns into a meal greater than the sum of its parts. Chef Dominic Ierfino's directions guarantee that you get all the best flavor of the clams absorbed into the pasta.

Serves 2

- **Kosher salt**
- **6 ounces spaghetti**
- **4 tablespoons extra-virgin olive oil, divided**
- **1 garlic clove, thinly sliced**
- **¼ teaspoon crushed red pepper flakes**
- **¼ cup dry white wine**
- **2 pounds cockles, Manila clams, or littlenecks, scrubbed**
- **2 tablespoons roughly chopped fresh flat-leaf parsley**

Bring 3 quarts water to boil in a 5-quart pot. Season lightly with salt; add pasta and cook, stirring occasionally, until about 2 minutes before tender. Reserve ½ cup pasta water and add enough cold water to pot to stop pasta from further cooking.

Meanwhile, heat 3 tablespoons olive oil in a large skillet over medium heat. Add garlic and cook, swirling pan often, until just golden. Add red pepper flakes and continue cooking 15 more seconds. Add wine, then clams; increase heat to high. Cover skillet and cook until clams open and release their juices, 3 to 6 minutes, depending on size of clams. As clams open, use tongs to transfer them to a bowl.

Add ¼ cup of the reserved pasta water to skillet; bring to a boil. Drain pasta and add to pan. Cook over high heat, tossing constantly, until pasta is al dente and has soaked up some of the sauce from the pan. Add clams and any juices from bowl to pan, along with parsley, and toss to combine. (Add more pasta water if sauce seems dry.) Transfer pasta to warm bowls and drizzle with remaining oil.

Adapted recipe courtesy of Chef Domenic Ierfino
of Trattoria Roma and the Original Roma Marketplace in Providence (p. 68).

Farmstead's Macaroni with Heirloom Tomato Sauce & Fresh Chèvre

This dish is great for entertaining because it can be made in advance. Chef Matt Jennings says that you can prepare the tomato sauce up to three days ahead and store it in the refrigerator. Reheat and stir in the cheese just before tossing with the pasta. The assembled macaroni can be covered and refrigerated for up to three days before baking.

Serves 4–6

2¾ pounds chopped heirloom tomatoes with their juices

2 tablespoons olive oil, divided

2 plump garlic cloves, minced

⅛ teaspoon sugar

Salt to taste

A couple of fresh basil sprigs (optional)

1 teaspoon fresh oregano, chopped, if not using basil

Freshly ground pepper to taste

4 ounces soft, mild goat cheese

½ cup freshly grated Parmesan cheese, of good quality

1 pound small pasta—penne or macaroni

½ cup breadcrumbs

Begin heating a large pot of water for the pasta. Meanwhile make the tomato sauce. Pulse the chopped tomatoes in a food processor fitted with the steel blade, or pass through the medium blade of a food mill before you begin.

Heat 1 tablespoon of the olive oil over medium heat in a large, wide, nonstick skillet or saucepan and add the garlic. Cook, stirring, for 30 seconds to a minute, until it begins to smell fragrant, and add the tomatoes and their juices, the sugar, salt, oregano (if using) or basil sprigs. Stir and turn up the heat. When the tomatoes begin to bubble, lower the heat to medium and cook, stirring often, until thick and fragrant, 15 to 20 minutes, or longer if necessary. Remove the basil sprigs and wipe any sauce adhering to them back into the pan. Add freshly ground black pepper, stir in the goat cheese and Parmesan and combine well. Taste and adjust seasonings.

Preheat oven to 350°F and oil a 2-quart baking dish or gratin with olive oil.

When water for the pasta comes to a boil add a tablespoon of salt and cook the pasta for a minute or two less than the instructions on the package indicate. It should still be a little underdone as it will finish cooking in the oven. Drain and transfer to a large bowl. Add the tomato-goat cheese sauce and stir together until the pasta is thoroughly coated. Transfer to the baking dish.

Toss the breadcrumbs with the remaining tablespoon of olive oil and sprinkle over the top of the macaroni. Bake in preheated oven until the casserole is bubbly and the breadcrumbs are lightly browned, about 30 minutes. Let stand for 5 to 10 minutes before serving.

Adapted recipe courtesy of Matt Jennings, Owner/Chef of Farmstead in Providence (p. 61).

Screppelle m'busse

This typical Abruzzese recipe supplied by Chef Walter Potenza of Potenza Ristorante & Bar translates from dialect as "crepes filled in soup style." His wife, Carmela, tells us that on their last trip to Italy, they found a trattoria that made such terrific screppelle that in three visits, they ordered them each time before ordering main dishes. Chef Potenza focuses on authentic Italian dishes, mostly from central and northern Italy, but he is also the author of Federal Hill Flavors and Knowledge, *an account of the history, traditions, and recipes of the chief Italian-American neighborhood of Providence. It's available at his Providence restaurant (p. 47) and his Cranston cooking school (p. 126).*

Serves 8

For the crepes

4 large eggs
Pinch of kosher salt
¼ cup whole milk

½ cup all-purpose flour
½ cup water
1 tablespoon olive oil

Pulse the ingredients in a food processor until smooth, being careful not to overmix. Cover and allow to rest for 15 minutes.

For the filling

1 whole chicken (3-4 pounds)
1 celery stalk
1 small carrot, peeled
Pinch of nutmeg

¼ cup Parmigiano Reggiano cheese
Salt and white pepper to taste

Salt the cavity of the chicken. Rest for 5 minutes. Rinse chicken with cold water. Place the chicken in a large saucepan, fill with cold salted water 2 inches over the top of the flesh, and add celery and carrot. Bring water to a boil, lower heat to simmer for about 1 hour or until the chicken meat falls off the bone. With a slotted spoon, remove chicken. Allow to cool. Reserve the broth and the celery and carrot.

Meanwhile, make the crepes by buttering a nonstick skillet with a pastry brush. Pour batter, cook for 1 minute on each side and set on a platter for later use. Continue to make the crepes until the batter has been completely used.

Remove chicken meat from the bones, place in a bowl. Chop celery and carrot in small dice and add to chicken with nutmeg and the Parmigiano Reggiano. Adjust seasoning with salt and pepper if needed.

Fill each crepe with the chicken-vegetable filling. Place crepes in a large bowl, pour broth over top to moisten the crepes, drizzle with olive oil, and serve hot.

Adapted recipe courtesy Chef Walter Potenza
of Potenza Ristorante & Bar (p. 47) and Chef Walter's Cooking School (p. 126).

Sweet Sausage with Spinach Penne Pasta

This recipe uses many of the gourmet foods available at Costantino's Venda Ravioli on Federal Hill in Providence. Substitutions can obviously be made. Alan Costantino recommends Costa d'Oro olive oil, but another extra-virgin Italian olive oil will also work. We prefer to use pitted Greek olives, but unpitted Kalamata olives are more authentic.

Serves 6–8

- 2 pounds sweet sausage
- 1 (8-ounce) bag fresh spinach, washed
- 1 cup Costa d'Oro olive oil, divided
- 2 garlic cloves, chopped
- 2 small ripe tomatoes, chopped
- 1 pound spinach penne pasta
- 1½ cups Greek ripe olives
- 1 small can (3.25 ounce, drained weight) medium-size black olives, or omit and increase Greek ripe olives to 2 cups
- Red pepper flakes, to taste
- Salt and pepper, to taste
- ¼ cup grated Parmesan cheese

Heat oven to 375°F. Place sausage on a sheet pan and bake until golden, about 25 minutes. Set aside to cool, reserving the rendered fat.

Remove any stems from the spinach. Chop the spinach into pieces. Pour ¼ cup olive oil into a very large sauté pan. Add the garlic and sauté until golden brown. Add the chopped spinach and cook until it wilts. Add the chopped tomatoes and cook until tender.

In a pot of boiling salted water, cook the pasta al dente. Set aside.

Cut the sausage into ½-inch slices. Drain the pasta and add it to the sauté pan along with the sausage and olives. Add the remaining olive oil (and the rendered fat if desired). Toss to mix well. Season with red pepper flakes, salt and pepper. Sprinkle with grated cheese and serve.

Adapted recipe courtesy of Alan Costantino
of Costantino's Venda Ravioli in Providence (p. 59).

Moussaka

Many of the dishes served at the Grecian Festival at the Assumption of the Virgin Mary Greek Orthodox Church in Pawtucket are based on family recipes and are included in the church's new cookbook, A Greek Feast. *This moussaka is always a favorite at the festival.*

Serves 8–12

2 pounds white potatoes **4 to 5 large eggplants**

Peel potatoes but not eggplants. Slice both thinly—⅛ inch or thinner—and brush both sides of slices with olive oil. Bake on cookie sheets at 400°F until golden brown, about 30 minutes. Set aside.

Meat sauce

1½ cups chopped onions
¼ cup (½ stick) butter
3 pounds ground beef
3 tablespoons tomato paste
½ teaspoon cinnamon
2 teaspoons garlic powder
2 teaspoons oregano

½ teaspoon ground cloves, if desired
¼ cup chopped parsley
½ cup red wine
Salt and pepper to taste
½ cup Romano cheese

In large skillet or pot sauté onions in butter. Add ground beef and cook until browned. Add tomato paste, seasonings, and wine. Remove from heat. Skim off fat if necessary. Adjust seasoning with salt and pepper. Add cheese. Set aside.

Cream sauce

½ pound (2 sticks) butter

½ cup flour

Salt to taste

½ teaspoon nutmeg

½ gallon milk

6 eggs, beaten

½ cup Romano cheese

Salt and pepper to taste

Breadcrumbs to coat pan

Melt butter. Add flour, salt, and nutmeg. Stir until smooth. Slowly add milk, stirring constantly until thickened. Remove from heat and slowly add a cup of sauce to the beaten eggs to temper them. Then stir tempered eggs into sauce. Add Romano cheese and salt and pepper to taste.

Assembly:

Preheat oven to 350°F. Butter two 9 x 13-inch rectangular baking dishes and sprinkle bottom lightly with breadcrumbs. Layer cooked potatoes close together to make bottom layer. (Potatoes are bottom layer only. Leftover potatoes are delicious sprinkled with salt as a side dish.) Add a layer of eggplant, then meat sauce, then eggplant, continuing until meat sauce is used up. You must end with a layer of eggplant. Pour cream sauce over and bake for about 45 minutes until golden brown. Allow to sit 15 to 20 minutes before cutting into servings.

Adapted recipe courtesy of the St. Barbara Philoptochos Society
of the Assumption of the Virgin Mary Greek Orthodox Church in Pawtucket (p. 294).
Cookbooks can be ordered by e-mail at philoptochos@assumptionri.org
or by calling the church at (401) 725-3127.

Pasta with Italian Tuna, Snap Peas, Lemon & Toasted Bread Crumbs

Cindy Salvato, who leads walking and tasting tours of Federal Hill in Providence, likes to share this recipe with her guests since it highlights the neighborhood's Italian flavors. She prefers to use jarred Italian tuna, which usually contains the best cuts of Mediterranean yellowfin tuna packed in olive oil. Two 5½-ounce cans of Italian tuna packed in oil may be substituted for each jar. She says that vermicelli works better than any other pasta shape and emphasizes that the parsley should be fresh, "not the dried that tastes like grass."

Serves 4

Toasted bread crumbs

2 tablespoons extra-virgin olive oil

1 cup seasoned bread crumbs

Pasta

2 (10-ounce jars) Italian tuna in olive oil

Extra-virgin olive oil

½ cup chopped shallots

2 tablespoons capers

3 cups fresh snap peas (the smaller the better)

Grated zest and juice from one lemon

1 pound vermicelli

3 tablespoons chopped flat Italian parsley

In a small pan, warm the olive oil over medium heat. Add the bread crumbs and stir them constantly until browned. Immediately transfer them onto a plate so that the steam can escape and they will not become soggy. Transfer to a bowl when cooled.

While bread crumbs are cooling, drain the oil out of the tuna into a 2-cup measure. Add more olive oil to make 1¼ cups. Take the tuna out of the jars and set aside. Put the olive oil in a large sauté pan and warm over medium heat. Add the shallots and cook slowly for 5 minutes; the shallots should be soft and slightly transparent. Add the capers, snap peas, and tuna; cook slowly for 3 to 4 minutes. Add the lemon zest and juice. Remove from the heat and cover to keep warm.

Cook the pasta al dente. Drain the pasta and toss with the sauce. Transfer to a serving platter and sprinkle with parsley. Serve with lots of toasted bread crumbs.

Adapted recipe courtesy of Cindy Salvato of Savoring Rhode Island in Providence (p. 46).

Polish Latkes (Potato Pancakes)

For a refined pancake, Marta Samek of Krakow Deli Bakery Smokehouse uses a very fine grater to shred the potatoes. She begins to heat the oil in a large frying pan when she starts to make the pancakes. The oil should be ready as soon as the pancakes are formed because the potatoes turn brown if not cooked immediately. To make sure that the pancakes cook all the way through without burning, she cooks them very slowly with only a small amount of oil in the pan. She says the oil should be hot at first, then turned down. For variations, add finely chopped bacon or garlic, or shredded cheese. The traditional accompaniments are sour cream and applesauce. Some people like sugar, but Marta says her brother Krystian Przybylko, who bakes the bread and smokes the sausages, enjoys them with soy sauce.

Makes 8 pancakes

1 pound white potatoes	**½ teaspoon pepper**
1 small onion	**1 teaspoon salt**
2 eggs	**Canola oil for cooking**
3 tablespoons flour	

Peel potatoes and shred on a fine grater. Grate onion. Mix potato and onion with eggs, flour, pepper, and salt. The consistency will be a loose, not thick, batter.

Add large spoonfuls of batter to hot oil in pan. Press mixture lightly to flatten, but do not apply too much pressure or pancakes will stick to the pan. Cook on one side for about 5 minutes until edges start to brown. Flip pancakes and cook for 5 minutes on the other side.

Adapted recipe courtesy of Marta Samek
of Krakow Deli Bakery Smokehouse in Woonsocket (p. 102).

Banana Cream Pie

This recipe has been a standby dessert at Aunt Carrie's in Narragansett for decades. Owner Elsie Foy says she got the recipe from her mother-in-law. Foy advises using any baked pie crust—"whatever makes you happy"—and that homemade, freshly whipped cream is best.

Serves 8

¾ cup sugar	2 egg yolks
¾ teaspoon salt	2 tablespoons butter
2 tablespoons cornstarch	1 teaspoon vanilla
½ cup pastry flour	1 baked pie crust
1 cup whole milk	1 banana, sliced
2 cups boiling water	Whipped cream

Sift all dry ingredients into top pan of double boiler. Add cold milk a little at a time. Using a whisk, stir constantly. When mixture is smooth, place over boiling water in double boiler base, add boiling water to mixture, and stir constantly. Continue stirring so mixture does not turn to paste and stick to bottom of pan. Cook until it comes to a full roaring bubble. It will thicken quickly.

When thick, take off heat, mix in egg yolks and butter. Stir well and add vanilla. Pour half of the mixture into pie crust, add half of the sliced banana. Add remaining mixture. Cool completely before topping generously with whipped cream. Garnish with remaining banana slices. Chill before serving.

Adapted recipe courtesy of Elsie Foy of Aunt Carrie's in Narragansett (p. 163).

Sin's Brownies

Jennifer Luxmoore of Sin Desserts often makes these unusual brown sugar brownies in individual round molds. Do not overmix the batter or brownies will be tough. Lining the pan with parchment paper makes it much easier to remove cooled brownies from pan.

Makes 16 2-inch squares

1¼ sticks butter
½ cup plus 1 teaspoon beaten eggs
1½ teaspoons vanilla extract
¾ cup plus 1 tablespoon sugar

1⅓ cups dark brown sugar
1½ cups cocoa
¼ teaspoon salt
¾ cup flour

Preheat oven to 350°F.

Melt butter.

Combine eggs and vanilla and mix. Set aside.

Combine sugars in mixing bowl or bowl of electric mixer and either by hand or on low speed, mix together until there are no lumps. Add in cocoa, salt, and flour. Mix on low speed until combined.

Keeping mixer on low, slowly pour in half of the butter, then half of the eggs, stopping to scrape bottom of mixer. Add other half of butter, then eggs. Scrape down again. Mix until just incorporated.

Spread into parchment-lined 8 x 8-inch pan. Bake for 25–30 minutes, or until brownies begin to pull from sides of pan. (Cake tester may still come out damp.)

Adapted recipe courtesy of Jennifer Luxmoore of Sin Desserts in Providence (p. 70).

Blueberry Cream Cheese Pie

At Rocky Point Farm, about 10 tons of blueberries are harvested each year and Rhonda Shumaker and Joe Gouveia are happy to share recipes with their PYO customers. This is a version of a classic midsummer treat. Use either a conventional pastry crust or graham cracker crust.

Serves 8

- **3 ounce package cream cheese, softened**
- **15 ounce can sweetened condensed milk**
- **⅓ cup fresh lemon juice**
- **1 teaspoon vanilla**
- **9-inch pastry shell, baked**

Whip cream cheese until fluffy. Gradually add condensed milk; blend in lemon juice and vanilla. Pour into pastry shell. Chill for 2-3 hours.

- **1 cup sugar**
- **2 tablespoons cornstarch**
- **¾ cup water**
- **2 cups fresh blueberries**

In a small saucepan, combine sugar, cornstarch, and water. Add ½ cup of blueberries; crush. Cook over medium heat, stirring constantly until mixture boils and thickens. Lower heat and simmer until milky mixture turns clear blue. Strain and cool.

Arrange remaining 1½ cups blueberries over top of chilled pie. Pour cooled glaze evenly over berries. Chill. Serve plain or with whipped cream.

Adapted recipe courtesy of Rocky Point Farm, Warwick (p. 139).

Appendices

Appendix A: Eateries by Cuisine

Codes for Corresponding Regional Chapters:

Asian

Barbecue

Casual American

Japanese

Mediterranean

Mexican

Iggy's Doughboys &
   Chowderhouse, (CW), 122;
   (SC), 170
Jamestown Fish, (NJ), 211
Jamestown Oyster Bar, (NJ), 211
Jim's Dock, (SC), 170
Landing, The, (NJ), 212
Matunuck Oyster Farm, (SC), 173
Mooring, The, (NJ), 213
Narragansett Grill, (SC), 174
Providence Oyster Bar,
   Providence, 48
Quito's Seafood Restaurant,
   (EB), 149
Red Parrot, The, (NJ), 217
Scales and Shells Restaurant,
   (NJ), 219
Seven Seas Chowder House,
   (CW), 128
Spain of Narragansett, (SC), 181
Tara's Tipperary Tavern, (SC), 182
22 Bowen's, (NJ), 185
Tyler Point Grille, (EB), 153

Spanish

Flan y Ajo, Providence, 32
Spain of Narragansett, (SC), 181

Thai

Siam Square, (EB), 151
Tong-D, (EB), 152

Traditional American

American, The, Providence, 20
Bay Voyage Inn, (NJ), 204
Benjamin's Restaurant and Raw
   Bar, (NJ), 204
Black Pearl, The, (NJ), 205
Brick Alley Pub & Restaurant,
   (NJ), 206
Coast Guard House, The, (SC), 166
Edgewood Cafe, (CW), 120
15 Point Road Restaurant,
   (NC), 235
Landing, The, (NJ), 212
Remington House Inn, (CW), 128
River Falls Restaurant & Lounge,
   (BV), 92
Safari Room at OceanCliff,
   (NJ), 217
Shelter Harbor Inn, (SC), 178
Tavern by the Sea, (SC), 183
Tavern on Main, (BV), 95
22 Bowen's, (NJ), 185
Twin Oaks, (CW), 130

Wright's Farm Restaurant, (BV), 97

Vegetarian Friendly
Eva Ruth's, (NC), 238
Foo(d) at AS220, Providence, 32
Julian's, Providence, 37
Perks & Corks, (SC), 176
Rasoi, (BV), 91
Small Axe Cafe, (SC), 180
Wild Flour Bakery, (BV), 106

Appendix B: Dishes, Specialties & Purveyors

Codes for Corresponding Regional Chapters:

(BV)	Blackstone Valley & Northwest Rhode Island
(CW)	Cranston & Warwick
(EB)	East Bay
(NC)	Newport County
(NJ)	Newport & Jamestown
(SC)	South County

Bakery

Allie's Donuts, (SC), 186

Calvitto's Pizza & Bakery, (CW), 131; (SC), 186

City Girl Cupcake, Providence, 59

Crugnale Bakery, (EB), 132; (CW), 154; Providence, 60; (BV), 99

Cupcakerie, The, (CW), 132

DePetrillo's Pizza & Bakery, (CW), 133; (BV), 101; (SC), 188

Eva Ruth's, (NC), 238

Mad Hatter, (NJ), 227

Mapleville Farm, (BV), 104

Gray's Grist Mill, (NC), 239
Jonathan's Cafe, (NJ), 225
New Harvest Coffee Roasters,
    (BV), 104
White Electric Coffee,
    Providence, 73

LaSalle Bakery, Providence, 65
Leo's Ristorante, (EB), 148
Red Parrot, The, (NJ), 217
Remington House Inn, (CW), 128
Roma, Providence, 68
Siena Cucina-Enoteca, (SC), 179
Solitro's Bakery, (CW), 135
Superior Bakery, (CW), 136
Taso's, (BV), 94
Trattoria Romana, (BV), 95
Wine & Cheese Restaurant, (BV), 96
Zooma Trattoria, Providence, 56

Specialty Shop

Brown & Hopkins Country Store, (BV), 98
Gem Ravioli, (BV), 100
Gray's Grist Mill, (NC), 239
Hartley's Pork Pies of Rhode Island, (BV), 101
Kenyon's Grist Mill, (SC), 190
Newport Spice Company, (NJ), 227
Virgin & Aged, (NJ), 229
Virginia & Spanish Peanut Co., Providence, 72
Yacht Club Bottling Works, (BV), 107

Wieners

Ferrucci's Original New York System, (CW), 121
Fidas Restaurant, Providence, 31
Nacho Mamma's, (EB), 148
New York Lunch, Inc., (BV), 89
Olneyville New York System, Providence, 44; (CW), 90; (BV), 125
Original New York System Hot Weiners, Providence, 45
Peter's Coney Island System, (CW), 127
Right Spot Diner, (BV), 91
Rod's Grille, (EB), 151
Sam's New York System, (BV), 93
Spike's Junkyard Dogs, (CW), 128; Providence, 51
Stykee's New York System, (CW), 129
Taso's, (BV), 94
Weiner Genie, (BV), 96
Wein-O-Rama, (CW), 131

Wine, Beer & Spirits

Bottles, Providence, 58

Appendix C: Rhode Island Food Events

January

Providence Restaurant Weeks, providencerestaurantweeks
.com. This 2-week event features about 90 restaurants offering
3-course *prix-fixe* menus at lunch and/or dinner. (See also July.)

February

Food & Wine Festival at the Rhode Island Flower Show,
flowershow.com. Once you've had your fill of horticulture, you
can sample wines and watch cooking demonstrations by local and
regional chefs.

March

Narragansett Restaurant Week, narragansettcoc.com. For 10 days in March, about 30 local restaurants offer 3-course *prix-fixe* menus for lunch and/or dinner.

Newport Restaurant Week, gonewportrestaurantweek.com. Almost 50 restaurants in Newport, Bristol, and surrounding towns lure diners with 3-course *prix-fixe* menus for lunch and/or dinner in the early spring. (See also November.)

April

Great International Spring Beer Festival, beerfestamerica .com. Held at the Rhode Island Convention Center in Providence, this event allows participants to sample the products from 70 or more brewers.

May

May Breakfasts. Since the 1860s, Rhode Island churches have held fund-raising breakfasts on or around May 1. One of the oldest continuous annual breakfasts is held at the Oaklawn Community Baptist Church (229 Wilbur Ave., Cranston, RI 02921, 401-944-0864). It always takes place on May 1 unless the date falls on a Sunday. For a list of some other May Breakfasts, visit golocalprov .com/food/statewide-guide-to-may-breakfasts.

June

Federal Hill Stroll, goprovidence.com/federal-hill-stroll. As Italians know, nothing beats a leisurely promenade on a beautiful summer evening—especially when you can listen to live music and stop for samples at participating restaurants. This evening event takes place on Federal Hill in Providence, where galleries, shops and restaurants also offer special discounts to participants.

Great Chowder Cook-Off, newportwaterfrontevents.com. Newport's self-proclaimed "largest and longest running chowder bonanza" features about 20 restaurants from New England and beyond competing for top prizes for clam, seafood, and "creative" chowders.

Taste of Block Island Weekend, blockislandchamber.com. Island-wide celebration of the beginning of summer includes special discounts at local restaurants.

July

Cape Verdean Festival, ricapeverdeanheritage.com. Many people come looking for the taste of home at this annual event held in India Point Park in Providence. Most popular is *catchupa,* the Cape Verdean national dish of beans and hominy long-simmered with pork, *linguiça,* and collard greens. For something less filling, try an empanada-like *pastel* filled with tuna, tomato, and garlic.

Providence Restaurant Weeks, providencerestaurantweeks
.com. This 2-week event is so popular that it takes place twice a
year (see January). About 100 restaurants offer 3-course *prix-fixe*
menus for lunch and/or dinner.

Public Clambake, newportclambakes.com. Once a year,
Kempenaar's Clambake Club in Newport invites the public to an
old-fashioned clambake featuring clam chowder, steamed clams and
mussels, a whole lobster, and *chouriço*. This being Rhode Island, the
meal begins, of course, with clamcakes.

Warren Quahog Festival, eastbaychamberri.org. Clams star
in this 2-day event that features clam boils, clam chowder, and
clamcakes. But you'll also find lobster, scallops, fish-and-chips,
and calamari. It's held at Burrs Hill Park, across from Warren Town
Beach where there's also plenty of room for arts and crafts vendors
and live entertainment.

August

Annual Grecian Festival, greekfestivalri.com. This festival held
at the Assumption of the Virgin Mary Greek Orthodox Church in
Pawtucket celebrated its centennial in 2012. The quality and variety
of the food has surely contributed to its success: roasted lamb, lamb
shanks, chicken, moussaka, pastitsio, spanikopita. . . . And then
there are the homemade Greek pastries and the specialty baklava
cheesecake to enjoy with a cup of Greek coffee or a glass of ouzo.

For the festival recipe for **Moussaka,** see p. 265.

Charlestown Chamber of Commerce Annual Seafood Festival, charlestownrichamber.com. Charlestown is the site of the state's largest seafood event, which features about 45 vendors serving boiled lobsters, lobster rolls, steamers, clamcakes, clam chowder, and fish-and-chips. There are also amusement rides, craft exhibits, live entertainment, and fireworks.

Clambake at the Lighthouse, roseislandlighthouse.org. There is hardly a better spot for a clambake than Rose Island in Newport Harbor, the site of an 1869 lighthouse. Bring a blanket or a folding chair and prepare to feast on a generous serving of steamers, mussels, Portuguese and Italian sausages, red and sweet potatoes, onions, carrots, corn on the cob, and seasoned fish. For a few dollars more, you can even throw in a lobster.

Newport WineFest, newportwinefest.com. This 3-day event in Newport features wine tastings and seminars along with a full schedule of cooking demonstrations and displays of gourmet foods, beer, and spirits.

Washington County Fair, washingtoncountyfair-ri.com. This 5-day event in Richmond is known for its country music performances, but livestock and agricultural displays celebrate agricultural traditions. Cooks vie for top prizes for their baked goods (cakes, pies, muffins, and scones) and for their canned goods (jams, jellies, vegetables, pickles, maple syrup, and honey).

September

Newport Mansions Wine & Food Festival, newportmansions .org. It seems only fitting that Newport's luxurious historic mansions would be the setting for this sophisticated 3-day event that brings together more than 100 vintners and top chefs from New England and beyond for tastings, dinners, seminars, cooking demonstrations, and other activities.

Taste of Block Island, blockislandchamber.com. Island-wide celebration of the fall season includes special discounts at local restaurants.

October

Bowen's Wharf Seafood Festival, bowenswharf.com. At this popular Newport event, restaurants and fishermen's associations present their specialties, including clam chowder, stuffed quahogs, clamcakes, shrimp, scallops, and lobster dinners. Live musical entertainment ranges from sea shanties to the blues.

International Oktoberfest, newportwaterfrontevents.com. The Newport Yachting Center is the setting for this 2-day event that features such German specialties as bratwurst, wiener schnitzel, potato salad, and sauerkraut—and plenty of beer to wash it all down. Live music, dancing, and even yodelers make for a rousing atmosphere.

Johnny Cake Festival, kenyonsgristmill.com. This annual event at **Kenyon's Grist Mill** in West Kingston (see p. 190) brings together about 75 farmers, artisans, and restaurants to celebrate the harvest season. Johnny cakes will, of course, be offered as well as other food specialties. Live entertainment and tours of the 1886 mill round out the day.

November

Great International Fall Beer Festival, beerfestamerica.com. In addition to tastings from 70 or more brewers, this event features an annual competition of ales, lagers, and ciders from the United States and abroad.

Newport Restaurant Week, gonewportrestaurantweek.com. Once the tourists have left for the season, local residents enjoy the second round of this popular event that includes almost 50 restaurants in Newport, Bristol, and surrounding towns offering 3-course *prix-fixe* menus for lunch and/or dinner. (See also March.)

Index